Quality Peace

Quality Peace

Peacebuilding, Victory, and World Order

PETER WALLENSTEEN

OXFORD
UNIVERSITY PRESS

OXFORD
UNIVERSITY PRESS

Oxford University Press is a department of the University of Oxford.
It furthers the University's objective of excellence in research, scholarship,
and education by publishing worldwide. Oxford is a registered trade mark
of Oxford University Press in the UK and in certain other countries

Published in the United States of America by
Oxford University Press
198 Madison Avenue, New York, NY 10016,
United States of America

Library of Congress Cataloging-in-Publication Data
Wallensteen, Peter, 1945–
  Quality peace : peacebuilding, victory, and world order / Peter Wallensteen.
     p.   cm.
  Includes bibliographical references and index.
  ISBN 978–0–19–021554–5 (hardcover : alk. paper) — ISBN 978–0–19–021555–2
(pbk. : alk. paper) — ISBN 978–0–19–021556–9 (ebook) — ISBN 978–0–19–027094–0
(Oxford Scholarship Online) 1. Peace-building. 2. Peace. 3. Conflict management.
4. International relations. 5. World politics. I. Title.
 JZ5538.W36 2015
 327.1'72—dc23
                              2015016047

Dedicated to my grandchildren

Etta, Aron, Morris, Nina, Tage and Holly

Motto: Pax Omnium Inter Omnes

(Everybody's peace with everybody else)

CONTENTS

PREFACE

Throughout history, concerns about war and peace have been viewed in terms of conflict. To many philosophers and writers there is a continuous and inevitable war among all. Thomas Hobbes pointedly formulated this in the 17th century. In Latin it was described as "bellum omnium contra omnes"—that is, everybody's war with everybody else. This was the state of affairs from the beginning of humankind, today, and, thus, forever. The only way out, the philosopher argued, was through an overwhelming power, which he called the Leviathan. This power—mostly identified with State, King or Government—emerges through a deal among rational humans making this authority their protector against violence and war: Power in exchange for Protection. Certainly, Hobbes was saying something more than merely reflecting the turbulent times of his native England. The image that he drew has appealed to many—in particular, to absolute leaders throughout history and probably without knowing Hobbes' sophisticated arguments. Power holders have projected themselves as the ultimate security for groups, entire populations, regions, or even for the planet as a whole. Certainly, their power has not been negotiated in a real sense between representatives, but simply been usurped, or awarded to them, by fate, supreme authority, or history.

Hobbes' solution has not worked. The world has continued to be plagued by wars and civil wars. There has been a struggle to be the Leviathan, to attain the commanding position. Power not only repels; it also attracts.

Thus thinking about war and peace has evolved and needs further development. There have been thoughts that appeared utopian at the time, but have still been successful; for example, notions of democratic rule (which does not involve a contract but gives more power to the people), inter-governmental unions (federations, global organizations), limitations on armaments, integration among peoples, confidence-building, and nonviolence measures. These are ideas associated with thinkers as diverse as Immanuel Kant, Alfred Nobel,

Bertha von Suttner, and Karl W. Deutsch, or practitioners as far apart as Emmeline Pankhurst, Woodrow Wilson, Mahatma Gandhi, and Mikhail Gorbachev. They all suggest that the idea of universal peace is relevant, achievable, and will come about in a different way than the one envisioned by Hobbes. These are traditions to which this work also aspires to contribute. By introducing the notion of Quality Peace it aims at finding the conditions beyond direct settlement of disputes that reassure the world that war will not appear again. Thus, it is time to revise the old Hobbesian notion into a modern variety where "war" is exchanged with "peace." Accordingly, the motto for this volume is: Pax Omnium Inter Omnes, that is, everybody's peace with everybody else.

The repetition of war has been a concern since the end of the Cold War. International strategies under the labels of conflict prevention and peacebuilding have been developed. They all assume that war does not have to be repeated in particular conflictual relations. By implication, this would apply to the planet as a whole. Such strategies are here subsumed under the concept of Quality Peace. By specifying the conditions for a peace after war that has certain qualities, it would then also be possible to reduce and, in the end, eliminate war from the human experience. In that sense local developments contribute to a world order that provides for more dignity, safety and predictability. There is no illusion that this is easily achieved. There is, however, evidence that this *is* possible and that it *has* happened, within and between states and regions. It will take place step-by-step.

This work has benefited from my two major affiliations in the past ten years—Uppsala University, Sweden, and the University of Notre Dame, USA—and in particular, the Department of Peace and Conflict Research in the former and the Kroc Institute for International Peace Studies in the latter. The resources collected in these two places on thinking about war and peace demonstrate the importance of particular milieus for peace research. These two institutions also provided financial support. At Uppsala, my work has rested primarily on the Uppsala Conflict Data Program and, at Notre Dame, in the group associated with the Peace Accords Matrix.

A number of persons have read parts of this. I am most grateful for input on whole chapters or sections from David Cortright, John Darby, Gary Goertz, Kristine Höglund, Madhav Joshi, John Paul Lederach, Erik Melander, Michaela Racovirta, Monica Toft, Jason Quinn, Pat Regan, and two anonymous reviewers. In unforeseen ways, my colleague in the struggle for peace research, Björn Hettne, and my late father Ivar Wallensteen contributed to this volume through many discussions.

Various parts have been examined at research seminars at the Department in Uppsala, at the Kroc Institute, and at conferences such as the one of Ethics of War and Peace by the Societas Ethica, Maribor, Slovenia, August 24–25,

2014. Two persons have read most of the manuscript and come up with a host of useful additions, comments, and corrections: Audrey Faber, who was my assistant in the autumn of 2014, and by my good friend Bill Montross, always willing to take up the challenge of making sense of my writing.

Certainly, my wife during fifty years, Lena Wallensteen, has contributed in ways that are impossible to measure. This work is dedicated to our six grandchildren. The oldest was born in 2006, meaning that they all belong to the new millennium. Let us hope that they will experience what this book is all about: a world of peace with quality.

Peter Wallensteen
January 2015

CHAPTER 1

Peacebuilding, Victory, and Quality Peace

1.1 The Challenge of Peace after War

History is scarred by war and the recurrence of war, even between the same parties. In a European context, the possibility of a repetition of wars in different constellations between England, Spain, France, Germany, Austria, Poland, and Russia has been taken for granted for centuries. Policies of alliances, counteralliances, arms races, and interventions have been seen in this light. The outcome of the Second World War and the end of the Cold War suggest that such patterns do not have to repeat themselves. Rivalries can cease and more constructive relations be built. Indeed, Denmark and Sweden had repeated wars in the Nordic areas through centuries, but since the early 1800s peace between these countries has been taken for granted. The same has now happened between Germany and France, as well as in a number of other civil conflicts. Close to two hundred peace agreements in the past twenty-five years serve to underline the importance of finding new relations between formerly warring parties. That said, not all have worked to durably terminate conflicts.

Historical rivalries remain. In East Asia, the relations between China, the Koreas, and Japan are still fraught with tension, conflict, and fear of war. In Africa the repetitions of conflicts between Hutus and Tutsis in neighboring Rwanda, Burundi, and Eastern Congo appear to be 'doomed' to repetition. The Israeli–Palestinian-Arab relations have similar properties. Indeed, there are also for the Balkans sinister scenarios for the future of relations among Serbs, Croats, Bosniaks, and Albanians. In Eastern Europe conflicts between Ukrainians and Russians have come to the fore again in 2014. Enduring rivalries appear part of the human experience.

Typically when a renewed conflict is observed in such complex relationships commentators are quick to describe this as "not unexpected," "wars waiting to happen," or "predestined." The fact is, however, that few relationships are always and continuously characterized by tension and fear. There are also spells of cooperation, exchange, and even integration. Neighbors cooperate with each other as much as they quarrel with each other. There are periods of cooperation—during the Cold War described as "détente"—and such periods provide opportunities for profoundly changing relationships. Indeed, this is also how the Cold War ended, in ways that were largely unpredicted by observers and political leaders alike. The fall of the Berlin Wall was seen as a "surprise" to observers at the time, but was a logical outcome of the relaxation of tension that preceded it and that deliberately aimed at reducing the risk of a major war. The change of dynamics in the Cold War unleashed popular energy that led much further than the parties themselves had anticipated. Indeed, it helped to reduce fear and build a more reasonable relationship between the West and Russia for the following quarter of a century. It set a new pattern of interaction, appearing entrenched. This, then, made the events in Ukraine in 2014 unexpected and challenging.

Also in other instances there have been conscious strategies of building peace to avoid repetition of conflict. The Nordic cooperation that emerged in the nineteenth century is an example; the European Union of the late twentieth century is another. These were political projects with elements of peacebuilding where an explicit purpose was the prevention of war recurrence. However, such cooperation may also be beneficial for more immediate and tangible reasons—not the least trade, employment, and investment. By focusing on matters that do not immediately invoke concerns of security, survival, and sovereignty it may be easier to initiate cooperation and change conflicting dynamics into constructive relations. Peace, then, becomes a spin-off from other activities.

This book maintains that the postwar condition of any relationship has to be dealt with between the parties directly and placed on a national as well as international agenda. Strategies such as "peacebuilding" have a specific role in this phase of a relationship, legitimately termed strategic peacebuilding.[1] It is typically reflected in a peace agreement that regulates the relations between the warring parties, most importantly by dealing with the disagreement that gave rise to the war in the first place. Removing the incompatibility is a necessary first step; a peace agreement can do that (Wallensteen 2015). Implementation of the agreement is what needs to follow (Joshi and Darby 2013) as a central element in post-conflict peacebuilding.

However, we also have to consider alternative war endings, notably victories, and the way they are secured. This is a matter of victory consolidation. This may include purposeful strategies by victors against the defeated, and might be supported by the outside community. It ends the disagreement by one side prevailing, but the other side may still not cease to exist or become irrelevant. Thus there is a choice of strategies also for a victor in relations to the defeated opponent.

In addition to the relations between the (formerly warring) parties in the postwar period there is the global context in which all conflicts, peace efforts, and victories are played out, a "world order." It refers to the way the world is "ruled" at a particular time. It is not only a matter of power relations and existing institutions but also prevailing norms for diplomacy and negotiations as well as the emphasis given to the use of violence and armaments. In a more integrated world, the order would be a matter of global governance; in a fragmented world it may be a system resting on balancing of power. Thus different "orders" may have different preferences for how challenging issues are treated. The order, in that way, affects all other actors, although the extent of this can be debated. Influence goes in different directions (Wallensteen 1984, Wallensteen 2011a).

With respect to the concept of peace, this book approaches postwar conditions, no matter what type of outcome, with the help of the notion of "quality peace."[2] This means it asks if the postwar conditions regulate the incompatibility and also meet standards of dignity, security, and predictability, factors that reduce the likelihood of war recurrence. "Quality peace" is a concept for breaking out of the dichotomy of negative versus positive peace that long has been taken for granted. It simply says that peace has to have a particular quality beyond the absence of war (the typical definition of negative peace), but it remains to specify what the critical elements of quality are.[3] The standards suggested here are those to be tested throughout this book.

The purpose of concepts and strategies of peacebuilding is to find postwar routes that do not lead to renewed fighting between the same parties. Peacebuilding aims to make the previous war the final one. At the same time peacebuilding mostly stems from a peace process, a peace agreement, and thus an arrangement (often supported by the international community) that is different from one party's victory over the other(s). The point of departure for peacebuilding is that neither side of the conflict has "won." Instead, the opposing sides have found reasons to settle for less than their maximum demands, and in the form of a public commitment, a peace agreement. There is a need for peacebuilding strategies, which, at a minimum, include the implementation of the agreement, but optimally also aim at removing some of the major causes of the previous conflict(s). The concept of peacebuilding is logically and empirically connected to a situation that emerges after a peace deal.

As this makes clear, the alternative to peacebuilding is not only the continuation of the same war; it is also the victory by one side, something that is habitually neglected in the discussion. The reasons for restarting a war may be just this: the perceived inability at a particular time to achieve the long-term goal of victory. A peace agreement may—by one party or sections of that party—be regarded only as a temporary break ("pause") in the ultimate pursuit of complete victory. Furthermore, this may well be understood by the opposing side, and thus tension remains after the agreement. Both sides continue to be insecure, as they still fear the "real" intentions of the other. A peace agreement may aim at bridging this dilemma—the origins of insecurity—but still have flaws in its formulation or implementation so that the dilemma remains. The agreed provisions may not be carried out in practice as planned. There may be unexpected factors (or actors) that change the relationships in challenging ways. Important components of the original incompatibility remain, and thus so does the security dilemma, which in turn is often the ultimate trigger of an armed conflict. It remains a strong force working on the parties pushing them toward escalation and renewed fighting.

The reality of peacebuilding is located between the danger of renewed war and the hope of victory of one of the sides. It is an uneasy state of affairs, and our concern is whether the postwar period can turn into a relationship with sustainable qualities. Furthermore, this means that peacebuilding writings and peacebuilding practices have to be assessed in a different way. It is not just a comparison between different peacebuilding strategies. The peace agreement outcome needs to be related to its most obvious alternative: victory, the domination and control by one side over the society or the relationship.

That is why this book takes up the challenge of victory and the way the victor consolidates power over society. For the winner this is also a matter of developing a peaceful situation after a war, but on the terms of the victor. Sometimes there may be an agreement of capitulation with stipulations on the distribution of power. Many victories, however, will have no such formal ending but simply create new conditions in a society. The opponent just disappears. If it is a government victory, it means little change in the established social order, except with respect to the defeated group and its supporters. If it is a rebel victory, it is likely to result in revolutionary transformations, with repercussions throughout society. If the winner is a separatist group, it means instituting new national territorial conditions, or even the creation of two separate states, where there previously was only one. In an inter-state setting the winner may have occupied the defeated nation(s), partially or fully, with far-reaching consequences for governance as well as territorial issues. Whatever the outcome, the winner is likely to be concerned about maintaining the *status quo* that the war has generated. This is what is called victory consolidation: the way the victor manages the victory, particularly in relation to the defeated party.

Consequently, we ask if processes of peacebuilding and victory consolidation meet the criteria of quality peace and, thus, result in a situation that will not lead to the recurrence of war.

There are many challenges that are the same in both these postwar situations. Whether the result of a victory or a joint arrangement, the security issue remains. As we just mentioned some actors may be insecure and thus the war may be reignited either as an offensive or a defensive move to enhance one party's security vis-à-vis the other. The respect of the other side and that side's right to live a secure existence is a central aspect of peacebuilding. This is the point where "dignity" enters this discussion: Does the postwar situation include respect for the equal rights of the opponent, in commitment and in practice? Without a positive response to this question, the dynamics of insecurity continue to operate and may at any moment turn a normal dispute into an escalating conflict and, sometimes, a war. A key issue in peacebuilding and victory consolidation, as a consequence, has to be its ability to reassure the opposing side of their equal rights, or respect for their dignity. This is a key consideration in quality peace.

This is not without precedent. The UN Charter mentions human dignity in its preamble. It is also possible to develop indicators of human dignity (Schachter 1983). Human dignity, in other words, has to be a central concern, whether based on class, identity, gender, or other dimensions.[4] This is an issue that has been given little explicit attention in the dominant peacebuilding literature and seldom approached systematically in studies of victory.[5] Violations of dignity in the form of discrimination, repression, and persecution may have sparked the war that the world much later tries to prevent from recurring.

Obviously, the postwar situation also involves an immediate security problem for the former warring parties. In a peace agreement they may ask for security guarantees (by keeping some of their own forces, by inviting international peacekeepers, or other forms of protection). In a victory the defeated leadership may sometimes be allowed to leave the country, at other times have to face criminal charges, or even execution. The security issue, however, also involves followers as well as security in the country at large. If there are groups fearing a restart of war, they may take action that may make such a recurrence more likely. There is also an important gender aspect, captured by the notion of security equality: Security for women is not always the same as for men in a postwar setting (Olsson 2011). Thus quality peace includes the notion of security for all.

Furthermore, there is a time dimension. The examples of strategies for postwar conditions mentioned initially—Nordic regional cooperation and the European Union—all work with long-term perspectives, where decisions are expected to create stable conditions for the future. The idea is to tie countries and peoples together in such a way that they no longer fear war from the other side while remaining respected as autonomous, equal actors—*and* that this state of affairs is stable. This means that there is a certainty about the new conditions and that they are unlikely to be reversed in the foreseeable future (i.e., predictability). The stability makes possible investments in the postwar situation that in turn strengthen the peace. It makes the new conditions sustainable. For how long? Normally, the question is not asked. If peace remains for a period, this increases the chances that it will remain in the next period as well. If, on the other hand, a significant actor regards the situation only as a period for its own recuperation, reorganization, and learning of lessons for pursuit of its previous ambition, fear remains. The future becomes unpredictable. Such ambitions are easily discovered in relationships that have seen enduring rivalries. The security dilemma returns in full force and the postwar arrangement is challenged. This is to say that peacebuilding, like victory consolidation, is a long-term project without a clear end point. Both situations aim at creating a new normality, where the peaceful pursuit of goals is taken for granted. A key indicator for both could be the peaceful transfer of power from the leaders at the end of the war to a new generation or even from one side to the other. If this happens it means that basic methods and rules are not questioned. When peacebuilding and victory consolidation work, they are no longer seen as peacebuilding or victory, only as a typical human undertaking to build a society that is "good" for all. The situation is turned into a new "normal" or "natural" state of affairs.[6]

From this we can surmise that there is an underlying peace concept that guides the work of this volume. Quality peace means the creation of postwar conditions that make the inhabitants of a society (be it an area, a country, a region, a continent, or a planet) secure in life and dignity now and for the foreseeable future.[7] Together these factors draw attention to the quality of the relationships following a war and the regulation of the disagreements that led to the war. Peace is not simply a matter of being without war for a period of time. It is a matter of maintaining conditions that do not produce war in the first place or—as some form of "peace" has failed previously—not repeating the same failures. The failure of one period of "peace" suggests that it did not meet the quality standards of "peace." Thus the postwar conditions that this book focuses on constitute the quality of that peace. The question asked and to be answered is: Will the postwar conditions be able to handle the strains in a society and thus not see a relapse into the same conflict, or the start of another conflict? When that question can be answered in the affirmative, then there is "quality peace." Otherwise there is not; there is simply a postwar period, or, even worse, an interwar period.

At the outset, it may appear that strategies of peacebuilding and victory consolidation are each other's opposites. They are different ways of regulating incompatibility, no doubt. However, both aim at achieving a lasting peace and preventing the recurrence of war, but the relationship between the formerly warring parties is built in entirely different ways. There are observers who see victory and its consolidation as the only stable situation: let the conflict take its course. It will create a "natural" end point. Third-party interventions and peace deals will only prevent this and negotiated solutions will be "artificial." From this perspective, settlements result in postponing the ultimate confrontation and a lasting victory. The idea is that, after victory, all actors will accommodate to the new situation, and thus stability will be secured. The typical example in the post–World War II period is, of course, the fate of the defeated Axis powers. The peace that was imposed has demonstrated the importance of thoroughly defeating the enemy. The costs, the proponents of the victory strategy argue, may have been high but the results are more durable. Germany and Japan have, for seventy years, been cooperative and constructive in relations to the former enemies and the world has made enormous strides in technological development, economic well-being, and peace.

These are powerful arguments. We will return to them throughout this book. However, they have to be considered parallel to peacebuilding strategies. Is it true that victory typically results in more lasting peace and that it also generates a higher quality peace than does the peacebuilding strategy? The underlying idea of this book is to contrast peaceful peacebuilding with consolidation of military victory in terms of their ability to generate quality peace. Is it at all reasonable to compare such different outcomes and postwar strategies? The debate suggests that it should be possible as examples are used in both directions; the different elements of quality peace conditions are applicable to both peacebuilding situations and victory consolidation outcomes. It may seem more reasonable that a shared peace agreement would result in "higher" quality peace, as all parties are involved in building the peaceful conditions. But logically there could also be high-quality outcomes of victory if, for instance, this outcome also can respect the security and dignity of the loser and thus reduce the security dilemma. The actual and contemporary experience should be the judge of this.

Furthermore, in this formulation it is clear that the evaluation of the quality of peace applies to a great many situations. The present peacebuilding paradigm almost exclusively deals with internal conflict in the post–Cold War setting. This includes pertinent issues of failed states, corruption, poverty, resource exploitation, and lack of democracy. In short, these are wars that deal with governance issues: rule by whom, for whom, with what means, and with which results? In contrast, the victory paradigm has often been more focused on inter-state war, be they the World Wars, the Gulf War, the Iraq War of 2003, or others. Here we suggest an approach that enables an enlightened conversation.

This is done by looking for quality peace in a comprehensive manner and by including three major types of armed conflicts (Wallensteen 2015). First, there are the intra-state relations that the peacebuilding literature typically addresses, the traditional civil wars. They are numerous and thus constitute an important element in this book. Second, there are the inter-state relations that we just touched upon. They involve regional rivalries, interventions, and border wars, as well as major power struggles and world wars. The post–Cold War era has seen little of such conflict and, thus, it may easily drop from the analytical horizon. This should not be allowed: Nuclear weapons-equipped India and Pakistan seriously confronted each other in 1999, and Ethiopia and Eritrea saw a nasty regional conflict, which ended in a peace agreement in 2000, still to be implemented. These should not be considered exclusively inter-state conflicts; similar rivalries affect other countries as well. For instance both India and Pakistan have been engaged on their own terms in Afghanistan as this country's fate affects their military calculations. Similarly Ethiopia and Eritrea have been concerned about the influence of the other in Somalia, not the least for strategic reasons. Obviously Afghanistan and Somalia, at this time, are not only regional issues, but also elements in global campaigns against terrorism and piracy. This points to the need to be attentive to regional and global peacemaking, as the outcome in one country will affect populations and countries outside the core rivalries. Regional and global conditions will receive separate attention in this book, as they bring us to the issues of world order. The notion of quality peace applies to all these complexities.

It also applies to the third category: internal conflicts over territorial disagreements, where the issue is the status of a particular area of the state, an intra-state region, and whether it is to remain within an existing state or become an independent entity of its own. It is a conflict type logically located between the previous two: it can be seen as internal, but it can also turn into an inter-state conflict, for instance, if the rebels are internationally recognized. This category involves classic dignity concerns: Will a particular segment of society (ethnic, national, linguistic, etc.) get the respect to which it is entitled within the present state formation, or does it require a fundamental reformation? To the actors themselves such conflicts are seen as "separatism" (the government) or "liberation" (the rebels). The different conceptions reflect the motivations of the parties, but in practice there is no disagreement between them about what the incompatibility concerns. In much analysis such conflicts have been subsumed under internal conflict in general. This is unsatisfactory. They highlight territorial issues and security dilemmas that are different from battles over governance in one country or the rivalry between two states (Wallensteen 2015). They require their own analysis. This book gives specific attention to such state formation conflicts.

Thus the book deals with three types of post-conflict situations (chapters 3, 4, and 5) and the issues of security, dignity, and durability. This, then, is placed in world order and institutional perspectives (chapters 6 and 7). Finally,

Table 1.1

Peacebuilding in Contemporary Scholarship

Share of Articles of a Journal Mentioning Key Words in Abstracts, with Full Text in Parentheses. Key Peace Research Journals, 2010–2014.

Journal	Peacebuilding	Victory	Peace Agreement	Total articles
Journal of Peace Research	2.5 (26.1)	0.8 (1.1)	2.8 (12.1)	356
Conflict Management and Peace Science	2.5 (14.7)	1.2 (1.2)	1.8 (20.2)	163
Journal of Conflict Resolution	1.1 (12.7)	0.5 (1.1)	1.6 (11.6)	189
International Studies Quarterly	2.3 (5.2)	0.6 (1.5)	0.3 (4.1)	344
World Politics	0 (3.9)	0 (0.7)	0.7 (21.7)	152
Total, %	1.9 (13.7)	0.7 (1.2)	1.5 (12)	1,204
Total, no of articles	23 (165)	8 (14)	18 (145)	1,204

Note Includes peacebuilding, peace building, and peace-building. Victory is used only when the term is used in conjunction with war. Done by Audrey Ann Faber, November 25, 2014.

chapter 8 draws quality peace conclusions for strategic peacebuilding and victory consolidation. In this way, this book will hopefully make a contribution to the development of peacebuilding studies, victory analysis, and world order approaches by demonstrating the interconnectedness of different fields of inquiry and political action.

The contribution of this work can be understood from Table 1.1. It describes the attention to central concepts—notably peacebuilding, victory, and peace agreement. In the five years 2010–2014 there were more than 1200 articles published in five highly regarded journals concerned with peace and conflict matters. It is remarkable that these three concepts were infrequently mentioned. There was somewhat more attention to "peace" in journals dealing specifically with "peace" and "conflict resolution" than in those dealing with "international" and "world" studies, as more than 10% of the articles mentioned this notion in the text of the articles. However, in the abstracts it was clear that this notion was only central to 1% or 2% of the articles. This translates into twenty-three articles. Surprisingly "victory" and "peace agreement" achieved even less attention. This book hopes to develop these concepts by empirically "confronting" them to post–Cold War conditions.

However, before embarking on this we need to review the history of peacebuilding and situate this study in existing literature. Peacebuilding is a novel concept and requires closer scrutiny, but so do the traditional policies of victory consolidation, and the two need to be related to each other. The remainder of this chapter and chapter 2 will do just that.

1.2 Peacebuilding: A Conceptual History

Peacebuilding clearly has become a post–Cold War issue and the term does not go far back in history. The reconstruction of Western Europe after the Second World War could today have been classified as a regional peacebuilding project, but the term was not used at the time. In fact the conditions in Europe were the result of a victory, and there was no general peace agreement after the Second World War between the allied countries and their enemies. Instead there was occupation, domination and, after a while, more narrow agreements. The Western European situation does not fit perfectly with peacebuilding notions, but it still provides stimulating applications of an idea that is in focus today: finding ways to integrate an economy in such a way that the former warriors no longer can confront each other. It was seen as a peace project, no doubt, but it was also a matter of economic development, reconstruction after the war, and building defenses against new threats. It was partially motivated by a fear from the Soviet Union from the outside, a fear of Communist takeover from the inside, and a fear from history of Nazism and fascism again becoming powerful. The specter was not only the Second World War, but also the Great Depression that preceded it and the instabilities created after the First World War. Thus the relations between the victorious West and the World War II losers fit within our analysis, as do those between the Soviet Union and the same actors. They were structured in different ways and thus improve our understanding of postwar conditions. These are issues that seldom appear in the discussions on peacebuilding, but this concept as well as victory consolidation is general and thus applicable across time and space. Consequently we will deal with these matters, notably in chapters 6 and 7.[8]

It is remarkable to see that textbooks presenting the scholarly subject of peace in the 1970s, 1980s or the early 1990s do not include peacebuilding as a concept (e.g., Curle 1971, Barash 1991). The very first use of the term, as far as this author has been able to find, was in an article by peace researcher Johan Galtung in 1976.[9] He presented peacebuilding as an alternative to peacekeeping and peacemaking. His article does not contain succinct definitions but his reasoning may be summarized as saying that peacebuilding is an associative structure of self-supporting conflict resolution building on specific peace-enhancing principles such as equity and symbiosis (Galtung 1976: 297–304, Gawerc 2006: 439). The article was not widely circulated and is now available only in Galtung's collected work from a publisher in Denmark.[10] It did not have an impact at the time but has since been rediscovered. It was written in the midst of the Cold War, when more comprehensive concepts beyond the established notion of peacekeeping had difficulties in gaining attention.

Only after the end of the Cold War could international organizations such as the UN squarely confront wars that had gone on for a longer period of time. During the Cold War these conflicts were often inaccessible to international concern. Superpower rivalry dominated and precluded third parties from getting involved. After becoming personally engaged in one of the conflicts on the UN agenda, UN Secretary-General Boutros Boutros-Ghali highlighted the importance of peacebuilding in his report to the UN Security Council, *An Agenda for Peace*, in June 1992. This text is today the starting point for much conceptual analysis of the term peacebuilding. It did not build on Galtung's terminologies, although there are similarities. A key adviser to Boutros-Ghali at the time, Ambassador Alvaro de Soto, tells how the concept emerged. The Secretary-General searched for an appropriate way to describe what the UN was planning to do following the peace agreement in El Salvador (Box 1.1 gives de Soto's full account), in which de Soto was a crucial mediator. They realized that it was not enough to bring about an end to the war and then leave the parties to themselves. Measures had to be initiated to prevent the two-decades-long war from restarting. Boutros-Ghali identified the word "peacebuilding" as an appropriate way for describing what El Salvador now needed. With such a general formulation the concept would also help to point to the need of major UN efforts elsewhere. Thus, Boutros-Ghali's seminal report included the first UN definition of peacebuilding: It is described as:

> . . . action to identify and support structures which will tend to strengthen and solidify peace in order to avoid a relapse into conflict (UN Secretary-General 1992: *An Agenda for Peace,* paragraph 21).

Boutros-Ghali gave examples based on his and the organization's practical orientation, when transferred also to an inter-state context (which was the framework within which the UN was still thinking; after all the Cold War was barely over):

> . . . to develop agriculture, improve transportation or utilize resources such as water or electricity that they need to share, or joint programmes through which barriers between nations are brought down by means of freer travel, cultural exchanges, and mutually beneficial youth and educational projects. Reducing hostile perceptions through educational exchanges and curriculum reform . . . (UN Secretary-General 1992: *An Agenda for Peace,* paragraphs 56 and 58)

Box 1.1 **UN Secretary-General Boutros Boutros-Ghali**
and Peacebuilding

Ambassador Alvaro de Soto, at the time Senior Political Adviser to the Secretary-General, recounts how the concept of peacebuilding emerged in the UN in 1992.

On January 31, 1992, the Security Council met for the first time ever at the summit level, convened by British Prime Minister John Major. The organizing idea was the opportunities offered by the end of the Cold War. The Council adopted a statement in which it mentioned El Salvador, asking Boutros Boutros-Ghali to provide recommendations on how to improve the capacity of the UN in peacemaking, peacekeeping, and preventive diplomacy. The Secretary-General created a task force chaired by Vladimir Petrovsky, of which I was a part, to prepare those recommendations. In June the same year, the Secretary-General went to the Environment and Development Conference/Earth Summit in Rio de Janeiro, Brazil, and for official visits to Brazil, Argentina, and Uruguay. I was traveling with him. While traveling we received a late draft of what became An Agenda for Peace. On a side trip to Iguazu, as he was reading it, he asked me: "Where does what we are doing in El Salvador fit here? It isn't peacemaking, since that's already done. It isn't peacekeeping as we know it because we are doing much more than simply monitoring a separation of forces and ceasefire. It isn't preventive diplomacy either. In fact, what we are doing is *post*-conflict, and it is more like peace *building*." He saw that what we were embarking on was likely to be a conceptually new set of activities and that there would likely be a lot of it as the Cold War wound down, and that it would be as important as the three areas on which the Council had asked him to make recommendations. So I followed up by cabling Virendra Dayal (interim Chef de Cabinet with the Secretary-General) reporting on what he had said, adding that he wanted to make this a new category, elevated to the same rank as the other three.

Alvaro de Soto, communication to the author, November 1, 2008.

Many of these issues are as much a matter of development and economic integration as peacebuilding. In that sense, it is reminiscent of the programs of reconstruction and development after the Second World War. From the very beginning there was a problem afflicting this concept: How could peacebuilding be separated from other concerns, notably economic growth or social justice? Boutros-Ghali did not draw a strict line, and probably did not see the need. El Salvador was poor and tired of war. The government would be happy for almost anything it could get in terms of international assistance. The parties in El Salvador were not likely to be fussy about the labeling.

However, in his following work—simply termed "Supplement to An Agenda for Peace" from January 1995, largely done by Ambassador de Soto— the concept achieved more precision, in particular a focus on security and institutional dimensions. It dealt with intra-state concerns specifically related to the war experience:

> Demilitarization, the control of small arms, institutional reform, improved police and judiciary systems, the monitoring of human rights, electoral reform and social and economic development . . . (UN Secretary-General 1995: *Supplement*, paragraph 47)

Although the framework was still wide, not the least in incorporating development concerns, attention was given to the capacities of states to operate legitimately and responsibly in the post-conflict environment.

The UN conceptualization, as we can see, has been highly practical, indeed operative. It was, from the beginning, centered on post-conflict situations. This is now an entrenched UN tradition. This is reflected in later documents, notably the World Summit Outcome in 2005, which, more than a decade later, advocated the creation of a United Nations Peacebuilding Commission with the purpose to:

> . . . focus attention to the reconstruction and institution building efforts necessary for recovery from conflict and support the development of integrated strategies in order to lay the foundation for sustainable development . . . [and] extend the period of attention by the international community to post-conflict recovery. (World Summit Outcome 2005: paragraphs 97–98)

As the World Summit statement makes clear, the international community had by now also discovered other problems not apparent earlier: Different actors were doing different "peacebuilding" activities, thus requiring coordination and integration. It also noted that the attention to particular conflicts had a tendency to go away, thus requiring an institutional structure in the UN itself to keep a consistent focus on the same cases of potential war renewal. An explicit reason for the UN to keep up its interest was the high frequency of a return to war in many intra-state conflicts, sometimes being as high as 50% within a few years of the previous conflict being terminated.

Still, this means that, conceptually, peacebuilding had become a more complicated undertaking. The focus remained on the "recovery from conflict" (i.e., on the postwar phase). It was largely concerned with internal development and one country at a time. But the question of who should carry the responsibility for peacebuilding and how coordination should be done had become a problem for decision-makers beyond the war-torn state.

In the World Summit Outcome formulation peacebuilding as a concept is removed from what Boutros-Ghali also had in mind: the inter-state relationships. In the UN parlance peacebuilding had by now become firmly anchored as a concept of post-conflict *internal* developments of societies (Call 2008: 4–6). This means that situations in Western Europe after the Second World War find themselves outside this conceptualization. However, nobody would deny the need for preventing a return to traditional war-prone rivalries. Indeed, if we are concerned with such broader peacebuilding issues, inter-state matters also have to be included, as well as major power relations. It is a definite peacebuilding question to ask how one should make sure that, for instance, the Cold War between the West and Russia does not return. What options are there for turning rivalries into constructive relations?

Furthermore, the Western European experience was regional, not just a bilateral development. With the strong focus of peacebuilding as a matter of dealing with internal affairs, the interconnections between countries and societies can easily be lost from analysis and political action. This conceptual development in the UN means that the focus of peacebuilding has been dramatically narrowed. It is not difficult to understand why this is so, as it may make the concept more efficient on an operative level (responding to questions such as, for example, regarding practical measures) and on an organizational one (whether, for example, the Peacebuilding Commission can do something that is not done by the "normal" development agencies). Both these concerns serve to limit the peacebuilding concept. In connection to this book, however, with its focus on quality peace and applying it to all types of postwar situations, peacebuilding may regain some of its original content.

This, furthermore, can also be seen when introducing the concept of conflict prevention into the discussion. In some situations post-conflict activities are in fact pre-conflict prevention work: to prevent a conflict from restarting. If a conflict nevertheless breaks out again, it is likely to challenge the strategies of peacebuilding that were there to prevent this. Then peacebuilding after one war becomes a matter of conflict prevention before the (possible) next one. It is obviously not easy to draw a strict line between what is post-conflict and what is pre-conflict. That is a chief reason why other conceptions of peacebuilding are more focused on continued cycles of conflict. Lederach summarizes this strand of thinking when stating that peacebuilding involves the transformation of relationships: Sustainable reconciliation, he says, requires both structural and relational transformations (Lederach 1997: 20, 82–83). That obviously enlarges the perspective even further. There are many relationships to transform. It is also possible that even "dysfunctional" relationships may not give rise to conflict, breakdowns, or wars. But it points to a broader understanding of social interaction that is involved in peacebuilding.

In one sense this was also part of the original concept. The idea has consistently been to prevent the recurrence of conflict. Relationships are seen as continuous, almost eternal. The end of one war does not preclude that the same relationship may see a recurrence. Consequently peacebuilding has to change that particular relationship, that is arrive at some form of relational transformation. Galtung's conception included the idea of self-supporting conflict resolution. This implies that the potentially conflicting parties have found a shared framework within which to manage their relationships. To Galtung this equals a "structure," to Lederach a transformation of relations.

However, there is nothing to say that such transformation of relationships only takes place after a peace agreement between the parties. A victory also results in a transformation of relations, and it may even open up possibilities for the construction of self-supporting structures for conflict resolution. It could be part of the victors' consolidation of their hold of power. This is a point with introducing the concept of quality peace, no matter what form of war outcome we are concerned with (peacebuilding or victory consolidation): it will bring in a tougher comparison between what can be done with peaceful means and what is the result of the use of violence. With this more holistic and long-term perspective the challenge to peacebuilding becomes not one of a particular measure of post-conflict peacebuilding but one of dealing with cycles of violence. From the quality peace perspective these cycles have to be broken or even turned into constructive peace-reinforcing dynamics. Such an approach to quality peace is supported by the fact that the same country may experience repeated events of violence, even to the point where each conflict can be described as phases and periods in a continuing relationship. Thus the same relationship may experience both peacebuilding and victory consolidation. The same may afflict particular regions that seem trapped in repetitive wars and armed conflicts. As such situations are like infected wounds, they attract a host of other interests that see opportunities for their particular agendas. Regional conflicts easily become entangled with global networks, alliances, and issues. What appears initially as a task for local efforts may quickly become a matter of global dimensions. From a UN perspective, such enlarged conceptions of peacebuilding may lead to a broad and complicated program not likely to appeal to practitioners or finance ministers.

Even so, this approach points to interesting possibilities. Conflictual regions may change, as can be seen also in recent times. East Asia as a region has not seen wars in thirty years, suggesting that something has changed in regional relations. This is the point of departure in a large project on East Asian Peace based at Uppsala University (Tønnesson 2011). In formerly war-torn and coup-prone countries (such as Bolivia, Greece, Turkey, Liberia, and Bangladesh) the absence of war and even military coups is increasingly taken for granted. Indeed countries in the midst of regional turmoil, war, and genocide have still remained peaceful (Costa Rica in Central America in the 1980s; Botswana in Southern Africa; Tanzania despite neighboring Rwanda and Uganda; Zambia situated between war-torn Angola, Congo, and repression in Rhodesia/Zim-babwe); what can be learned from such experiences and how are they different from those in less fortunate regions (such as Central and Western Africa, Horn of Africa, Middle East, Central Asia, and Indochina)? An analysis building on dimensions of quality peace, in other words, can rest on a comparison of cases with and without war, and also on comparisons among regions with different experiences and where there are important changes over time. This is a vast topic of its own, largely beyond the scope of this book, but pertinent inter-state regional issues are dealt with, notably in Section 7.2.

Galtung's general conception moves the searchlight further, with its empha-sis on equity and symbiosis: Interactions on equal levels create linkages and prevent isolation, particularly if they also include people-to-people exchanges (Galtung 1976: 298–300). Lederach does not detail the kind of changed rela-tionship he has in mind, while Doyle and Sambanis, in one of the first quan-titative studies on the subject, point to local capacity for conflict resolution as a central factor in their model, in a dynamic interaction with international capabilities (Doyle and Sambanis 2000). The role of democracy has become increasingly central but sometimes more as a hope for "participatory politics" (Call 2008: 6) than in terms of particular forms of governance. In some way, all these conceptions point to the possibility of large parts of the population being engaged in control of their own destiny. It comes close to the notion of "dig-nity" that is important here, and for which democracy is one possible organiza-tional expression. It is of central concern in thinking about quality peace.

This means that a simple negative definition of "no renewal of war" is not enough as a target for peace after a war. The negative formulation has the ad-vantage of being clear, easy to understand, and even to measure universally over time and space. But the postwar situation may still be unsatisfactory in other respects, and elements in this may actually spur new conflicts. Thus the quality of the relationships is of importance. Equity may mean deliberate re-distribution of resources from rich to poor, for the purpose of improving qual-ity of life for the latter (which could be a value in itself, but also instrumental in making impoverished young people less susceptible to recruitment into armies). It may serve to reduce ostentatious inequalities in society that otherwise may prompt opposition and, ultimately, armed rebellion. With improved access to resources (education, basic material needs, employment, influence), more people have a chance to say no to "jobs" that negate their humanity (be it rebel armies, bonded labor, prostitution, or drug trade). This means, in fact, providing dignity.

In particular, we should note that quality peace is a relational concept. Primarily, it concerns the relations between the (formerly) warring parties, their supporters, or their entire "sides," be they, for instance, combatants, the identity groups to which they relate, or their funders. When quality peace focuses on dignity, it means dignity accorded to the former warring parties, but also to actors and populations within the society at large, or to relevant inter-state interactions.

Furthermore, postwar efforts must be carried out with an eye to the future. It has to be a long-term development that provides security to life (i.e., no wars or other forms of violence-induced insecurity) as well as dignity (as just described). These are the post-conflict conditions that make the inhabitants of a society secure in life and dignity now and for the foreseeable future. Here, we move one step further and apply the same criteria to a postwar situation that results from victory. Life after a war must have such a strong quality that there will remain few compelling reasons to restart the terminated armed conflict. The higher the quality of the peace for the many, the more likely it is that there will be an interest among sufficiently large segments of a population to prevent the recurrence of war.

This definition may appear to apply only to one society at a time, but this is not so. Having one society that is internally secure next to a neighbor that is not brings insecurity to both. The threat of conflict spilling over or leading to a dispute with the neighbor is a threat to the inhabitants of both societies. They are no longer secure in life and dignity. The Cold War balance of terror (deterrence) rested on the deliberate and mutual infliction of insecurity on East and West by the West and the East, respectively. Contrary to this, neighbors have an interest in the well-being of each other, whether they are strongly integrated or not. The concept of quality peace thus incorporates inter-societal relationships. With increased integration across the borders the chances of maintaining peace may also increase. Once the neighbors are more closely integrated they may come to constitute a shared society (as the EU is presently attempting). Cooperation is a way of reducing uncertainty, but does not require complete integration. There can be regional peace-creating strategies without removing the particularity of the constituent units. Dignity means diversity without discrimination.

This is important, as "cooperation" could be another way of describing exploitation, where one side benefits more from the relationship than the other. Exploitative cooperation can become a seed of conflict, and to structure cooperation so that it is mutually advantageous is likely to be difficult. In a world without central government it is close to impossible to structure cooperation in ways that makes it universally true that all benefit and no one loses, and at the same moment in time. This is also an observation that is valid for an intra-state setting, as well as a challenge to governance. As a result of deliberate policies some areas may benefit, while others may lose. The close "cooperation" that a shared state may imply may in fact reflect domination by some sectors or regions over others; such integration is likely to lead to continuous friction and, eventually, a desire to break away from either those benefiting from the arrangement (not wanting to share with the others) or those losing (seeing the situation as unfair and biased). Thus the logic of separatism/liberation that we have pointed to is an integral part of what peacebuilding as well as victory consolidation has to deal with. Autonomy, independence, and reduced integration may be ways to establish dignity. If this can be done in peaceful ways, it is likely to be another route to quality peace. It is as legitimate as the one of integration. A generic definition of quality peace also has to include the possibility of the parties terminating their relationship.

Thus academically the definitions of peacebuilding as well as quality peace remain wider than the operative ones of the practitioners and social engineers. There are valid practical considerations for limiting the concept of peacebuilding to intra-state conditions after a war. It is more possible to handle, as the states constitute the basic units of the UN system, international law, and international transactions. However, even so, attention to inter-state and regional affairs is important and should not be underestimated. Peacebuilding cannot be an isolated activity, even less so in today's highly interconnected world. What happens in Afghanistan affects distant United States as well as neighboring China. Events in Sri Lanka, Pakistan, Iraq, Southern Africa, or Latin America influence diasporas residing in North America and Europe. What happens in Burma and Bangladesh has an impact on peoples in Indonesia and Australia. Indeed, one of the most diverse peace missions presently in operation is the international naval flotilla that protects the shipping lanes through the Bay of Aden and the Indian Ocean from pirates based in Somalia. Seemingly "distant" waters have become a common concern.

As we have made clear, peacebuilding refers to concerted efforts after a war that has been ended through a peace deal. The concept stands in an uneasy relationship to war itself. If countries were building peace without having recently been at war, would this not constitute peacebuilding? Galtung's definition does not have the element of "post-conflict" in it. Peacebuilding is then a general reconstruction of society so that it will remain at peace with itself and with the surrounding world, whether or not it has recent experiences of war, coups, rebellions, genocide, repression, or other forms of systematic violence. However, very few countries are without either of these experiences. Sweden most recently fought a war in 1809 with Russia and an armed conflict in 1814 with Norway. It is a uniquely long period. Does it contain elements of a peacebuilding strategy? One could argue that. The country at the same time went through a peaceful transformation from an authoritarian monarchy to a democratic welfare state, providing more dignity to the individuals and reasonable parliamentary barriers against new wars (as seen in the opposition to a possible war with Norway when it unilaterally broke with Sweden in 1905). It also moved from an agricultural society to a leading industrial nation, where it became more valuable to be an Executive Director or a Director General than a Major General. There was a shift in structural conditions as well as in values of life. Thus most countries will have an interest in peacebuilding, whether or not they have a very recent experience of war. To most people, war is a traumatic and violent encounter. For some states, it is part of their national—and often distant—history, but for half the countries of the world today, it is a very recent experience.

Galtung uses the Nordic countries as an example of inter-state peacebuilding, and their recent war experiences among each other date back to the early 19th century. Their cooperation may have less to do with a history of war and more with the increasing commonality of being geographically peripheral and subject to similar pressures from stronger powers. Their cooperation may in fact have been a preemptive strategy to avoid future entanglements with major actors rather than a post-conflict strategy reconciling previous wars. Nevertheless it has a lot to say about peacebuilding, under conditions when states are similar in strength, can easily communicate with one another, share many values, and trade closely. For instance, cooperation included a currency union that lasted for several decades, and partly explains why these three countries (Denmark, Norway, and Sweden) still cling to their national krona, in spite of pressures to join the euro zone. It was once tried.

The experience of the European Union is another example frequently cited, being closer to a conscious post-conflict peacebuilding effort, albeit under other labels. Actually, in the terminology developed here, it is more a matter of victory consolidation, at least in its early phases. There had been two wars and the engineers behind European integration obviously wanted to find ways to prevent this from repeating itself. At the same time, as in the Scandinavian context, it had a *Realpolitik* dimension: The Western European countries were pushed together to face the threat from the Soviet bloc and the dangers of a nuclear war. It was not conflict prevention, as it did not aim at dealing directly with that threat, but community building to be stronger against the shared enemy. In a sense these two efforts (the Nordic and the European ones) were as much strategies of deterrence and unity against possible future threats as of post-conflict reconciliation.

The intra-state peacebuilding efforts that are focused on today by the international community are markedly different from the Nordic and European examples. Contemporary cases build on a peace agreement, which often has involved sizable international engagement (with third parties, peacekeepers, sanctions, etc.) and may include international understandings of what is a "good," "positive" peace (respect for human rights, dealing with war crimes issues, etc.). The former warring parties may remain as political actors but are now expected to act within a shared framework and no longer be polarized against each other. Rules have been shaped for the conduct of future disputes and conflicts.

The peace agreements since 1989 are—in some ways—pacts between former warring actors, committing themselves to construct a state, a society, a relationship, and/or basic policies together. As this was not their reason for engaging in conflict, it means both (or all) sides have to adjust their goals to new conditions. There are likely to be actors who will not easily accommodate to this turn of events. In the early literature, such actors were often termed "spoilers," as their primary ambition was seen to undermine or dilute the agreements (Stedman 1997, Stedman 1998). Later such vocabulary has been avoided or not been seen as sufficiently precise (Höglund 2008). To many actors, the peace agreement is the second best outcome, compared to the original hope for a decisive victory. These actors may not necessarily be happy about the post-conflict situations and may yearn for an opportunity to continue the battle until the "root cause" of the conflict has been removed. To have them also participate in a conscious effort of peacebuilding aimed at preventing exactly this may not be without problems. This means that peacebuilding is not only an effort to prevent war; it also aims at keeping actors from winning, at least by military means. In fact, building the rules of conduct, including for political change, is one of the chief goals of peacebuilding. Thus it is not surprising to find that postwar situations are conflict-ridden. Perhaps the best one can hope for is that all the actors begin to see their disagreements as political rivalries rather than military battles, and that the previous war is replaced by mutually regulated ways of continuing the conflict. Reformulating a famous edict of Carl von Clausewitz, in these circumstances peace becomes the continuation of war by other means. That in itself may prevent future wars, if the "peace" that is built is reasonably successful, and meets certain quality standards (Clausewitz 1832, Clausewitz 1984). This is also the motto of this book. Instead of Thomas Hobbes' "*bellum omnium contra omnes*" or "the war of all against war" which necessitates one centralized power to achieve peace (Hobbes [1651] 1991), the present work points to a way of achieving everybody's peace with everybody, or *pax omnium inter omnes* (Wallensteen 2008a).

1.3 Victory, World Order, and Quality Peace

The joint efforts of building peace from a peace agreement in an internal conflict differ markedly from what is likely to happen after a victory. Victory means that one side takes power with armed action, imposes its preferred policy, rewards its supporters and, often, does not deal with the followers of the opponents in an integrative way. Their fate may in fact be severe. As the war is a struggle over power, and as one side wins, it means this side is in a superior position and believes it is able to impose whatever policy change it wants. It is also a radically different outcome for the international community. The external allies of a victorious side are likely to celebrate; they now expect some "return" on their "investment." The international friends of the losers are likely to lose more than a cause: They end up in an uneasy relationship to the victors (be they the incumbent regime that has defeated a rebel movement, or a rebel movement that has taken over control of the country, or a government that has prevailed in an inter-state confrontation). Victory, in that way, is unsettling for a series of relationships. In fact, much peacemaking and peacebuilding may stem from exactly this fact: It may appear "better" for regional or international order if nobody wins a protracted and costly war. This was a logic that existed during the Cold War, when East and West could sustain conflicts in Afghanistan, in Angola, between Iran and Iraq, in Central America, and in Indochina with this ambition. It was more important to deny the other side a victory than ending the war. The result was devastating for the countries concerned. It was also a cynical approach to conflict, life, and liberty.[11] In times when such major power strategic concerns are less significant, there may be a preference for having wars end in negotiations stemming from a perceived stalemate.

Nevertheless, victories do occur. It is important to analyze how the international community deals with them. We would expect the approach to be different from outcomes building on a peace agreement. The pattern of victory and the following consolidation period vary in interesting ways. Victories may, in fact, be more diverse than peacebuilding efforts. A quick overview demonstrates this:

- In the post-Cold War era one of the first victories was the one in Ethiopia and Eritrea, where the rebels took over and divided the country into two states (1991). Thus the war was followed by two processes of consolidation, or even nationbuilding. But then there was a war again, between the same actors, but this time both being states (1998–2000).

- In Afghanistan, the Pakistan-supported Taliban rebels won in 1996, imposed their rule, allowed al-Qaeda to take up a base, and thus came into conflict with the United States, particularly after September 11, 2001. The regime was defeated by the internationally assisted Northern Alliance in late 2001. A protracted period of a different form of victory consolidation followed, as did a renewed conflict with regrouped Taliban fighters.

- The United States occupied Iraq in 2003 in an inter-state war that removed the government and captured the leader, Saddam Hussein, who was hanged some years later. The United States withdrew its regular troops by 2010, after a national government had been formed under a semblance of democratic procedures, in a period of war and victory consolidation. By 2014 tensions had again resulted in an intensified challenge from a new rebel group, ISIS, based in the estranged Sunni communities of both Iraq and Syria. ISIS simultaneously challenged two governments and also the two states. It led to renewed commitments to Iraq from Western and Arab states.

- In Sri Lanka the government defeated the Tamil Tiger rebels in 2009, thus preventing the creation of a separate Tamil state in parts of the island. The leader was killed and an uncertain period followed for the sizable Tamil minority population. The government did not allow international human rights investigations.

- The winner of the presidential elections in Côte d'Ivoire won a short armed conflict in 2011 to be able to take up his seat. The captured predecessor was sent to the International Criminal Court in The Hague and a period of victory consolidation followed.

- In August 2011 rebels drove Muammar Gadaffi from the capital and, in effect, from power in Libya. Gadaffi was killed in October. A first election took place in 2012, consolidating the victory but still not bringing stability to the country. After a couple of years the country appeared fragmented with different groups controlling different parts, with no effective central government.

The review demonstrates that victories have been consolidated by local allies taking over power from the international intervener. However, this will affect the legitimacy of the new power holders (for instance, in present-day Afghanistan, Iraq, Côte d'Ivoire, and Libya). The consolidation process seems to require internal legitimacy, which is less of a challenge, one might surmise, in a victory based on internal resources (as exemplified by Ethiopia and Eritrea after 1991 and Sri Lanka after 2009). Even so, international efforts may have been crucial for many of these outcomes (delivery of weapons, finding exits for the incumbent, etc.).

It is remarkable to note that in much of the peacebuilding literature, the victory option has rarely been considered explicitly.[12] "Victory" may not even be listed in the book index. However, victory is the most obvious alternative to peacebuilding. It poses the question if the peace approach is a "better" option in terms of making quality peace. Obviously the international community often believes so, as it engages itself to find peace agreements. But we have already seen some examples of internationally supported victories. Critics of international peacebuilding practice may still not argue for a victorious outcome. The critics may prefer to see a shift in peacebuilding strategies from one set of measures to another, where a basic stalemate is maintained or gradually evaporates. Thus a particularly pertinent question for this book is this issue, which can be put in the following way: Is internationally supported peacebuilding more effective in building quality peace than the consolidation of victory by one side? This means setting the marks very high for strategies of peacebuilding as well as victory consolidation. We would expect that the negotiated ending to a war would result in a different set of postwar actions by governments and the international community than the military victory. Thus peacebuilding can be juxtaposed to victory consolidation.

In the study of inter-state conflicts, victory is a more typical concern, and how it affects the period after war. Thus there is more to build on in this regard, although developments are often understood in terms of distribution of power, and rarely with regard to peacebuilding aspects. The connection to world order is, however, often close.[13]

This leads us to a number of additional assertions. First, are the strategies applied in peacebuilding strikingly different from those used in victory consolidation? Second, is it possible to specify which strategies are the more effective in preventing recurrence of war? Third, will the strategies result in relations that meet the three criteria of quality peace—that is, dignity, security, and predictability? However, this also has to be seen in the larger international context and whether it is conducive to the prevention of war recurrence or not, making the existing world order an important dimension. This means that we may now add a fourth question: Does it matter under which historical period (or order) the war ending takes place? We will explore this in the following section.

As we will see in section 1.4, there is considerable academic discussion on peacebuilding, not the least whether the efforts by the international community can be seen as "liberal" or not, and what the alternatives could be (Richmond 2006, Paris 2010, Joshi et al. 2014). For the most part, peacebuilding concerns have been central only in the post-Cold War period. Thus there is a similarity in that this discussion refers to the same, particular world conditions or, as we would like to label it here, world order. It is expressed well in the formulation "liberal" peacebuilding. During the post-Cold War period there has been a predominance of liberal thinking in international affairs in general. The international market forces have been unleashed in an unprecedented manner, not least with the new market opportunities in formerly "closed" parts of the world, such as Russia, China, India, and South America, as well as parts of Africa. Investments for exports have also resulted in domestic economic growth but, at the same time, global and local inequalities have increased. There is also an increase in the number of democracies, and multiparty politics have gradually become the international norm for internal affairs. Particularly important in this context, there has been a concern for humanitarian conditions in situations of war, repression, and genocide. The perspective on war and the political use of violence in general has changed.

Thus it also seems important to pay attention to the type of world order. This relates particularly to the relationships between major powers and their impact on the national or local conflicts. We will introduce this global perspective in chapters 6 and 7, to demonstrate the complexities in which quality peace is being constructed. What happens on the ground in one conflict will be impacted by the surrounding world and, to a more limited extent, will also have an impact on global developments. The most important issue, then, is to ask what types of world order there are and what they mean for the building of quality peace. For the most part these questions, as well as the others mentioned in this chapter, will be addressed by studying the literature to ascertain the state of the art of the discipline. However, some of the questions require original work that will also be included in this volume.

1.4 Perspectives on Peace after War

The experience of wars and peacebuilding efforts since 1989 has sparked a vast scholarly and policy-oriented debate. The investments in peacebuilding have been heavy, and one may legitimately ask if the taxpayers footing the bills have received value for their money. Why should Swedes maintain international efforts in Liberia or Americans support peace agreements in Burundi? If the efforts succeed it may suffice but the reports are many on the breakdown of peace and the restart of conflicts. Thus the "investments" seem lost. Indeed there is truth in such assertions. A number of peace agreements have failed and wars do reignite. It may suggest that the peacemaking task was "hopeless" from the beginning. In a destructive and protracted war the chance of peace is often worth the effort and the price. But more likely the question will be asked if the "right" strategies were used, and the errors are likely to be highlighted. Some voices, however, would advocate nonintervention or even intervention on a particular side to contribute to victory and, hopefully, a lasting peace. Thus the debate becomes intense, and has generated at least three basic perspectives on peacebuilding in literature and practice. Only some of them bring in the issue of victory and victory consolidation.

Let us first, however, note the lack of the systematic collection of information on the postwar conditions that can be seen in the literature. The *Uppsala Conflict Data Program* (UCDP) contains a wealth of information on conflict dynamics, including the resort to negotiations and the conclusion of peace agreements. Some attention is also given to analysis of the peace agreements (Harbom et al. 2006, Högbladh 2006, Högbladh 2012). However, the deeper analysis will require additional information on the implementation of the agreements. This is the task that the Kroc Institute's *Peace Accord Matrix* (PAM) (Joshi and Darby 2013) has set out to do, by including a large set of peace agreements and some fifty variables on issues addressed in these agreements, and by following them for a period of ten years. This is going to be a most significant tool for the analysis of peacebuilding and quality peace. In doing so, the analysis can build on the three perspectives, but also bring them together, as they may not be entirely contradictory. The differences may be more a matter of emphasis.

First, there is research based on the idea that the fighting sides are rational actors making deliberate, calculated decisions to militarize a conflict that may otherwise continue on an unarmed, nonviolent level. A war is expected to determine a distribution of power between the belligerents. As many wars since the end of the Cold War have been protracted, it means that the parties arrive at situations that they had not anticipated, and so they have to negotiate with the opposing side. Numerous post-conflict situations, in other words, are in an uneasy balance between groups that may still have reasons to restart the conflict at a moment in time which is conducive for victory. Peacebuilding strategies emerging from such considerations have to focus on finding ways in which former belligerents are unable to restart the conflict. This is most appropriately done through institutional change. New societal structures are at the same time strong enough to prevent a new outbreak of war and valuable enough for the former belligerents to give them the opportunity they need to pursue their goals, without starting the war again.

This first strand of research deals with *policies for institutional change and development*. Which are the *strategies* that would enhance the role of state structures and find an agreeable way of representation and making the state capable of effective action? The construction of state machinery and democratically inspired forms of government is central to this. The idea is that actors will always have choices and only when the strength of the structures are such that they cannot break out will they also remain within the framework: The costs of challenging the existing structures will be greater than the costs of starting a new war. If all (or most) actors benefit from the new institutional arrangements, then there is less incentive for challenging them, not the least as the actors may fear to become more isolated and marginalized. This is basic in arguments such as the "institutionalization before liberalism" that has been advocated by Roland Paris, building on his analysis of a set of peacebuilding experiences in the 1990s. His seminal work, *At War's End*, will thus have to be scrutinized in some detail in the following chapter, where a reanalysis of his work yields interesting results. This is peacebuilding as institution building— finding checks and balances, rule of law, and ways of representation, at some stage leading to democracy. The same, of course, would apply to wars that end in victory. Also in this case there is a need for institution reform, legal systems, possibly also elements of democracy.

This leads us to a second perspective that deals with conflict dynamics itself. A trigger to conflicts is the insecurity they generate, as outlined earlier in this chapter. Conflicts are formed by actors with incompatible goals and with sufficient resources to create their own military means (building small or large armies, creating bases, purchasing of arms) to pursue their goals. The disbanding of such assets is often a first element in peacebuilding strategies and probably also in victory consolidation. In a post-civil war situation, for instance, the government has been part of the conflict. Rebels rose against that government for a particular reason. They are not likely to trust those institutions unless they are in (sufficient) control of them, in some form of power sharing, representation, or other way.

The core of most conflict is a *security* dilemma. Actors gain support to organize conflicts, not just by intimidating people, but also by building on an idea of defending one group against another. Intimidation, in fact, can be selective, to achieve just that. Fear of others sparks defensive measures that the others may perceive as preparations for conflict, and thus take similar measures to protect themselves. Relationships can deteriorate quickly. The central issue in this perspective is for peacebuilding to find ways to deal with the underlying security concerns. That not only includes the disarming of groups or giving their leaders influence in society. It also has to do with solving some underlying dynamics of conflict, creating new frameworks for viewing the relationships in the future. It may, in fact, mean empowering local leadership to take responsibility, not reducing the role of such leadership. This is *peacebuilding through the creation of systems that enhance security* in ways that yields local control, dignity, and predictability.

A third line of thought emphasizes *economic structures and issues of development*. It builds on the idea that the conflicts largely start from economic considerations, sometimes captured in the word "greed" rather than "grievance," although the debate now has moved beyond that simple dichotomy (Ballentine and Sherman 2003). In his best-selling 2007 book *The Bottom Billion*, Paul Collier has popularized economic concerns and "conflict traps" in which countries may end up. A complex interplay of factors—such as conflicts, natural resources, geographical features, and bad governance—tends to trap countries into continuous repetition of conflict. This results in a distortion of societies away from the needs of the majority to meet only the desires of the few. Collier integrates greed with grievance. The net result is his observation that approximately one billion people are located in around fifty countries which are stagnating, while other parts of the world have seen economic growth during an extended period of time. Thus creating the social and political conditions for sustained economic growth, will, in Collier's perspective, be a necessary approach. Transparency, national control over revenues, and use of resources in a responsible way are all ingredients in such an economy-building policy. One may say that the creation of political leadership that is self-confident enough to engage in the world market for the benefit of national development is what is required. This perspective has less to say on institutional constraints on belligerents or finding confidence-building measures. It is more an argument that economic growth under particular conditions will generate satisfaction for a sufficient number of actors for them not to restart a conflict. It certainly gives a role to the international community, particularly in the field of security provision, something we will return to below. It does not neglect the aspect of democracy, but points to its weaknesses (Collier 2009).

Although some economists have objected to such argument, notably William Easterly (2006), this is more on the basis of critique of development aid through governments rather than questioning the needs for economic policies that reduce the danger of another war. By reducing the strength of government, Easterly argues, and in a corresponding way increasing the role of private, "homegrown" initiatives—finding the entrepreneurs—economic growth can be generated. This is probably true, but it does not help us to know what to do to contain the warlords that still may be around. Indeed many warlords are happy to portray themselves as entrepreneurs, and they do have some of the same features: taking risk, creating networks, and generating income, but often far outside the boundaries of morality and legality. The problem is who gains from what kind of investment. The dilemma, in other words, is that there is a need for a stronger state at the same time that there is a need for freedom for the entrepreneurs. Finding the balance that will generate both is the real problem. Together the work of Collier, Easterly, and others provides us with a third perspective: *peace through economy building*, finding the routes to a self-sustainable economy that generate opportunity for a life in security and dignity. In fact, to these political economists, the outcome of the war is less of a concern. Whether the policies are pursued as peacebuilding or victory consolidation does not matter. The important dimension is the construction of a functioning postwar economy.

As mentioned, the three perspectives are not contradictory. For instance, Collier concludes that governments in the Bottom Billion countries are incapable as well as unwilling to act in a nonpartisan way. Thus an international presence for a long period of time is necessary: "Both sending and recipient governments should expect this presence to last for around a decade and must commit to it" (Collier 2007: 177). This is a dramatic conclusion and not likely to be popular on either side. But it demonstrates that institution-building is part of the equation, as are international guarantees for security. However, we do not know how this works when we deal with victory consolidation.

An example will help to illustrate the arguments. The international community has been engaged for nearly two decades in Bosnia-Herzegovina. Indeed, violence has ceased; the actors act under the rules agreed in the Dayton Accord from 1995. The international presence has been heavy. The armies of the parties have been reduced. An infusion of outside capital has led to reconstruction and economic gains. Still, it appears to be a dependent growth. It rests on the continued international presence and the willingness of donor countries to continue international support. Recent studies show that the feelings of insecurity among the groups have not been reduced. The social, cultural, and political distances between them remain considerable. The three constituent national identities have been cemented rather than dissolved. The de facto separation imposed by the war has continued to predominate in the postwar lives of the population. There is no common understanding of what the war was all about. There appears to be only one point of convergence: All groups object to the way the international control has been exerted. Certainly there are some variations, but the consensus is striking (Kostic 2007). These findings provide a dramatic challenge to the post-conflict peacebuilding strategies. Bosnia-Herzegovina, after all, is a prime example of international achievements. The war was stopped in 1995 after three years. An agreement was worked out by the international actors, mostly the United States. American troops were in place for a period. The EU built an entire program for the integration of former Yugoslav countries into the Union. The costs for the non-war situation are staggering. Still the world hesitates: Can it withdraw or will that result in renewed fighting? How to transcend the security dilemma in such a situation?

Interestingly Collier in his later writing makes this into an important point. The provision of security is necessary, even in the form of a guarantee against coups, for instance, to democratically elected heads of state (Collier 2009). This is very much in line with this book. This means that the postwar setting can be seen from three perspectives: strategies for institution-building, security-building, and economy-building. Although this categorization is drawn from the literature on peacebuilding, it largely also applies to victory consolidation. In security building, the key is the relationship between winners and vanquished, a dynamic where the conditions after a war might be challenged. Thus, the dimensions of quality peace will be of assistance in formulating the conditions for preventing the recurrence of war, whether the war ended through a negotiated settlement or victory.

1.5 Organizing this Book

Now we are equipped with three particular topics on peace in the aftermath of war: how the efforts relate to security, to the dignity of those involved, and to predictability, the elements of quality peace. In addition we have pointed to three chief concerns for overcoming the dynamics of war, namely by building institutions (including democracy), security (to transcend the security dilemma), and an economy that can be sustained. These three sets of literature are presented in some depth in chapter 2. In chapter 3 we face the question of quality peace after a civil war, while chapter 4 takes up internal territorial conflicts and chapter 5 asks questions for inter-state relations. Chapter 6 deals with the world order dimension and chapter 7 adds the international institutions into the equation, while chapter 8 brings together what seem to be reasonable paths to quality peace, hoping to stimulate policy as well as research.

CHAPTER 2

Quality Peace and Contemporary Scholarship

2.1 Peace in Post-Cold War Conditions

As shown in chapter 1, an important concern in the search for international peace and security since the end of the Cold War has been to identify working strategies in postwar conditions. By now there are practical experiences and academic analyses that shed light on what has been done and what can be learned. Still there is no consolidated knowledge to draw on. Scholarly inquiry is going in different directions, without systematically responding to pertinent challenges. The same seems to be true for the practice, although some evolution can be seen, for example, in the work of the UN Peacebuilding Commission. There is still a need for a reasonable manual for the strategies that are deemed most optimal. There is a need, as well, for "best practices" drawing on insights from practitioners and academics.

This is even more marked when we approach the second of the two war outcomes that we have identified: victory consolidation. There is no book with a title that includes these two words. There is literature on the consolidation of democracy and regimes (Alexander 2002; Diamond et al. 2010; Hadenius 1997; and Pridham 1990), but the victory discussed has seldom to do with war. An exception is the work by Monica Toft, to which consequently we pay particular attention (Toft 2010a, Toft 2010b). There is little study of what victors actually do after a victory; there are anecdotal information and case studies, but there is not much statistical analysis.

A third key notion in this book is "world order." Again there is a literature that is specific, and in particular with a focus on global strategic concerns. However, rarely is it connected to particular war patterns and, most notably, not to the ways societies and relations are (re)constructed under different world order conditions. The concept has a ring to it of status quo and power politics (Kissinger 2014). Matters of hegemony and balance of power are in the forefront, sometimes also institutions (Ikenberry 2001). For example, the wealth of data in the Correlates of War project, covering wars since 1816, would invite a discussion of variations in orders, but it has only begun (Sarkees and Wayman 2010, Wallensteen 2011a, Wallensteen 2012). This means that, for now, only with respect to peacebuilding is there a comprehensive litera- ture directly relevant for a discussion on quality peace, as we could understand from Table 1.1. This explains the bias of this chapter toward peacebuilding studies. However, the purpose of the following review is not only to evaluate the state of the field but also to draw conclusions that are helpful in approach- ing quality peace. Thus, we will conclude chapter 2 with ideas on indicators and possible measures, some of which will be used in the rest of the book.

No doubt the peacebuilding literature demonstrates that something of great relevance for international peace and security has changed. A first indication is the large number of peace agreements. Table 2.1 brings together pertinent in- formation stored in the Uppsala Conflict Data Program (UCDP) conflict data- base on this topic. As can be seen in this table, the record includes twenty-eight peace agreements in the latter part of the Cold War and 178 in the period that has followed. Although the latter is longer, it is still safe to say that reaching agreement between warring parties has become a completely new and central task for negotiators, foreign ministries, international organizations, and non- governmental bodies. Here is a first sign that world order does matter: There is a difference in emphasis on how to terminate wars during and after the Cold War period. Negotiations are now a more common way of concluding ongo- ing wars. Indeed, the study of peacebuilding, as we saw in chapter 1, is related to actual settlement activity. During the Cold War period, there was a focus on victory by one's own side or the prevention of victory for the other side. Also, as can be seen in Table 2.2, the number of conflicts has been somewhat higher for the post-Cold War period, which makes this even more pronounced (Themnér and Wallensteen 2014). Many more conflicts saw attempts at peace agreements, but there were also experiences in conflicts of a series of accords interspersed with wars, in the best of circumstances approaching protracted peace processes. Not shown in Table 2.1 but possible to retrieve from the same database, we can note that there was at least one peace agreement in fifty-two armed conflicts in the post-Cold War period (40% of all conflicts) compared to twelve in the Cold War era (about 14%). As the total number of peace agree- ments is 206, we can also deduce that there are many conflicts with repeated attempts at forging negotiated endings. There is a failure rate. It is one of the reasons for the scholarly and policy interest; there is an intellectual and practi- cal problem to be solved at the same time.

Important in our particular context is the observation that the frequency of peace agreements varies between the three categories of conflict that are

Table 2.1

Peace Agreements and Types of Conflict 1975–2010

Type of conflict	1975–1988			1989–2010		
	Number	Peace agreements	Number of conflicts with peace agreement	Number	Peace agreements	Number of conflicts with peace agreement
Inter-state armed conflict	16	14	3	8	4	4
Intra-state conflict over government	40	9	5	60	139	28
Intra-state conflict over territory	31	5	4	65	35	20
Overall number	87	28	12	133	178	52

Source: UCDP customized report, 2011; website: ucdp.uu.se.

identified by UCDP and reproduced in Table 2.1. For the full period, 148 of the peace agreements dealt with internal conflicts over government (nine in the first period, 139 in the second). These situations can thus be seen as the cases where the peacebuilding issues are the most difficult and the most acute. Another forty agreements concerned territorial conflicts inside existing states (state formation conflicts—that is situations where the basic incompatibility is about control over territory within a state) and eighteen were concluded in armed conflicts between internationally recognized states. As the number of internal conflicts over territory and government is roughly equal throughout the period, it means that considerably more peacemaking energy has been devoted to internal conflict dealing with matters of governance. It suggests that the dynamics of these conflicts differ from those of inter-state and internal disputes. However, the focus in much peacebuilding literature is on internal armed conflicts. These data justify that particular focus, but also point to the importance of not neglecting other types of conflict. That gives a reason for discussing them separately, as will be done in chapters 3, 4, and 5.

The most obvious and radical alternative outcome to peace deals is victory: one side wins, the other is defeated. The agenda after such a war will be different, as it is no longer a matter of negotiations among the fighting parties.

Table 2.2

Victory and Type of Armed Conflict, 1975–2010

Type of conflict	1975–1988			1989–2010		
	Number	Victories	Number of conflicts with victory	Number	Victories	Number of conflicts with victory
Inter-state armed conflict	16	5	5	8	2	2
Intra-state conflict over government	40	26	20	60	32	23
Intra-state conflict over territory	31	1	1	65	11	11
Overall number	87	32	26	133	45	36

Source: UCDP conflict database, customized report.

The point of a victory is, of course, for the victor to take all power and give no role for the losing party in governance of society. It means that only one side has a say in the postwar situation, the victorious party, and the path the victor chooses will also be the way a state moves for a considerable period of time. Table 2.2 gives us pertinent information on this aspect of the termination of armed conflict.

Table 2.2 shows the number of victories in the same categories of armed conflicts for the same period as for the peace agreements in Table 2.1. Victories in the post-Cold War period occur in thirty-six of 133 armed conflicts—that is in 27% of all conflicts, compared to the latter part of the Cold War with 30% of the armed conflicts. This is only a small difference between the two periods. Victory has not ceased to be an important outcome. However, taking Tables 2.1 and 2.2 together, we may note that peace agreements have become more common in the second period, going from twelve out of eighty-seven (14%) to fifty-two out of 133 (39%), while the rate of victory remained the same. This also means that in the Cold War years close to 60% of all conflicts were protracted, without any form of ending. This is a number that is down to about 40% after 1989.[1] Certainly this underscores the interest in peacemaking and peacebuilding in recent years. Victory is not a novelty, and thus has not received the same attention.

These trends are supported in studies using other definitions of conflict. For example, Toft (2010a) finds that negotiated endings have increased and in the 1990s constituted 41% of all endings, equal to the number of victories. To this should probably be added ceasefire agreements, which constituted the remaining share (18%). Looking at conflict episodes since 1946, Kreutz reports that until 1989 peace agreements were 8.4% of all terminations and victories 58.2%. Since 1990 the percentage shares are 18.4% and 13.6% respectively (Kreutz 2010: 246). Negotiations for ending armed conflicts have introduced a new dimension, making the question of the quality of different outcomes a pertinent one.

These results demonstrate the utility of contrasting victory outcomes with peace agreements. It is likely that most actors strive for victory and only reluctantly engage in peace agreements. Thus the dream of victory may persist even if the conflict is ended by an agreement. An agreement can be regarded as a stepping stone for some. Others may see the agreement as a measure to prevent the other from winning, and thus be a preferred outcome. To many actors the possibility of victory is important, and in particular what might happen after a victory. That makes it remarkable to find that the literature on peacebuilding has given victory and its consolidation a minimal role. The argument in the present book is that its importance is underestimated, that such outcomes will generate different conditions from those of peace agreements, and that this has effects, in particular for the quality of peace and for recurrence of war. This further underscores the importance of comparing different types of post-conflict efforts. The narrow path of peacebuilding is not only one taken to avoid a return to war after a conflict because the sides of an agreement are dissatisfied with the accords and their implementation. The challenge is that, to some actors, a victory may remain more desirable. Even if a peace agreement is properly implemented, groups may still prefer to restart the war, arguing that only a complete victory will yield a peace with the traits that party advocates. Furthermore, this may be attractive to outside actors. Thus we have to observe whether a victory actually results in a postwar situation that is more compatible to the criteria of quality peace than is the one following a peace agreement.

Let us proceed to consider the literature and what can be learned from it for our purposes.

2.2. Postwar Conditions in Contemporary Writing

In chapter 1 it was noted that there are three sets of literature that are particularly significant for this work. First, there are studies on international peacebuilding experiences, in the form of peacekeeping missions, international aid programs, and programs launched under headings such as peacebuilding. The concern in this literature is on the postwar period, rather than the causes of a war as such. A typical question is: Do peacebuilding efforts result in a durable peace? The answer is often given in the form of institutional reforms. Did particular strategies give the result that the initiators expected? Peacebuilding strategies are at the forefront and peacebuilding missions constitute the unit of analysis. A set of authors relates to Roland Paris and his work, which voices a strategic concern in peacebuilding: Which strategies of peacebuilding achieve the goals set by those mandating the various operations? It has an evaluative and critical approach to dominant trends in international peacebuilding strategies. These questions are close to decision-making concerns. It is an actor-oriented approach where policy options are evaluated. A result may be suggestions for alternative strategies. There is, in other words, a normative foundation in this work. It deals with policy choices and easily leads into a discussion on desirable conditions from a normative and ethical point of view.[2] Here these studies are brought together under the heading of strategic analyses (Section 2.3).

A second set of authors builds on quantitative research traditions, sometimes with accompanying case studies. The series of works by Michael Doyle and Nicholas Sambanis is typical in their use of statistical work and a large number of cases (large-N approaches). Often political variables dominate in this tradition, many of them relating to security. This approach is more systemic, identifying variables that statistically correlate with success and failure in peacebuilding. The countries with or without peacebuilding missions are selected for the study, providing for a broader comparability than the first approach. The methodology warrants labeling these studies "systematic," alluding to an emphasis on selecting a broader collection of cases than those just involved in international peacebuilding efforts. In effect, victory outcomes are also covered, although seldom in focus. There might also be illustrations in the form of case studies (Section 2.4).

There is a third group considered in relevant scholarship. It deals with structural causes of the recurrence of war. There is no concern with the decisions that led to the wars or with the actors themselves. The focus is on structural conditions that foster the start and return of war: By understanding the causes appropriate peacebuilding policies can be inferred. Peacebuilding strategies emerge as implications of research results. Many of these studies have a basis in economic theory and they are almost entirely quantitative in nature. Leading authors in this group are researchers associated with Paul Collier. The empirically based conclusions also form the basis for policy implications. As the spotlight is on economic and political structures rather than individual missions or countries, these studies can be labeled structural, where war is a reflection of instability or state failure (Section 2.5).

Remarkably the three types of literature hardly intersect. For example, in his recent critical and informative evaluation of the field, Roger Mac Ginty (2011) deals entirely with the discussions initiated by Roland Paris and followed up by Oliver Richmond (2009) and others critiquing the notion of a "liberal peace." Mac Ginty raises new and interesting challenges to this field. However, there is not a single reference to the work associated with scholars such as Michael Doyle, Nicholas Sambanis, Paul Collier, James Fearon, and Monica Toft, although they address the same issues. Similarly in the edited volume on peacebuilding by Tom Keating and W. Andy Knight (2004), there is no reference to the systematic or structural analyses available at the time. Not unexpectedly the same is true the other way around. Apart from courteous references to the contributions of Roland Paris, there is seldom a deeper look into the comparative literature by the researchers using quantitative methodologies. There are probably many reasons for this state of affairs, one being the methodological divide (comparative vs. statistical analysis), another shifting disciplinary backgrounds (economics vs. political science vs. peace research), but perhaps also different understandings of what is important in world affairs. A focus on political variables, such as state institutions, authority, and legitimacy, implies a particular concern with power and its distribution as necessities for change. A concentration on economic variables, such as resources, fiscal policies, and development strategies, may suggest a basic concern with economic development as a major way for improving living conditions. From a peace research perspective, however, all these approaches seem equally valid and should all be considered.

This debate deals with civil war situations. There has been very little discussion on peacebuilding in inter-state relations, although many would be willing to acknowledge the importance for one country of what happens in another. There are spillover effects from wars in the form of refugees, arms flows, smuggling, and destruction of infrastructure, to name a few consequences. Countries that are landlocked have particular difficulties in developing and securing peace. However, the specific dangers of inter-state conflict have been left aside from the discussion. A partial explanation can be found in Tables 2.1 and 2.2: The inter-state armed conflicts have been few since the end of the Cold War. Still several of them have been highly threatening to international peace and security, notably India vs. Pakistan, or extremely destructive with long-term consequences for an entire region, as exemplified by the war between Ethiopia and Eritrea from 1998 to 2000. Implications of these conflicts for peacebuilding have not taken center stage. For that we have to go to an entirely different literature, the one on the causes of inter-state wars, where in particular the work on democratic peace is relevant but also the studies on the role of territory as well as external intervention. Thus we will scrutinize this literature and relate it to the concerns for quality peace (Section 2.6).

Perhaps unexpectedly the notion of "liberal" peacebuilding connects some approaches to world order issues. The discussion that has surrounded the early work of Roland Paris seems more often to concern "liberal" policies in general, rather than the specific peacebuilding situations or strategies. Similarly Paul Collier has met criticism associated with his World Bank affiliation or his emphasis on the state, rather than the peacebuilding implications as such. Many of these observations are matters of world order (Section 2.7). The concern here is different: What do these studies suggest in terms of postwar strategies that will enhance quality peace? Furthermore, the literature also suggests possible ways to measure quality peace, something to be pursued throughout the book, starting in section 2.8.

This means that in the following, these approaches to postwar conditions are evaluated with respect to (1) what they define as "success" and "failure"; (2) their classification of conflicts (notably territorial vs. governmental incompatibilities) and its implication for conclusions; (3) whether they bring up the issue of peacebuilding versus victory consolidation, and if that would affect their conclusions; and (4) what they have to say with respect to the criteria for quality peace, as identified here (security, dignity, and predictablity for all segments of society). With these four questions in mind we can now present and discuss the leading empirical contributions to peacebuilding.

2.3 The Strategic Approach: At War's End

It is appropriate to start by revisiting the well-known work of Roland Paris, *At War's End*. Paris works in a traditional style of case studies with comparative elements. There are also other contributions in this approach and they also will be highlighted. Paris's book has become a "must-read" on contemporary peacebuilding; he has continued to write on this and in a later article he points out that his critique of liberal peacebuilding was not meant to discard the importance of liberal measures in general (Paris 2010). Still his work became a starting point for a critique of "liberal" peacebuilding approaches, often focusing on the international dominance in local peace processes resulting in a political adaptation of local efforts to a global capitalist framework.

At War's End was published in 2004 and immediately drew international attention. It raised pertinent issues in the peacebuilding strategies that were applied during the 1990s. In particular, Paris points to the failure of peacebuilding missions he has scrutinized. He finds that this is due to a disregard for the importance of building institutions first and proceeding to democracy promotion later. Democracy, he suggests, in the form of elections, should be referred to a later phase of peacebuilding. Also internationalizing of the economy should wait until institutions are in place.

Paris selects his cases with care, and thus finds eleven comparable cases in the post-Cold War period. He proceeds to add three later cases to demonstrate the utility of his findings (Paris 2004: 61–62). His assessment is that there are two cases of "clear success" (Namibia and Croatia) and two equally "obvious failures" (Angola and Rwanda) (Paris 2004: 151). The remaining cases fall in a broad category in between. We can note that the success rate is low, but so is the failure rate. Let us here concentrate on the clear-cut cases, and relate Paris's analysis to the questions mentioned above (meaning of success, type conflict, peacebuilding vs. victory, and quality peace measurements).

A first difficult issue is how to understand the "success" and "failure" rate. There is no yardstick with which to compare. Possibly the failure rate is high in any international operation, and thus two out of eleven might not be objectionable in a world without a central government. In studies of sanctions success rates often vary between one-fifth and one-third of the cases (Wallensteen and Grusell 2012: 225). There are many reasons why international actions in general would be more likely to fail than, say, domestic government measures. The international bodies do not have the same coercive, legal, and remunerative power as national governments. It may be reasonable to expect a mixed success rate. However, that is something that is politically unacceptable, indeed normatively as well, as it may mean the continuation of violent conditions. Learning from failures may make the failures meaningful. In that regard, Paris does the right thing.

We should also note that the chosen method does not allow for comparison to non-cases—that is, cases where there were no peacebuilding operations. Such a control group would be valuable, and it might have included cases of victory. As indicated in the discussion above on Tables 2.1 and 2.2, there are many situations without clear outcomes. They may enrich the discussion.

However, it is possible to contrast successful and failed cases.[3] Paris identifies success as cases where the conflict has not resumed and there has been reasonable economic and social development. This brings him to two cases from the 1990s: Namibia and Croatia. A reason for the successful endings to the armed conflicts is related to the fact that the opposing actors withdrew (South Africa and Serbia, respectively—see Paris 2004: 153). In Paris's words "international liberalization efforts had a largely positive outcome" in these two cases but in addition they "offered unusually propitious conditions for postconflict stabilization" (Paris 2004: 153). Let us look a little closer at these cases. This is useful as they are also mentioned in other studies and constitute formative experiences for peacebuilding policy and scholarship alike.

The first successful case is the UN mission that resulted in Namibia's independence in 1990 (led by Martti Ahtisaari, later President of Finland and Nobel Peace Prize laureate in 2008). It was a matter of implementing an international agreement negotiated between South Africa, the United States, and the Soviet Union, as part of the unwinding of the Cold War. The Namibia issue had been stalemated for more than forty years when South Africa finally began to accept a solution in line with UN demands. A UN mission (called UNTAG) was mandated to carry out the agreement. There is general agreement that this mission was carried out in a professional way.

The second operation with a "positive" outcome, the one in Croatia, UNTAES, dealt with the Serb-populated areas in East Slavonia that were controlled by Croatia. In 1995 the UN helped negotiate and administer the handing over to Croatian authorities of this territory (in a way that left the Serb population in place; a good account is given by the UN mediator, former Norwegian Minister of Foreign Affairs, Thorvald Stoltenberg, in Stoltenberg 2001). This was, again, regulated in a peace agreement. Following the implementation of the agreements, the two international missions were closed down shortly thereafter. From the UN perspective, these are textbook cases of successful missions: There was an agreement, all leading parties supported them, there were UN troops available, and the missions were accomplished in a reasonable time and without unexpected costs.

Thus we can establish that Paris has singled out cases where there is little disagreement about their success. However, the generalizations from this may be more limited, as will be seen when relating this to the second of the four questions posed, since both these conflicts dealt with territorial issues and the agreements were on the status of the contested territory. Thus they have a significantly different character from the remainder of the cases in the sample. Paris observes this but does not separate them from cases that solely concern governance issues. In terms of success, these cases actually involved less complex peacebuilding challenges. Once it was agreed among the warring parties which of them was to control the territory, there remained few incentives to pursue the conflict. It could have been done, for example, by encouraging internal dissent, but none of them resorted to such strategies.

Admittedly both cases exhibit some governance issues as well. For Namibia it was a matter of building a new government, which also gave a role to the white minority that was fearful of its fate under African majority rule. For the Croatian case this was more challenging, as the Serbs would constitute a minority subject to a more hostile government that it could not influence. Serbia chose not to defend its minority in the neighboring country. However, both Namibia and Croatia remained open societies and the fate of the minorities could be followed from the outside, if need arose, even if not stipulated in the agreements. The governance aspects were less significant for the ending of the conflicts than were the territorial dimensions.

In terms of the third question, the outcomes were negotiated with clear guidelines for the implementation of the agreement. They were not military victories. The UN missions participated in the first round of elections in Namibia before withdrawing. Thus what followed was a peacebuilding mission, not a process of victory consolidating as a result of military superiority. In another sense, of course, it could still be seen as a peacefully gained victory for the opposition. The main opposition, the liberation movement SWAPO (South West Africa People's Organization),[4] expected to win the elections and actually did so. SWAPO formed the new government, and the same party is still in control, twenty-five years later. This may reflect its ability to mobilize its own constituency, but at the same time it has not antagonized other sectors of the society. It has probably helped that the economy has been doing well. Looking at the situation today, the white minority seems still to be safe in the country. Thus Namibia is a case of successfully building peace on an agreement that was implemented with international support. The outcome may have favored the liberation movement, but it was not a militarily achieved victory. Applying the three quality peace criteria—security, dignity, and predictability—post-conflict Namibia scores high. Central, however, was an agreement on the status of the territory, not the peacebuilding mission as such or the economic policies pursued following independence.

Let us turn to Paris's second case. Integrating East Slavonia into Croatia was less rewarding from this perspective. The Serbs became a minority in a highly nationalistic Croatia. It is likely that more Serbs have left Croatia than whites left Namibia. For Paris, as well as for many others working on peacebuilding, the fact that there were no more wars between the same parties and that fairly capable governments were in place would suffice to call this a "positive" outcome. However, if we add the notion of dignity there is possibly a difference: The Serbs have had more to fear and less to win from their inclusion into Croatia than the whites had with respect to Namibia. The democratic principle of majority rule was upheld in both cases, but democracy also involves the issue of the treatment of the minority.

East Slavonia was, like the Namibia settlement, a matter of defining the ownership of the territory. Croatia demanded that sovereignty over East Slavonia. That followed the generally applied principles for dissolving the Yugoslav union by using the administrative borders that existed before the conflict (in the same way that the Namibian solution followed the general principles of decolonization). It was a peaceful transfer of sovereignty, thus making this a case of peacebuilding. It may have worked out better in the long run than anticipated. The accession of Croatia to EU in 2013, and the possibility of Serbia following suit, open new opportunities also for the minority.

The story of these two cases suggests, however, that Paris's main explanation, that international liberalization really worked, is beside the point. The conflicts have not restarted, as the potential belligerents have accepted the new status quo. The government of Serbia did not pursue the issue of the Serbs in Croatia. The government of South Africa did not interfere in Namibia. Both these governments had other concerns. Serbia was engaged in wars, first in Bosnia and later in Kosovo. South Africa concentrated on ending *apartheid*, building democratic rule, and adhering to the decolonization principles. The agreements gained legitimacy and would thus have been difficult to revoke. The policies pursued for domestic development (in Croatia or Serbia, or in Namibia or South Africa) were not a concern of the conflicting parties; they were not an element in the incompatibility and not regulated in the agreement. One may note, however, that all the states turned out to be fairly open societies ("liberal," if one likes that terminology) at the time, and are definitely even more so today. In fact, the theories of democratic peace may have more to say about this. The lack of conflict could be due to increased intra-state and regional transparency as well as the creation of channels for dissent in the domestic societies. Going a step further, the outcomes were also in line with the new world order emerging after the Cold War (see more in chapter 7).

Let us move to the two cases Paris has identified as "obvious failures" (Paris 2004: 151) where the wars restarted and the peacebuilding missions did not accomplish their goals: Angola and Rwanda. They are particularly interesting for the framework applied here, as they are, at the same time, also cases of victory and victory consolidation. They are comparable as both are wars over the control of government, thus being different from the two cases we have just discussed. Also in the history of UN peace operations, they are seen as failures. But they may still have much to say about peacebuilding as well as victory consolidation.

The first failure refers to Angola in the early 1990s, with a fairly large peacekeeping mission and elections that were cut short when the opposition movement UNITA (União Nacional para a Independência Total de Angola, or National Union for the Total Independence of Angola) feared it would lose, and thus restarted the war. By any standard this was a failure of the UN mission. The war went on until 2002, when it was terminated with the killing of UNITA leader Jonas Savimbi. Until that moment, no durable agreement was possible. The actors on both sides (the government made up by MPLA [Movimento Popular de Libertação de Angola, or Popular Movement for the Liberation of Angola] vs. UNITA) were in the conflict for one outcome: victory of one over the other. The war stopped when one side won.

However, in the agreed ending, a capitulation of sorts, the remaining UNITA leadership was allowed to take up positions in the parliament and, in fact, included into the ruling elite. Interestingly they could do this by referring to the revised peace agreement that had been negotiated previously; it actually provided a framework for ending the war, reuniting the country. True, at the time of Paris's research, the peacekeeping effort was a clear-cut failure. But the story did not end there; for example, the peace accords had continued utility. Post-2002 Angola is an interesting case of victory consolidation, where the previous peace process played a role. This is worth some additional consideration.

The initial efforts by the Angolan government pointed to an open-minded approach. The intransigence of UNITA was built on Savimbi's power, and his approach was not shared by the whole leadership. Cooperation was possible once he left the scene. Six years later, in 2008, parliamentary elections were again held, with UNITA as the main opposition party; MPLA received the bulk of the votes. These are late elections by any standard, and perhaps later than would have been advocated by Paris. The inclusiveness may also have been a costly strategy as Angola is regularly cited as one of the world's most corrupt states.[5] In 2010 the parliament changed the constitution, abolishing the presidential elections and stipulating that no president could serve more than two terms. This rule, however, was to take effect when the incumbent's term expired, in effect giving the serving president a chance to rule for another ten years. The victor cemented the victory, but elections were still allowed, and new elections were held in 2012. In reality, we may say, democracy was technically adhered to but in practice manipulated.

Importantly, there was no restart of war, but what was the quality of the peace that had been established? Angola could be said to have gone from "failure" in peacebuilding in one decade to "success" in the next, but then more as a form of victory consolidation. A central issue for future evaluation of quality peace is, for example, the ability of the regime to manage a transition from one leader to another, or even from one party to another. The same leader, Jose Eduardo dos Santos, had, by 2014, been at the helm for thirty-five years, continuously based on the support of MPLA. It is a situation that does not meet the quality peace criteria set up here.

The second case of failure is Rwanda, which saw a sequence of civil war, a peace agreement with international peacebuilding elements, a continued war accompanied by a unique genocide, a French intervention, and in 1994 the victory of one side, the RPF [Rwandan Patriotic Front], dominated by the Tutsi, the identity group that was most targeted during the genocide. The conflict ended in victory for one side and that side remains in control twenty years later. The most recent presidential elections were held in 2010 and the incumbent,

Paul Kagame, was reelected with more than 90% of the votes. Kagame was the leader of RPF that initiated the civil war in 1990, and has thus been critical for Rwandan politics for a quarter of a century.

In Rwanda, as in Angola, the party winning the war has remained firmly in control of the government. The civil war has subsided, but neither country has been without armed conflict since the major war ended. The security situation is still far from satisfactory. Rwanda is continuously and heavily involved in the conflicts in Eastern Congo, and the Angolan government battles a separatist group in the Cabinda enclave, a different and territorial conflict at that. Military expenditures remain high, particularly in Rwanda, where the government in fact continues the same war as in the early 1990s, but now on the neighbor's territory. On democracy scores, both countries are located at the low end.[6] However, both countries enjoy good international relations and Rwanda is sometimes mentioned as a model for economic growth (incidentally as it was in the 1980s, before the civil war and the genocide).

There is no doubt that these are "failures" in peacebuilding as stated by Paris. The issue is instead that the explanation for the early failure (i.e., the restart of the wars after 1992 and 1994) is found in early political liberalization (Paris 2004: 154). This refers to the early Angolan elections, where the failure of carrying out the second round restarted the war. It may also refer to the failed idea of a broad-based government that was in the Rwandan peace agreement of 1993. There is a parallel, no doubt. The alternative in Angola could have been some form of power-sharing without elections, but that is also difficult to conceive of in reality: Savimbi seemed bent on winning all in Angola, not sharing power with MPLA, while in Rwanda the hard line Hutu establishment was not open to sharing power with Tutsis and RPF. This Hutu group was early on contemplating another solution, what became the genocide of 1994. There was an uncompromising position and it seemed only vaguely related to political liberalization. There were difficult security dilemmas that were not confronted by the international missions.

This can also be seen in the pursuit of postwar policies. MPLA's postwar inclusive approach to UNITA is remarkable, and is a way of diffusing the security dilemma. It has no parallel in Rwanda. The victors consolidated their victory in different ways. Although Rwanda allowed Hutu refugees back into the country, it has maintained strict control over the majority. Rwanda's wars in neighboring Congo largely focused the Hutu opposition and its supporters. "Peace" inside Rwanda is maintained through interventions against the armed opposition outside the country. Furthermore, the opposition has not capitulated in any way, and definitely not through a peace agreement, as was the case in Angola. The security situation has not improved, but sharpened and intertwined with the complexities of the Great Lakes region. The armed conflict in

Angola is at an end, as long as UNITA's supporters feel secure, exert influence, and benefit from oil revenue. None of this is the case in Rwanda. The majority population has little say in the running of the country. Rwanda does not meet key elements of quality peace: the ability to provide security and dignity for all inhabitants. The consolidation of victory has taken different paths in the two cases, largely depending on different ways of maintaining internal security.

It is also interesting to observe that there have been no further international peacebuilding efforts in these two countries: The one in Angola was terminated in 1997, the one in Rwanda one year earlier. Victors do not want or need UN action. However, the losers may both desire and require it, not the least as international efforts lead to more transparency. This may in fact be an important difference between peacebuilding and victory consolidation. The peacebuilding approach involves normative commitment and parties that are willing to accept such conditions. In victory consolidation, however, the victor is likely to resent international involvement and transparency, perhaps stimulated by the failure of previous international efforts. From an international perspective the reasons for failure may have been that the international resources were too limited to protect potential losers and give credible assurances from war or genocide. A more robust peacebuilding and peacekeeping mission would have been more appropriate, particularly in situations with sharp local dividing lines. In the general discussion on lessons of peacekeeping, this is the more common conclusion.

Angola demonstrates more inclusiveness by having UNITA in the Parliament. It may be costly if it is related to the country's high level of corruption. Interestingly, Rwanda is perceived to be significantly less corrupt. In 2011, Angola finds itself in the low place of 165, while Rwanda is ranked 49, among 188 countries, according to Transparency International.[7] Corruption may contribute to keeping conflicts at a low level.[8] The strategies for victory consolidation are definitely contrasting and instructive for our further deliberations.

In other words, the factor of liberalization that Paris pointed to may not have been the ultimate element that failed in the international response. More likely it was the inability to provide convincing external security guarantees. Indeed both Angola and Rwanda have continued to be highly integrated into the international economy. Both are examples of economic growth. Both adhere technically to electoral principles and ideas of openness. The preference for economic liberalization does not separate between periods of peacebuilding and victory consolidation, nor between these "failed" cases and the "successes" discussed previously.

There are other relevant themes of inquiry in this context, also using a case study or comparative approach. Many have emerged after Paris published his work. To these themes belong the importance of reconciliation and war crime tribunals. These are measures that often gain attention in postwar conditions and are judged to be important for the future. Rwanda stands out as a country with a specific and comprehensive approach to this. Studies illustrate problems, for instance, in the *gacaca* process, the village courts used in Rwanda (Brounéus 2008, Brounéus 2010). The case of Rwanda has drawn a rich literature on roots of evil as well as measures of reconciliation, particularly associated with the work of Ervin Staub (Staub 2011, Staub 2013). Other forms of documentation and reconciliations have also been used (Hayner 2011). Special courts have been set up for certain intra-state conflicts (Cambodia, Rwanda, Sierra Leone) to complement the more general approach of the International Criminal Court. The impact of these courts on the future of war recurrence remains to be studied (Mendeloff 2004).

An additional issue relates to gender and gender equality in postwar situations, which also is germane to our discussion on dignity. It has been demonstrated that peacebuilding operations often miss this particular dimension, as described in the case of East Timor (Olsson 2009, Olsson 2011). Also other victories have drawn attention: An interesting case is the territorial conflict in Sri Lanka, where there are pertinent warnings for the long-term effects of the postwar policies pursued (Höglund and Orjuela 2011).

To summarize, the four cases on the extreme in Paris's sample point to the challenges identified in chapter 1. The two "successes" turn out to be a result of withdrawal of a former ruler from the contested area, as both were territorial cases. The UN missions were proportionally significant to the size of the populations and the level of violence. The state of affairs that was agreed upon and implemented has remained intact since the missions were ended. This is interesting also as the former rulers have seen dramatic changes in governance, but still have not demonstrated an interest in reestablishing control. The peace that has resulted appears lasting and meets the quality requirements, particularly in the case of Namibia.

The "failures" are found in two very polarized situations with extreme violence where, for now, one side has prevailed and consolidated its victory. The international efforts were small in relation to the level of violence and size of the populations. The UN missions were terminated early on. The victors pursued different policies in these two cases. One exemplified a more inclusive approach, the other an interventionist one, striking militarily at the opponents in neighboring countries, while keeping strict controls domestically. In both victories the same leaders remained long after taking power and both countries still face the delicacy of a significant shift of government. Only at that juncture will it be possible to assess if they have arrived at a degree of quality peace. This affects the duration of the arrangement. The international peacebuilding efforts were dismantled quickly in all four cases and the status quo has remained the same ever since the armed conflicts ended.

We have also noted that entirely new issues have emerged, notably reconciliation and gender equality. There are also works that deal with the problems resulting from victory. The studies by Paris and others in the comparative case study approach illustrate the importance of the four questions we have raised for this review: What is the meaning of success and failure? Is there a difference between conflicts over government and territory? Is there a differentiation between peacebuilding and victory consolidation? Does the analysis yield conclusions of value for quality peace criteria? There are important observations on all these counts. Let us proceed and ask the same of other approaches.

2.4 The Systemic Approach: Works by Doyle and Sambanis

So far we have spent considerable time looking at the work of Roland Paris; his work requires that, and is also a way to introduce the examples that figure prominently in the peacebuilding discourse. Equally influential is the article in the 2000 volume of the *American Political Science Review* by Michael W. Doyle and Nicholas Sambanis. This was further elaborated upon in their book *Making War and Building Peace* (2006) and in other instances (Sambanis 2000, Sambanis 2010), without revising earlier conclusions. This scholarship is concerned with the impact of two types of peace operations, termed "strict" versus "lenient" in the 2000 article, renamed "sovereign" and "participatory" in their 2006 book (Doyle and Sambanis 2000: 783; 2006: 18fn35; 2006: 73, respectively). They study civil wars since the Second World War, and their book adds case studies, some being the same as those referred to by Paris, but with different narratives; their comprehensive and statistical study has become a standard reference point for quantitative studies of peacebuilding. Their conclusions are more positive than those reached by Paris, but the questions asked are not entirely the same. Paris is concerned about the particular methods used (political and economic liberalization, democratization, etc.) whereas Doyle and Sambanis ask about the role of local capacity for overcoming the strains in a post-conflict setting and whether it can be augmented by international cooperation.

The authors present a theoretical approach where what they term "the peacebuilding triangle" connects hostility, local capacity, and international capacity (Doyle and Sambanis 2000: 782; 2006: 63–68). Hostility refers to the relations between local factions, and these are matters that "normally" should have been dealt with through local resources and competence in solving conflicts. When this is insufficient or ineffective, hostility between factions increases and international capacity (for example, in the form of international monitoring, although the authors do not exclude the use of force) is brought into the situation. The success of peacebuilding will be a function of a country's indigenous capacity, the international assistance that can be mustered, and the level of hostility in the country. The argument is that if local capacity is low and no international intervention is to be expected, levels of hostility will increase. However, if it is high, we would surmise there is no need for international support on a major scale and the country would be able to deal with its internal issues itself. This means that the writers are not studying peacebuilding operations per se, but the effects of a capacity problem. The measurement of success is the non-recurrence of conflict and war. An element of "success" thus is the same as the one suggested by Paris, but the causal chain differs.

Doyle and Sambanis's measurements of local capacity refer to economic resources—that is GDP per capita, energy consumption, and natural resource dependence (Doyle and Sambanis 2000: 783; 2006: chapter 3), all seen as proxies for the capacity a country can mobilize. Our main line of scrutiny here is the same as for Paris's work: What happens to the result if we take into account the distinction between types of internal conflict? What about their measure of "success," which is very specific and only constitutes of two or five years of nonwar (2000: 783; 2006: 73)? From a policy perspective this may suffice, but hardly from the perspective of long-term change. Furthermore, we will connect the results to the distinction between peacebuilding and victory consolidation, as well as the three criteria for quality peace.

Following the authors we use the "strict" definition of peacebuilding (also "participatory," see Doyle and Sambanis 2006: 73), which they prefer "because it reflects a higher order of peace but requires only a minimum standard of political openness," compared to their "lenient" version which largely only refers to the absence of violence. The success rate, they establish, is lower with the stricter requirements, but it also results in the stronger findings. The authors code the postwar situation both two and five years after the war (2000: 783). In all they study 124 conflicts that started between 1944 and 1997 and their status at the end of the 1990s. For some cases, being close to the time the research was done, this means there are only two years without conflict; for others there will be longer periods to consider. Table 2.3 gives the result when adding the distinction between government and territorial conflict, drawn from the Uppsala Conflict Data Program.[9]

Table 2.3 is challenging to peacebuilding, as the failure rate is high using the strict definition: eighty-one out of a total of 124 cases, or two-thirds of the cases, are categorized as failed. This in itself should be seen as alarming. However, this provides a yardstick against which to measure "success" and "failure." If two-thirds of them are likely to fail, categories of operations that do

Table 2.3

Strict Peacebuilding and Incompatibility in Internal Conflicts since the Second World War.
"Success" as defined by the "strict" definition.

	Success	*Failure*	*Total*
Incompatibility			
over government	34	53	87
over territory	9	28	37
Total	43	81	124

Source: Conflicts and success rate according to Doyle and Sambanis 2000, incompatibility according to the Uppsala Conflict Data Program.

better than this should be seen in a more favorable light. If this yardstick is also applied to Paris's eleven or fourteen cases, the results are not very different. Paris classified two cases (of eleven) or four (of fourteen) as "success," making for a maximum of 29% success. This parallels the rates demonstrated by Doyle and Sambanis. It serves to underline the difficulties in achieving desired results in international affairs.

Building on the data used by Doyle and Sambanis, Virginia Fortna (2004) asks if peacekeeping keeps the peace? In getting to the answer she points to a couple of significant selection effects. Peacekeepers are not sent to the easier cases, notably where the parties have already signed an agreement and declared a ceasefire. They are also not sent to the situations where there are decisive victories. In neither of these cases is peacekeeping necessary or wanted. In what Fortna calls "a second look" she finds that in cases that end without a clear winner, peace fails in half the cases without peacekeepers, while the same is true for only a third in those with peacekeepers (Fortna 2004: 273). In particular, peacekeepers are sent to situations where there is a truce to be upheld (Fortna 2004: 278), which implies that the conditions are fraught with challenges. Performing a duration analysis, Fortna estimates the risks of recurrence of war for different types of peacekeeping missions. For the post-Cold War period traditional peacekeeping missions and observer missions have been the most successful, reducing the risk of war by a remarkable 86% and 81% respectively (Fortna 2004: 283). In conclusion, she writes that "Despite a number of well-publicized peacekeeping fiascos in the early and mid-1990s, peacekeeping is an effective conflict management tool . . . well worth it" (Fortna 2004: 288). Thus the success rate increases if one takes into account the degree of difficulty involved in the assignments.

We can also note that in the original study by Doyle and Sambanis, the ratios of success vary in an important way. Table 2.3 presents a higher failure rate for the territorial conflicts, where three-fourths do not meet the standards of "strict" peacebuilding. Also with the more "lenient" definition, the territorial conflicts stand out as the more troubling for peacebuilding.[10] They clearly are subject to a dynamic not easily captured by the traditional tools of peacebuilding, such as those mentioned by Paris. Also, the Doyle and Sambanis notion of "local capacity" takes on a different meaning in these situations, if the "locals" are acting in the same state or have a completely different territorial basis for their action.

Moving to our second question, relating to the types of conflict, Sambanis uses the same data to deal specifically with territorial conflict in a separate article. He does this by discussing the utility of partition as a solution. He points to a number of problems with such solutions and also demonstrates that they do not necessarily enhance democracy or provide for stable relations after the war (Sambanis 2000). His hesitancy regarding such solutions is warranted and largely shared by an international community where the states are the building blocks. Still we find that new states are created at times and thus will confront international peacebuilding with difficult issues. If the measures (including autonomy or granting independence) are agreed among the parties, the outcome is fairly straightforward. There is a treaty and a political understanding to work from. This has been the case for Sudan in 2011 implementing the peace agreement of 2005, East Timor after the referendum in 1999, or the dissolution of the Soviet Union in 1991.[11] In this perspective, an international peacebuilding operation can work from a basic agreement among the parties. The cases mentioned by Sambanis largely confirm this: Namibia, Croatia, East Timor, and Bosnia, where the peace arrangements ultimately were supported by the parties, and it is also after this the peacebuilding missions were sent in. As the reader will recall, these are cases that figure prominently in the work by Paris as well. More problematic are cases where there is limited or no agreement on the new state of affairs. This includes cases such as those of Kosovo, where almost all EU and Western countries have extended recognition now amounting to about half of all states in the world, but there continues to be opposition from Serbia and Russia, among others. Particularly dubious, of course, are the cases of North Cyprus, Abkhazia, and South Ossetia, where only the strong external military power present on these territories has recognized them as states. Still this means that territorial conflicts and their post-conflict periods require particular scrutiny.

We may ask, in line with this observation, if some results would have been different if the territorial issue had been taken fully into account in the work of Doyle and Sambanis. Table 2.3 indicates that. This is also reinforced by the 2001 work of Harzell, Hoddie, and Rothchild, who investigate peace agreements after civil wars. They note that peace agreements that include territorial autonomy have a greater likelihood of lasting longer. They also point to third-party enforcement as such a factor (Harzell et al. 2001: 199–201). This gives us additional food for thought: Territorial disputes may not only end in partition; autonomy may have attraction and special qualities.

Coming to our third concern, we can note that Harzell, Hoddie, and Rothchild are satisfied with reporting that there were forty-nine victories in their data, compared to forty-one negotiated settlements, and that "only" 37% returned to war (Ibid 2001: 195). Doyle and Sambanis make more out of this, when they note that "treaties do the heavy lifting, however, and we must acknowledge that simple UN involvement is not enough to strengthen a peaceful transition. The operation's mandate is critical." They also find that "treaties are positively correlated with [peacebuilding] success" and that military victory is "completely nonsignificant" and that this "does not change if we discriminate between government and rebel victory" (Doyle and Sambanis 2000: 789). It should be recalled that "success" here is the nonrecurrence of war within two to five years. Still, the results are strong. They suggest that victory does not generate conditions for a lasting peace.

As we could observe with respect to Paris's work, there are new dimensions that have emerged, based on systematic statistical approaches. This is striking with respect to gender equality, where there are convincing data demonstrating that it correlates with duration of nonwar conditions and human rights (Caprioli 2005, Melander 2005a, Melander 2005b). Also there is work on the importance of amnesty for nonrecurrence of war (Melander 2010), creating problems in interpretation, particularly for the criterion of respect for dignity in postwar conditions.

In terms of the three quality peace criteria, the notion of a participatory peace is of special interest. However, Doyle and Sambanis do not report strong correlations between this type of peace and local capacity. Rather they find that "negative" peace is associated with local capacity (Doyle and Sambanis 2006: 132). Other elements in quality peace are not covered—for example, matters of dignity and security in the postwar period. The concern in the studies has been to demonstrate that international peace missions actually do contribute to peace in the short and long run. However, the qualities of that peace are separate issues. Let us, then, move on to an additional set of studies, with different points of departure.

2.5 Structural Approaches: Civil War as Instability

There is an increasing and relevant study of the recurrence of civil war that has direct implications for peacebuilding, victory consolidation, and quality peace. A central author in the field is Paul Collier, who has popularized his works in books such as *The Bottom Billion* (2007) and *Wars, Guns and Votes* (2009). They summarize his and his colleagues' efforts over a decade studying the economics of the recurrence of war. The World Bank report *Breaking the Conflict Trap: Civil War and Development Policy* (2003) and the recent *World Development Report 2011* (referred to as WDR below) with its focus on conflict, security, and development follow this path. The advanced statistical techniques used by many authors and their ambition to relate to development policy make these studies different from those reviewed so far. In particular, there is less concern with peacebuilding strategies or war outcomes. The approach is instead one of macro-economics looking at where war experience functions as a measure of instability.[12] It still is relevant.

The World Development Report notes that 90% of the countries with armed conflicts taking place in the first decade of the 2000s also had a major armed conflict in the preceding thirty years (WDR Overview 2011: 2–3). It is not a perfect measure of recurrence, as many of the situations never ended but saw continuous warfare, but it still points to both the prevalence of violent conflict and the urgency of dealing with them.

Let us take a closer look at this and the recurrence measure. In the period 1989–2010 there were 133 armed conflicts, as reported in Tables 2.1 and 2.2; for one year, 2011, 37 were going on (Themnér and Wallensteen 2014). One way to read this is that about one hundred had been ended in some way. However, entirely new armed conflicts occur. In 2011 the world saw renewed fighting after almost ten years without war in Côte d'Ivoire, and an entirely new war took place in Libya, a country previously known for one-sided violence and repression, not organized armed conflict. In 2012 the protests and repression in Syria also resulted in a new civil war. In 2014 Ukraine was a new location of armed conflicts. The world, in other words, has to deal with the possibility of new conflicts, not just repetitions of previous conflicts. Peacebuilding after a previous war may assist in preventing recurrence, but may say little about preventing new disputes in the same country from emerging and escalating into war. Thus the study of the causes of war is significant for the problem of quality peace. The concern in the WDR report is policies that could help reduce the high level of war in the world as a whole, no matter the outcome.

The World Development Report takes a broad look referring to a wide set of studies that point to the importance of institutions. The report gives less importance to elections and legitimacy. It stresses that the recurrence of war will be reduced if policies are in place—carried out by local, national, and international communities—that emphasize "citizen security, justice and jobs" (WDR Overview 2011: 11). "Citizen security" relates to the way the security sector operates and how confidence can be built in a society that incorporates all citizens. "Justice" refers to the needs for reforming the justice sector and anticorruption efforts, while "jobs" deals with economic policies and, in particular, the ability to provide for employment opportunities. This provides a stronger focus than we have seen in the previous approaches. Paris is observant of economic factors, but argues that liberalization of the economy "should be delayed" until political frameworks are in place (Paris 2004: 204). Doyle and Sambanis refer to economic matters, but more as proxies for local capacity than as indicators of economic development. There is little mention of economic reforms among their conclusions.

However, the importance of job creation has been underlined in a series of studies, and with different arguments. WDR reports on common perceptions that armies and violent gangs both find recruits because of unemployment (WDR 2011: 6, 9). Unemployment is also connected to loss of income, respect, and status (WDR 2011: 6). In this context, we should take note of the use of "respect" as this is close to the issue of "dignity" that is part of the present work's approach to understanding peace after war. Employment and personal income are basic resources for participation in society and thus for dignity. If this cannot be provided in a normal way, a portion of the population may come to believe that respect and dignity can only be gained with the use of weapons.

As pointed out by Collier (Collier 2009: 103–119), rebel weapons originate mostly from governments, which in turn often rely on external arms trade. This may be the way rebel movements start, until they become well versed in arms smuggling and in locating sources of income. A government's arms purchases, which may be a way of deterring aggression from the outside, have other functions in intra-state affairs. It is more likely that military challenges stem from within a society. In markedly resource-scarce countries it is more apparent that military expenditures take away funding from productive investments, such as infrastructure, education, and health. If such social expenses are handled by development assistance, they actually reinforce the government's ability to pursue violent repression and civil war. Collier refers to findings that high military expenditures are associated with increased risk of further conflict (Collier 2009: 113).[13] An obvious corollary to this is the importance of controlling arms trade and arms smuggling. A weak government will have difficulties in exerting control over its borders as well as over its own armed forces and dealings with nonstate actors. There are examples of how international peacekeeping could have a role in supervising international arms embargoes, alleviating some of these problems (Wallensteen 2011a: 206–228). These arguments suggest that government's spending on defense and police provides an indicator of insecurity in poor societies. Typically such vital statistics often remain unpublished, leaving the field to unhealthy speculation. Remarkably the issues of military expenditures and availability of weaponary are aspects rarely mentioned in standard work on peacebuilding.

The analysis of weak government is an additional, relevant theme stemming from the studies of the causes of war. Several writers point out that semidemocracies or countries in transition "away" from an authoritarian regime are more conflict prone. They may never reach the conditions of "mature" democracy but instead find themselves trapped in conditions that are difficult to break (Snyder 2000; Hegre et al. 2001). These studies bring us back to the importance of institutions, as emphasized by Paris, but also point to the difficulties in locating situations that are favorable to institution building. One might suggest that the possibilities of solving conflicts actually increase when societies emerge from authoritarian conditions. Again the distinction between governmental and territorial conflicts comes to mind. Locally or regionally based armed opposition to authoritarian regimes may have a higher likelihood of sustaining itself than a democratic opposition challenging the dictators in the capitals (Wallensteen et al. 2009). Thus nationalistic and authoritarian regimes may inadvertently breed more sons-of-the soil conflicts (Fearon 2004), and thus eventually contribute to the breakup of the very states they have set themselves to preserve. The collapse of authoritarian regimes seems often to be associated with strong separatist tendencies, as witnessed in the cases of the Yugoslav and Soviet unions, but also in Spain and Indonesia when the authoritarian regimes caved in. The study of the demise of authoritarian regimes would benefit from introducing the governance-territory distinction.

The economy-oriented literature relevant for durable peace takes a broader look than the previous two approaches. It is not focused on particular conflicts and how they end, or on particular peace operations and their degree of success and failure. The focus, notably in the Collier tradition, connects war and development in an intricate web, where the economic factors drive societies. However, in terms of our guiding questions, we find that this literature rarely distinguishes between conflicts with regard to incompatibility (territory vs. governance) or with respect to outcome (peace deal vs. victory). The insights are more general, not the least conclusions on regime transitions and citizen security. The emphasis on employment enriches our understanding of what dignity could mean in poor societies. In the following this literature plays a significant role.

2.6 Lessons from Inter-State War Studies

For the most part the literature on inter-state relations differs dramatically from that regarding intra-state conditions with respect to peacebuilding concerns. The concept of peacebuilding is rarely used, nor are matters such as "local capacity," "reconciliation," and "gender." Instead there is a focus on security dilemmas, balance of power, possibly also regional integration, and the role of international organizations. This means that "success" and "failure" are judged in different terms. The policy measures discussed often deal with deterrence, which are actions taken by one side in order to deter the other side. Being invaded would constitute a "failure" of that policy. Thus matters of military spending, possible alliances, and credible commitments come in the foreground, rather than matters that relate to both sides in a dispute. The focus is the particular state rather than the international system, as the latter lacks a single decision-making center. Furthermore the number of recent inter-state conflicts may be too small to really make possible a systematic evaluation of whether a particular policy worked or not. "Success" and "failure" become a matter of whether, and how, the opposing state responds to particular measures. Type of dispute may still matter, however, and the issue of victory may be even more prominent. Let us first compare the inter-state discourse to the intra-state discussion with respect to postwar conditions, then move on to implications for the study of quality peace in inter-state relations.

In much recent peacebuilding work on internal conflicts, reconciliation plays an important role, as a way of changing relations between formerly warring parties. The Truth and Reconciliation Commission in South Africa has been an inspiration. For international relations there seems to be little expectation of such measures playing a role, as they seldom are emphasized in mainstream literature. They are regarded as too "soft" for academics normally looking at "hard" matters such as weapons. However, there are some exceptions. For example, there is work on apologies, concluding rather cautiously about its importance (Lind 2009). The question has even been raised whether states can be offended (Dimitrova 2013). A unique contribution is the one by Long and Brecke studying reconciliation events in both civil wars and inter-state wars, where they note the different functions of reconciliation in the two types of wars (2003: 118–119). From the point of view of quality peace apologies and reconciliation moves are ways to extend respect to those victimized in war and are thus matters of dignity. It is a question of recognition (Lindemann 2011). Sometimes expectations of an apology take a central role in regional affairs, as witnessed in Japan's dilemmas in East and Southeast Asia (Lind 2009, Philpot and Hornsey 2011).

The same lack of attention can be seen in the discourse on the admission of guilt for the onset of a war and, as a consequence, economic compensation for damages during the war. There is a philosophical interest in "rectificatory justice" (Collste 2010), but that has translated into a host of empirical studies of postwar inter-state relations. This is remarkable, as these two matters featured prominently in the Versailles Treaty in 1919, forcing Germany to accept both. Particularly the issue of guilt for the war onset in 1914 continues to be debated, not the least in the scholarly community. With respect to compensation, remarkably, Germany restarted its obligations following the Nazi era. In October 2010 the country celebrated its payment of the last installment. Whether these measures really are important for future relations can be debated. Heavy war reparations will have an impact on a national economy, as experienced in Finland, subject to such payments to the Soviet Union following the Second World War. Rather than contributing to long-term positive sentiments, it demonstrated Soviet power and influence on the country. Still, similar demands do occur in other wars. It was a sticking point in the negotiations between Iraq and Iran in ending their devastating war. The Security Council found a solution to both problems at the same time: Separate teams of experts were to investigate the responsibility of the war and the issue of compensation (United Nations, Security Council, Resolution 598 (1987), paragraphs 6 and 7). Vaguely it also talked about finding measures "to enhance the security and stability of the region" (Ibid, paragraph 8). These provisions led to the end of the war. However, it did not result in regional cooperation. These examples testify to the role of "soft" issues. They may be as "hard" to solve as "harder" issues. In both these war terminations, the last issue to be solved was the one of guilt. These are matters that relate to the dignity of both sides and they are obviously important in ending of conflicts. But they are not systematically analyzed in postwar inter-state relations.

There is more attention to issues of institution building where the League of Nations, the United Nations, the Organizations for Security and Cooperation in Europe, and the EU have had on their agenda to bring peace and security to formerly belligerent major states (Ikenberry 2001). The two former were the result of cooperation among the victors; the two latter built relations among more complicated conflict outcomes. Thus there are insights that can be drawn from these experiences, which are relevant to our present undertaking.

Still it is remarkable to observe the much higher attention to issues of reconciliation and peacebuilding in intra-state conflict compared to the scholarship dealing with inter-state problems. They appear as two different worlds in terms of the questions asked and the ways they are answered. The mind-set seems also to be different. For many scholars writing on internal wars it seems obvious that reconciliation is both necessary and possible. For writers dealing with inter-state affairs it seems to be the opposite. The continuation of conflict is taken for granted. By introducing the concept of quality peace, the present work aims to bridge this barrier and demonstrate the utility of a more unified approach. What happens inside a country is clearly affected by its external relations (extending from colonial legacies to modern interventionism) as is the external situation by a country's internal relations (where a regime change may lead to fundamental policy revisions).

The traditional study of war and peace between states has been occupied by scholars, philosophers, and practitioners emphasizing the importance of military power as a key instrument for keeping peace, but also for explaining the outbreak of war (Blainey 1973). The focus has been on victory, and the ability of the victor to consolidate its superior position. If that is achieved, then the relationships will follow the logics of power. Machiavelli was a first in this area, writing down his observations in the early 1500s from the perspective of the powerholder. Unsolved issues will be contained or not raised. The breakdown of a peaceful situation into war is a matter of political mismanagement in the use of military resources and victory consolidation gone wrong.

However, long-term changes in relations between leading states can obviously be affected by other matters creating policy dilemmas, as witnessed in the event of power transitions (one state becoming stronger than others). Many of these notions have had difficulties in finding consistent empirical support beyond individual cases (Geller and Singer 1998, Vasquez 2012). Also major states are dependent on outsiders, notably through trade relations (integration reducing the autonomy of each actor versus the dangers of increasing competition and rivalry); experiences of cooperation (building confidence versus eroding trust); and alliances (short-term and opportunistic ones versus long-term and strategic ones). The results from large-scale data collections may yield insights for peacebuilding between states.

The fear of recurrence of war, furthermore, is a matter that plagues relations between major powers. This provides a bridge between intra-state and inter-state analysis. It is sufficient to remember the continuous experiences of conflict between Germany and France to realize that the conditions in Europe today are entirely different from those prevailing one hundred years ago (i.e., before the outbreak of the First World War). These two countries saw repeated and failed experiences of victory and victory consolidation. Such outcomes did not last for more than a generation and colored inter-state relations between the repeated wars. The victories were often associated not just with the cold calculations for a particular change, but also involved deliberate humiliation of the opponent, conscious infliction of human misery, purposely turning inhabitants into refugees, and intentionally thwarting national economic development by shifting scarce resources to military technology.

Thus the post-1945 change in the relationship between France and Germany is a matter of interest in a discussion on quality peace. As mentioned in chapter 1 this is not often referred to as a case of peacebuilding. In our terminology, it may more aptly be seen as a consolidation of defeat and victory, where neither side actually was the dominant one; more power had been vested in other actors. This suggests interesting parallels to other inter-state relations which have moved from rivalry to cooperation, notably the dyads of Denmark and Sweden, the United Kingdom and the United States, and Spain and Portugal. Historically there was a standard expectation of war in these relationships, but today that is not the case. Disagreements may exist, as do rivalries, misunderstandings, and contrasting interests. But this is not making war inevitable.

Not all parts of the world find themselves in such conditions. The Horn of Africa has seen considerable inter-state rivalry between Ethiopia and Eritrea, allies in a previous war. Both claimed victory and wanted to consolidate that victory on their own terms, despite international efforts to find solutions. This unsolved conflict has strong repercussions in the region, as witnessed by the difficulty of finding an agreement to reconstruct neighboring Somalia. The failure to establish reasonable regional peace conditions is one of the reasons for the pirate activity in the surrounding waters, a situation that has come to involve the world in unprecedented international maritime operations in the Indian Ocean.

The subcontinent of South Asia continues to see terrorist deeds linked to the unresolved conflicts between India and Pakistan going back to the creation of the two states in 1947.

The fact that both states in 1999 conducted tests of nuclear weapons did not deter them from engaging in a war the same year, contained only by concerted international efforts. It seems that the nuclear threat in itself is not sufficient to bring the parties to a peaceful settlement. The international community has to be party to the situation.

East and Southeast Asia find a situation without major war for the past thirty years, but there is a continuous concern with possible escalation of border skirmishes and maritime disputes in and around the unsolved issues of Korea, Taiwan, islands, and reefs. In 2011, the only inter-state armed conflict in the world that year was the one between Cambodia and Thailand, an unsolved territorial issue that goes back to colonialism.

Thus it is pertinent to investigate whether there are conclusions from the onset of inter-state war that have implications for inter-state peacebuilding as well as victory consolidation. A most remarkable breakthrough in the study of inter-state war in recent years is the so-called democratic peace hypothesis, which says that democracies do not fight wars with one another. This has now become an entrenched finding, as stated by Fred Chernoff in his review of the field: "[m]ore agreement exists regarding the observational generalizations than about the explanations for them" (Chernoff 2004: 54). There is room for continued work; the focus, however, is on the institutional aspects of democracies, and to some extent to their interactions (trade, organizations). Matters of deliberate inter-state peacebuilding have not been part of the discussion. In chapter 5 we will draw attention to this aspect.

There is also a discussion whether this applies only to "mature" democracies and not to countries finding themselves in a phase of democratization. Mansfield and Snyder (2005: 2) argue that there is a particular danger for international war in "transitional states that lack strong political institutions needed to make democracy work (such as an effective state, the rule of law, organized parties that compete in fair elections, and professional news media)." Thus the sequence of democratization becomes important. They also note that a period of democratization in great powers "has always been a moment of particular danger" (Mansfield and Snyder 2005: 15), alluding to the possibility of a democratization of China resulting in tensions or conflict with neighboring countries. A connection between such internal regime changes in major powers and external conflict has also been documented historically (Wallensteen 2011a: 68–73). This seems to be a pertinent observation with respect to peacebuilding, as the countries concerned are likely to find themselves in particularly difficult circumstances of transition after a war.

This conclusion is supported by the recent work of Fox and Hoelscher (2012) suggesting that "hybrid polities" (partial autocracies, partial democracies, and transitional regimes) are more prone to experience social violence. This is a type of violence that is broader than armed conflict, but still relevant in our discussion. Interestingly the authors raise the issue of the direction of the causal arrow: Is it the prevalence of violence that undermines a regime, or is it the development of the regime that leads to the violence (Fox and Hoelscher 2012)? This may relate to the situation inside a country, but is also likely to have an impact across the borders.

There is also important work on territorial disputes. John Vasquez has devoted considerable attention to this, and the book *The Steps to War* convincingly demonstrates the importance of territorial issues for the escalation of disputes to war. The fact that countries are neighbors is not significant for wars, but territorial issues have an impact of their own (Senese and Vasquez 2008). In related work Gibler shows that the territorial issues can be an important determinant factor behind the reported peaceful relations between democratic states: Stable borders reduce the importance of military institutions, and make democracy more likely, while unsolved border issues provide for external threats that enhance militarization, increase repression, and make states more autocratic. Gibler concludes: "Because borders are international institutions, they affect the development paths of both states in the dyad, and stabilized borders that decrease the need for militarization and centralization in one state also tend to demilitarize and decentralize the neighboring state" (Gibler 2007: 529, see also Gibler 2012). Thus democracies will have few disputes and also a greater chance to deal with those that remain through arbitration and mediation.

These studies on inter-state relations further point to the significance of different types of conflicts. As we have argued above, the distinction between government control and territorial control is important for intra-state peacebuilding. We can now see its significance in inter-state relations. In fact, Senese and Vasquez demonstrate this very clearly when they categorize the inter-state disputes they are analyzing for the period 1816–1992. Of the 1,671 disputes identified, 583 are categorized as dealing with territory— that is more than one-third of all disputes, and such disputes account for 55% of all that escalate to war (calculated from Senese and Vasquez 2008: 42). The remaining disputes are classified as "policy" and "regime," which are likely to be close to the UCDP category of disagreements over government. Escalation in inter-state relations more often connects to territorial disputes than disagreements over governance.

Still the interplay between type of regime and the onset of war gives considerable insight into possible peacebuilding conclusions for inter-state conflict. For example, two states characterized by "hybrid policies" next to each other are likely to generate internally driven insecurity as well as external threats, while a consolidated regime next to a fragile state may generate insecurities as well as incentives for cross-border incursions. This has direct implications for one of the central criteria of quality peace: the perception of security. Regime failure, whether in one's own country or in the neighboring country, may increase anxiety on both sides of the border. The security concerns are real.

Also inter-state relations create a particular challenge to the notion of dignity. National identity can sometimes turn into a chauvinist attitude denying the identity and dignity of others. Inter-state relations can increase such sentiments and complicate relations, particularly after a war and, more specifically, after a war outcome that means victory for one and defeat for the other. Victory in inter-state relations, in other words, may have negative implications for respect, tolerance, and dignity of a population segment that might be seen as connected to the other country (be it the victor or the loser). Together these factors undermine the prospects of a lasting nonwar situation. Thus there are ample reasons to take up inter-state relations when studying peacebuilding and victory consolidation after war. A relationship between countries will also have to involve a particular quality in order for this to provide for security, dignity, and predictability. The realist notion of deterring the other side does not generate that, but it remains to be determined what conditions can, no matter what the outcome. Consequently, our inquiry will have to address this in a more complete way. This is done in chapters 5 and 6.

The literature on inter-state wars gives more information on the governance-territory dimension than any of the other work. It also has more to say on the type of outcomes. However, the use of any form of quality peace criteria is rare.

A number of questions typically asked for peacebuilding in internal affairs are lacking, but could still be important for inter-state affairs. In this spirit we approach the question of world order.

2.7 The Post-Cold War Period as World Order

The literature on peacebuilding has grown dramatically but evidence is largely limited to the post-Cold War period. The special conditions created by the end of the Cold War may affect our ability to draw more general lessons that have historical applicability. This period may have too many special traits. Also, it is still a short one. Can we, with any degree of certainty, really conclude that there are systematic differences between peacebuilding and victory consolidation based on observations of such a short period? It can even be argued that it is a distinct experience as a world order and thus not comparable to other periods. Let us explore if this short period can be seen as a specific "world order," a special distribution of power and special ways of dealing with peace and security.

The references we have seen in Section 2.3 to "liberal peacebuilding" suggest that there is such an order. There are standard procedures in peacebuilding that warrant the concept of "liberal": democracy, personal freedom, market economies, corporate freedom, low taxes, free trade, social inequalities. These are all code words associated with a liberal approach. Institutions such as the World Bank and IMF are seen as the key actors in pursuing this approach around the world. From this perspective, there is a "world order," directed from a diffuse, but still seemingly coordinated center, connecting Washington, D.C. and Wall Street in New York with financial and political operators in London, Paris, Berlin, and Tokyo. This is the Bretton Woods world, to name it after the place where global economic policies were laid out for the post-World War II era. However, this is an "order" that has existed since 1944 and does not operate differently in the period after the Cold War; it only now covers a larger area. That is one meaning of globalization: It has created access to an enlarged market, but no principal differences from before. However, from the perspective of peacebuilding, the end of the Cold War may be more significant. The period would thus constitute a different era of managing armed conflicts, but not necessarily in the global economy.

First *the post-Cold War period has some features which are sufficiently unique* to make it an order of its own. The concept of world order is mostly associated with the distribution of power among the leading actors. In this regard, the post-1989 period is different. The end of the Cold War meant a shift from a contention between two powers that both claimed global reach and global relevance. After 1989 only one continued to make that claim, but even so, withdrew from a number of conflicts and areas, normally following peace agreements. All other leading states exhibited a regional reach, although the extent of that "region" could be debated, but the United States continued to be a global actor. The decade of the 1990s definitely was a unipolar moment (Krauthammer 1990).

Secondly, in terms of the peace concerns, it shifted from global consideration of all conflicts to a *focus on local and intra-state conflicts* (Wallensteen 2012a). This is how the international political commitment to peacebuilding emerged.

Third this could build on a *notable consensus on the importance of economic growth and the negative impact of armed conflict.* The globalization of the 1990s was a universal phenomenon, and meant more than just an expansion of economic opportunities. There was also a trend toward democratization as a value in itself. In fact, it may have run counter to the demands of the market, as it often resulted in instabilities that were detrimental to economic interests.

Fourth there were *surprisingly uniform reactions* to certain challenges, particularly terrorist deeds—notably on September 11, 2001—and to the danger of nuclear weapons in the hands of Iran and North Korea. Even divisive events, such as the US war on Iraq in 2003, Russia's involvement in Georgia in 2008, the recession beginning in 2008, the reactions to the Arab Spring 2011, or even the crisis over Ukraine in 2014, have not prevented cooperation in other areas. These are further reasons to see the period as separate from the Cold War, when disputes were quickly generalized into global confrontations.

Fifth there is also *internal coherence* in the approaches to conflict and peace: Peacekeeping troops, mediators, and arms embargoes have been standard in containing and solving localized conflicts. Lately the role of women has been part of this as well as the idea of the rule of law.

These five arguments make clear there is something special about the present era. Certainly we still have to ask if the world will see further learning and strengthening of international institutions, thus solidifying an era of cooperation. Or if the world is located between two Cold Wars where the old Cold War is gradually replaced by a global polarization between a rising China and a declining West? Or is it a time that soon will be described as an imprudent spending spree before the Great Global Climate Crisis, similarly to how the 1920s is now seen as the irresponsible period before the Great Depression? We cannot know. What can be done is to generate insights that are helpful for this particular situation, possibly contributing to preventing a more negative scenario.

Still the present period provides challenges to our understanding of its role in history. We have already noted that the present era, so far, is *a short one*, and that limits research and generalization of findings. The overview of literature has demonstrated a range of scholarship that is relevant for the issues of peace-building as well as the analysis of victory. For most scholars, whether searching for the impact of liberal, lenient, or strict peacebuilding, state failure or inter-state war, nonrecurrence of war is measured in the number of years that have passed without a new war. The time dimension works as a proxy for other matters. The time lines used are very brief, often no more than two or five years. By any standard this is very short. Its advantage is that there is a close temporal connection to the war ending and the policies pursued after that (peacebuilding or victory consolidation). It can be argued that the impact of such strategies should be measurable immediately—for example, when an international peace operation is present. However, many arguments pertain to policies that have to be sustained over longer periods of time. Thus a few calendar years will not suffice. In the structurally focused literature that has been presented in section 2.5, whether a war ends in a peace agreement or a victory is of little consequence. The war and its aftermath is the concern and so is the process of restoring the prewar situation (in terms of economic output, for example). The World Development Report is typical. Its—quite realistic—suggestion is that it may take fifteen to thirty years for a country to return to a situation that resembles key pre-war conditions (WDR 2011: 10–11). The strategic and systematic peacebuilding scholars operate within two to five years; these studies would benefit from incorporating longer time spans. Policies that seemingly failed in a short time may still have laid the groundwork for future recovery, as demonstrated in the case of Angola in section 2.3.

Thus the brevity of the present period—not more than twenty-five years—provides a natural barrier. It makes it tempting to incorporate materials from the period prior to 1989. This is legitimate, but will have an impact on the validity of the conclusions, and researchers need to be attentive to this. Some key conditions may simply not be comparable.

The short duration of the period has a particular *effect on the number of cases* that actually can be studied. This appears clearly in the 2010 article by Monica Toft in *International Security*. It created attention as it demonstrated the strength of rebel victories in civil war: Such victories are said to be more durable than other outcomes. Toft's work is important for this book and we will return to it. What is interesting right now is that the finding is based on an analysis of 137 civil wars from 1940 to 2007, thus incorporating cases before the idea of peacebuilding had become important as a deliberate policy concern. Negotiated endings have become more common and this is, of course, why peacebuilding turned into a major concern in the late 1990s: Can these endings be sustained? In actual fact, there are seventeen new wars starting after 1990 according to Toft, and at the same time there are thirty-seven war endings. This means that the 1990s saw the conclusion of a number of highly protracted conflicts that had begun during the Cold War. An example is the Namibia conflict that we have encountered earlier (in section 2.3), active from 1966 until 1990.[14] Even more interesting is that among the seventeen new conflicts, most were defined as ended by 2002, which suggests that the present period displays a record of terminating conflict quicker than during the Cold War period. Furthermore, only two of these new conflicts restarted (Burundi and Chechnya). In fact, the recurrences are remarkably few in Toft's data: only nineteen out of the total of 118 conflicts that were ended, that is 15%.

At this time our concern is that this means that the number of cases from which to generalize is small. It makes results vulnerable to minor changes in the categorizations. This can be demonstrated by noting that most of the victories were by governments, and 17% restarted compared to 6% of the rebel victories. The results are sensitive to the selection of cases. Removing the unique category of decolonization conflicts (which typically were won by liberation movements, here described as "rebels"), we arrive at a rate for rebel victory of 16%. The difference in rates of recurrence between government victory versus rebel victory disappears. The calculations are dependent on the number of cases, the period that they cover, and how cases are categorized.

There are ways to increase the number of observations. One is to go beyond major war and concentrate on all types of armed conflicts. This is what the Uppsala Conflict Data Program does. It also has information on separate types of conflicts, notably those between non-state actors and also one-sided violence. This enlarges the numbers. One can go even further as Joakim Kreutz (2010) does. The 231 armed conflicts reported for 1946–2005 are disaggregated into 403 "conflict episodes." It means the number of cases increases and the results are less vulnerable to the coding of particular cases. On this basis he demonstrates that more conflicts ended with peace agreements after the Cold War. It gives us more data points and thus a closer understanding of the present period. This is also consonant with the assertion that this period is different. Peacemaking has been more important than victory. Furthermore, Toft, as well as Kreutz, informs us that wars were more protracted during the Cold War. The changes of 1989 are associated with significant shifts in the approaches to conflict.

This is underscored by a further finding by Kreutz that government victory—not rebel wins —makes it less likely that a conflict will recur. Furthermore, the presence of peacekeeping troops reduces the likelihood of recurrence, and the most fragile situations are found in the first years after a conflict has ended. This brings us to an important point.

It makes it possible to calculate the rate of recurrence, even though the time spans are limited. Thus, taking all conflict episodes for the 1946–2009 period, 23% of the conflicts restarted after three years and 50% at some point during the reviewed period (Wallensteen 2015: 31). Peace agreements, however, had the lowest overall rate, 36%. This suggests not only that the first years after the ending of war are more crucial but also that victories may be consolidated quickly but encounter increasing difficulties after a period of time. Peace agreements show the opposite pattern: They are likely to be tested early in a postwar situation, and some may collapse, be renegotiated and, presumably, become better. For the victorious actors the tests may come later. Losers may bide time and reemerge as political forces when an opportunity presents itself. The type of outcome generates different effects for the postwar period, perhaps not only for the rate of recurrence.[15] It tells us that the result of a particular war outcome may wear off. The new status quo may become entrenched and acceptable, particularly under conditions that actually deal with some of the issues that led to the war in the first place.

In the post–Cold War period, the issue of recurrence has been important. A dominant ambition of leading actors has been to end conflicts quickly, finding ways in which local actors can work together and then reduce international involvement. There has been a preference for peace agreements, but when victories have been the fact, they have been exposed to pressure to apply some of the same measures. This makes the concern of the quality of the postwar conditions significant. This is also why the issues of respect to dignity are pertinent. Duration may be intimately linked to such respect and thus to long-term developments. An element in the postwar situations then is how the actors in the new status quo (whether achieved through peacebuilding or victory consolidation) handle new security threats. These are the further elements in the narrow path toward quality peace that we are investigating here.

There is one obvious exception to these concerns that marks the post-Cold War period. There is agreement on fighting terrorist threats with violent means; there seems to be less ability and willingness to negotiate such conflicts. The consensus, in other words, extends to peaceful approaches in dealing with non-terrorist conflicts, but also agreement on violent approaches to terrorism. Again this is a type of agreement that hardly existed during the Cold War. This also warrants labeling this period a different order than those we have seen before. Thus we will return to the issues of world order in chapter 7.

2.8 Measurements and Indicators

One of the purposes of this chapter is to find measurements of the various elements of quality peace. We have said in chapter 1 that quality peace means the creation of postwar conditions that make the inhabitants of a society (be it an area, a country, a region, a continent, or a planet) secure in life and dignity now and for the foreseeable future. We have seen a plethora of possible indicators in the reviewed studies.

The definition points us in two different directions for finding measures. One is to gauge the relationship between the (formerly) warring parties after the war. A second one is to portray the situation in the society as a whole, as new challenges may arise. In fact, the distinction will be blurred. It may not be easy to find measures of how former leaders relate to each other, particularly not in cases of victory. For peace agreements, meetings, further agreements, and the quality of electoral contests may be indicators of where the leadership as well as the society is going. Extension of amnesty, pursuit of war crimes, and the provision of security guarantees are further possible indicators.

Much of this has to do with the notion of *"foreseeable future."* The time horizons are likely to be different for leaders and for society. For society it is a matter of a generation. The central question is likely to be: Will my children and their children be able to live in peace or not? If an inhabitant is hopeful they will, many things follow that are good for society. If that inhabitant is not sure, he/she will take action to provide for such a future. If the inhabitant has access to resources, corruption may follow. As we have seen in the literature overview, academic studies have very short time-horizons (almost by necessity), but societies are likely to see matters in longer terms.

Clear indications of predictability are the duration of regimes and leaders. It may be that victors stay longer in power than do leaders who negotiate a peace agreement. Examples that were mentioned refer to Angola and Rwanda, with the same leaders in place for decades. It is not hard to suggest that important leadership changes are soon going to take place. They will constitute demanding tests of the new power arrangements. As such changes come closer, biologically speaking, tensions may rise in society. Many have an interest in peaceful transitions.

Another central notion is the one of *human dignity*, which is written into human rights conventions. The 1948 Universal Declaration of Human Rights starts by mentioning the "inherent dignity" of members of the human family. Paragraph 1 makes this abundantly clear:

> All human beings are born free and equal in dignity and rights. They are endowed with reason and conscience and should act towards one another in a spirit of brotherhood.

Thus respect for human rights might be the optimal indicator to apply to a situation after a war. But it may not be the only measure of dignity. There are also everyday expressions of discrimination that have to be observed (Schachter 1983).

To this belongs the official regard for minorities or other groups without power. Minority rights are a particular concern and we might expect that negotiated endings will have a stronger record on this. The same could be said of inclusiveness and gender equality. Still, the fate of ethnic groups that were aligned with the opposition may be most important to watch.

Reconciliations measures that include acknowledgment of victimization, apologies for discrimination, and investigations of crimes relating to this as well as forms of compensation would constitute indicators for how a society deals with dignity. Again this applies within as well as between societies.

A functioning democracy would be a measure of the ability of the population at large to exert influence, and giving all a chance to raise concerns and press for particular demands. Majority rule constrained by minority rights may well be the ideal construction of a society after a war, no matter how the war ended. The construction of antidiscrimination institutions would also indicate where a society is going.

Democracy, furthermore, provides a particular measure for seeing how a society moves over time: Do elections take place as stipulated, are all actors having a fair chance, is there access to media for all, is voting conducted in an appropriate way? These are all established indicators. Interestingly, in victorious countries elections are also important, however controlled they may be. The degree of control then provides for indicators of respect for different opinions in a society.

The definition also mentions "*secure in life,*" which here is used to refer to personal safety, not the full concept of human security.[16] This can be indicated by corruption levels, the rule of law, and other indicators of transparency. On a societal level we would be concerned about military spending and ideally this would also concern the expenditures for police and intelligence operations. The way the war ends is important, notably the access of all to disarmament provisions (men and women alike, or both sides in the war, for example). On a leadership level this is likely to be a particular concern and many demand to have the state provide for their own security, something that can be costly. Certainly demands for impunity will follow, something which in turn will create insecurity in other parts of society.

The review suggests additional ways to gauge the postwar situation. One is the leaders' ability to deal with new security threats (as can be seen in the size of the military budget, the country's involvement in new armed conflicts, national crime rates, etc.). Investment patterns inform us on the ability of the country to generate commitments from resource-rich groups.

Also more traditional measures have to be used, whether quantitative (such as economic development, conflict patterns, etc.) or qualitative (implementation of agreement, rise of new actors, changing global conditions, etc.). This particular work is not moving toward a composite index of quality peace, although that may be an ultimate goal.[17] Here it suffices to point to the importance of the notion of quality peace.

Finally, we should note that the challenge here, then, is to see if these measures are able to capture the peacebuilding efforts and victory consolidation practices taking place in three different types of conflict: between states, within states, and in internal conflicts over territory (state formation conflicts). This has to be done with an eye on the fact that *intra*-state conflicts may become *inter*-state as a result of separation of territory and, thus, generate valuable lessons on postwar conflict dynamics for all categories. In addition, the policies pursued will be related to the global conditions (the world order), notably the priorities of major powers, regional actors, and international institutions. From this it would also be possible to identify general strategies. Some of these will be dependent on the present world order; others may be more general. This is the complexity to which we now turn.

CHAPTER 3

Quality Peace after Civil War

3.1 Civil War Outcomes

Civil wars have been the focus of peace research as well as peacebuilding efforts only since the end of the Cold War. The literature has grown very quickly, although the term "civil" war is a misnomer. Most such wars in history and in recent time are neither very civil nor well organized. The "armies" that are involved could actually be anything from gangs of criminals under a political leadership to highly disciplined, well-resourced forces with state-like political functions. This type of warfare ranges from harassing civilians in hastily erected roadblocks to highly coordinated military campaigns over large territories over several years. The variation is large in weaponry and strategies as well. The issue that brings together these events into this particular category is that they all aim at keeping or unsettling the incumbent government. There are also other conflicts that are termed "civil war," notably the major war between the United States (the North) and the Confederate States (the South) in North America in the 1860s. In this context, it was a war about state formation, where the South wanted to secede and not take control over the capital, Washington, to run the whole country. It thus belongs to the category of conflicts that we deal with in chapter 4. The present chapter takes up the subject of internal government conflicts, by focusing on this particular category and by introducing a statistical analysis of key variables relating to the concepts introduced in chapters 1 and 2.[1]

As we have seen in Tables 2.1 and 2.2 in the Chapter 2, the civil war types of armed conflicts are numerous. UCDP records forty such conflicts in the 1975–1988 period, and sixty for 1989–2010, which constitute almost half of all armed conflicts in each period. There is reason to believe that intra-state conflicts have been more numerous than inter-state wars for a long time. For the period 1816–2007 Sarkees and Wayman (2010) report ninety-five inter-state wars and 334 intra-state wars, clearly giving preponderance to intra-state violence. In this case we talk about large-scale situations, as this refers to armed conflicts with more than one thousand killed in a year (Wallensteen 2015), not just the armed conflicts that UCDP covers. In spite of these statistics, early peace research concentrated on conflicts between states rather than within them; the destruction caused by inter-state wars such as the two World Wars makes that understandable. At the same time, however, it left intra-state wars untouched for a long time and may even have contributed to an illusion that intra-state conditions are more peaceful than inter-state relations. Indeed the idea of the state as a "model" for international order rests on the assumption that a government is more able to uphold law and order within its domains than outside it. That can be theoretically argued, notably using the state's monopoly of the legitimate use of violence as a point of departure. However, some further reflection suggests that there are more opportunities for internal conflict than external: Historically governments have had to deal with internal concerns on a daily basis, but only sporadically engage with threats from outside. Thus the historical neglect of intra-state war and violence in disciplines such as political science and sociology is remarkable. Here we focus on such intra-state conflicts that deal with government power. We will return to inter-state conflict in chapters 5 and 6.

Today, this previous bias is no longer possible. Chapters 1 and 2 showed that internal conflicts are the ones that draw most attention in the peacebuilding literature. There are some examples that have almost acquired the status of being seminal, even to be emulated by others. A typical case is the transition in South Africa from the *apartheid* system to democracy. It was, undoubtedly, one of the historical positive surprises, as the predictions of an inevitable racial war were many in the 1970s and 1980s. Finding a negotiated way out of this conflict also gave rise to hope for other situations. It is particularly interesting in this context, as it involved a minimum of peacebuilding efforts pursued by international actors. The South African peace agreements concluded in the early 1990s were not even described as such agreements in general commentary and analysis at the time, although they fit most definitions, including the one by UCDP. Perhaps this is because they had very little third-party involvement; they were conducted directly between the two main protagonists. It was an indigenously built peace, where the resulting process of change and special measures, notably the creation of the Truth and Reconciliation Commission, received international acclaim. It also illustrates the importance of the peaceful transfer of power. A military victory by one or the other side would most likely have created a completely different outcome. It is not hard to imagine what it could have looked like, but in retrospect it is difficult to conceive of such a situation, as the actual outcome now seems "natural." Of course it was not. Thus this thought experiment again underscores the importance of comparing different possible outcomes. Analysts have to guard against taking anything for granted. The "normal" conditions of today are the outcomes of a series of historical choices, agreements, and implemented decisions.

Another way to think of this stems from conflict statistics. Of the sixty civil armed conflicts since 1989, there was a peace agreement in twenty-eight—that is, close to half of all conflicts. Twenty-three cases had at least one experience of victory, while nineteen conflicts saw neither a victory nor a peace agreement. From this should be subtracted ten conflicts that saw both a peace agreement and a victory. Peace agreements have been somewhat more common than victory. Furthermore, the data show that the two outcomes do not necessarily exclude each other. A peace agreement can be followed by a victory, or the other way around (The Democratic Republic of Congo is one example). But almost a third of the civil conflicts saw neither a victory nor a negotiated settlement. This means that they continued, became protracted, possibly had temporary ceasefire agreements, but in principle, remained unsolved at the end of the period.

Still this is an impressive development. In all there are 139 agreements in civil wars since 1989 and, as mentioned, they concerned twenty-eight conflicts, which makes an average of close to five agreements for each. Comparing this to the 1975–1988 period we can see the difference. There were a total of nine peace agreements in five conflicts (out of the forty, that is one-eighth of all conflicts). This means that peace agreements have become markedly more common. The change from nine agreements to 139 is remarkable. At the end of the Cold War, there was only a small number of books and articles on peace agreements in international affairs. Today there is a vast body of scholarly and popular writings as well as considerable accumulated experience in the making of peace agreements.[2]

Still the post–Cold War peacemaking demonstrates significant variation among the conflicts, some taking a larger share of the efforts than others. There were sixteen agreements in Guatemala; the final one was concluded in 1996. These agreements were integrated into a comprehensive peace process continuously pursued by the same parties over several years. In this case, the parties may very well have learned a lot about what was possible to achieve through negotiations, and also which demands had to be dropped if there were to be an agreement. Guatemala's experience builds on a process, with many peace agreements between the same parties, and where none was to be implemented until the final one had been signed. This case tops the list of peace agreements. Together the results were comprehensive enough to fully end the violent conflict between the armed opposition and the government.

It is instructive also to look at the other cases. Chad is coded to have eleven agreements, but with different actors constituting the government. Liberia (also eleven agreements) saw two different wars where some actors were the same throughout the process. The development in Sudan involves a total of ten agreements, largely between the same actors. This case straddles the distinction between conflicts over government and those over territory. The solution, as expressed in the Comprehensive Peace Agreement of 2005, was a joint government for the whole country (the Unity Government, lasting for a time, but some actors may have preferred for it to continue much longer). However, the same agreement also provided for a process for dividing the country, which was the outcome of the January 2011 referendum making South Sudan the newest state in Africa by July 9, 2011 (we will return to this case in chapter 4). Continuing the account of peace agreement experiences, these four cases are followed by Côte d'Ivoire and El Salvador (nine each), and Burundi and Uganda (eight each). These eight countries have also been identified in studies of state fragility and ethnic conflict. They have a mixed record of "success" and "failure" in peacebuilding, as we can see in the work by Roland Paris (2004, see section 2.3). They are marked by repetitive experiences of conflict and peace and are the ones most frequently analyzed in international peacebuilding studies. We can also note that together these eight countries concluded three-fifths of all peace agreements in government conflicts since the end of the Cold War. There are another twenty conflicts with peace agreements which are not subject to the same intense scrutiny. There is a selection bias in cases that are discussed, but the possible effect of this on analysis is seldom spelled out.

Conflicts with only one agreement are as numerous as those with a large number. The list includes Cambodia (1991), Congo (Brazzaville, 1999), Guinea-Bissau (1998), Haiti (1993), Macedonia (2001), Mexico (1996), Nepal (2006), Niger (1993), and the Philippines (1995). It could be suggested that some of these are the most "successful" cases: There has only been one agreement, and the conflict has not been heard of much since. However, few of these have been heralded as successes of peacebuilding. Cambodia has received a fair amount of attention, not least as the agreement was connected to the ending of the Cold War and retained a locally based Communist party, although under a different name. Similarly Nepal's experiment in peacebuilding after the peace agreement has attracted much interest, no doubt because of the peaceful removal of the monarchy and the remarkable strength of the Maoist party in a post–Cold War setting. It has turned into a protracted peace process. An interesting case is Macedonia, a country located in the turbulent Balkan region, having a history as a constituent republic of the former Yugoslavia and with no major and immediate neighbors necessarily interested in its survival as a state. The odds for the survival of the peace agreement have been low in many of these cases, but still they have withstood test of the time.

Let us revisit the Doyle and Sambanis list of successful peacebuilding cases for civil wars (Doyle and Sambanis 2000: Table 1, p. 784). Using the authors' strict definition, we can now benefit from the passage of time. Two years of nonwar were identified by the authors as a peacebuilding success, if there was also a minimum standard of political openness. This can now be extended by looking at the situation after ten and fifteen years (in this case the end of 2008). The results are reproduced in Appendix 3.1.

After ten years the rate of success obviously goes down. In total, Doyle and Sambanis recorded 124 civil wars, of which eighty-one were defined as failures within two years (i.e., war restarted, the conflict had not ended by the time of coding, and the situation did not meet a minimum of democratic openness). A total of forty-three cases (those listed in Appendix 3.1) were assessed as "successes." Thus the success rate was 34.7%. If we remove (as in Table 2.2 in Chapter 2) territorial conflicts, which belong to a separate category to be dealt with in chapter 4, the success rate actually improves somewhat after two years to 39.1%.

Let us continue the history of all forty-three situations. After ten years, eleven had seen a return to war—that is, the success rate drops to 25.8% since the beginning (but is actually 74% of those that survived the first two years)—and after fifteen years an additional two went back to war (Colombia and Guatemala, both after a spell without war in the early 1970s according to Doyle and Sambanis 2006: 76–77), but almost 94% of those that survived ten years also continued after fifteen years, thus making the long-term success rate 24.2% of all cases. For the subcategory of peacebuilding in government conflicts the rates are somewhat better: 28.7% remain successful after ten years and 26.4% after fifteen years.

This demonstrates that the two-year cutoff is too crude for a full analysis; there are likely to be more failures as time passes. But our data also demonstrate that the rate of failure declines gradually. There is a high failure rate the first two years, when close to two-thirds of all endings recorded lead to renewed war. After ten years three-quarters of those that survived the first two years are likely to remain in place, and after fifteen years nine-tenths of the ten-year survivors are still without a new war. Even so, they were exposed to new dangers and two cases went back to war. Measuring from the initial conflict ending, we can conclude that about one-quarter of the peace arrangements still remained in force after fifteen years.[3]

Obviously it is urgent to stimulate more thinking about how repetitive conflicts can be brought to an end. This is partly a conflict resolution concern (Wallensteen 2015), but in particular a peacebuilding matter. Thus we now concentrate on the ways in which a lasting peace can be forged after a war, searching for the strategies of peacebuilding. The contrasts between the frequent failure cases and those with no such breakdowns, as well as those that continue or end in victory, are interesting for such an understanding. This means that we look for the conditions for peacebuilding, understood as lasting security and dignity of the inhabitants (i.e., quality peace). It can be achieved through an implemented peace agreement, but also through a victory. Our concern is the quality of either outcome.

3.2 After Civil War: Peacebuilding Strategies

The peacebuilding literature is focused on ways to permanently remove governmental wars from the conflict register. The approaches vary, however. Paris (2004) dealt with institutional reforms, largely meaning political changes associated with constitutions, democracy, and the rule of law. Many other researchers share this opinion, notably Barbara Walter, who in 2010 emphasized the ability of a government to credibly commit to an agreement. She describes this as follows: "Governments that are constrained by a formal constitution, and that follow the rule of law *are* much less likely to face renewed violence in any form. In fact, any measure that limits the government's ability to act outside the law and unilaterally usurp power makes the government a more attractive negotiating partner and offers combatants an alternative way out of war" (Walter 2010: 33, italics in original). Thus legal constraints, possibly building on power realities in the society, are what make it difficult for governments to restart war or create the type of insecurity that would give rebels a reason for doing so.

However, there are also other observations, for instance, on the use of resources for military purpose in the postwar period. A quote from economist Paul Collier illustrates this: ". . . the decision of the government to spend on the military inadvertently signals to citizens that it is planning to turn nasty, and that this signal forewarns those rebels who recently put down their arms that they were unwise to do so." (Collier 2009: 113). In other words, the credible commitment mentioned by Walter is by Collier seen in the military spending patterns: A reduction of military spending would signal the government's commitment to peace, an increase in military resources does the opposite. The way a government acts, rather than constitutional constraints, is what matters. Not the least it draws attention to how this action (or lack of action) is perceived by the potential rebels. It may also be an incentive for governments not to publish credible information on such spending.

This makes the work by Monica Toft particularly interesting as she emphasizes the importance of security sector reform for avoiding the recurrence of civil war. In her data on civil wars, this turns out to be a significant relationship, suggesting that an agreed and implemented amalgamation of armies reduces the likelihood of a war occurrence (Toft 2010: 59–60).

Although Collier points to actual behavior, he still has a focus on structural conditions that form the political actors and governments—that is, government institutions and the extent of corruption. There seems to be some convergence among researchers on the importance of credible commitments, notably from the actor which is normally the strongest in armed conflict, the government. Thus Metternich and Wucherpfennig demonstrate—based on civil wars rather than territorial conflicts (2011:14) —that "consolidated peace" lasts longer than "fragile peace." The authors' notion of a "consolidated peace" actually refers to a credible process of democratization—that is, a form of institutional change. Democracy building would, in itself, signal a commitment by governments and rebels alike to not restart a war.

There are other institutional factors to consider. The notion in Doyle and Sambanis of local capacity is an important one. As we saw in chapter 2, their operationalization of this concept can be questioned, but the idea may still be inherently correct. If there is, for instance, sufficient local capacity in dealing with conflicts at an early stage, the society may be spared new wars. In their conclusions, they distinguish between "difficult" cases, where there is little local capacity, and "easy" cases, where there is substantial local capacity (Doyle and Sambanis 2006: 336). The difficult cases can be contained through peacekeeping missions (as in Cambodia) and turned into a more positive development (where peace agreements do not break down).

One way to consider local capacity, not often looked at, is the gender dimension. In important contributions, Gizelis (2009) and Olsson (2009) find that, in societies with higher status for women, peacekeeping operations are also more effective. This gives rise to several reflections. One is that the social capital of women is a significant resource for peacebuilding, the other that peacebuilding operations in themselves may not be the crucial variable for peacebuilding success. Instead, underlying factors or policies in the societies may be decisive, such as the status of women. Gizelis demonstrates this with a statistical analysis building on Doyle and Sambanis, while Olsson documents this for one particular case, East Timor, a territorial conflict but still of general importance.

The local capacity is crucial and, in the view of many of the authors, such aspects are more important than immediate democratization. However, the importance of democracy for peace inside societies has also been documented, notably by Hegre et al. (2001), showing that semidemocracies are associated with more civil wars than either authoritarian or fully democratic societies. The best way forward is to democratize: "In the short run, a democratizing country will have to live through an unsettling period of change." But this is likely to be overcome and for the future the authors strike a positive note: "There *is* a democratic civil peace, and it may be achieved in the short run in some countries. In the long run most states, possibly all, may reach this condition, especially if we take into account the higher survival rate of open societies" (Hegre et al. 2001: 44, italics in original). The authors leave the readers on this positive note, and in line with a typical structural approach, do not suggest how this state of affairs could be achieved. Thus we do not know whether an international peacekeeping mission could be an advantage for stabilizing a semidemocracy, or whether building local capacity is a necessary and primary condition rather than having, say, national elections. Probably the routes may vary and the choices may be difficult to expose to quantitative analysis. The closest to a guideline the authors can give is to say that "The most reliable path to stable domestic peace in the long run is to democratize as much as possible." (Ibid. p. 44). How to pursue this path is the question that has to be faced by the researchers concerned with strategic peacebuilding. Furthermore, this optimism is not necessarily shared by all. In a study of democratic transitions and external wars from 1816 to 1992, Mansfield and Snyder observe cases where the transition resulted in reversions to autocracy apart from external and domestic war. Thus the authors argue for a step-by-step approach to democratization, building on effective administration rather than early democratization (Mansfield and Snyder 2005: 267–274).

Turning to the systemic peacebuilding analysis, democracy is important but there is also a concern for the sequence. Doyle and Sambanis conclude that "Elections must usually come after the institutional transformations that establish the foundations of the rule of law." Peacekeeping seems to be the way to retain order, eliminate insecurity, and provide for the transition (Doyle and Sambanis 2006: 336–341). In this work Doyle and Sambanis come close to the sequence suggested by Paris, but with the important addition of stimulating local capacity. As they also argue for international peacekeeping, there is an implicit admission of the importance of the military situation after the war. However, only Collier has gone so far as to point to the importance of a reduction of military expenditure as a signal of commitment.

This leads to the idea of a peace process and whether an element is present of the parties learning for post–civil war peace. We have already noted that some conflicts have a number of peace agreements, suggesting that there actually are some lessons being developed. What is it that needs to be learned and by whom? Paris, Doyle, and Sambanis give attention to the international community, in the belief that this is an important element in the success of peacebuilding after a civil war. Even the emphasis by Doyle and Sambanis on local capacity is seen in this light. If there is not enough local capacity to deal with a conflict, international resources have to be brought to the situation. In a way the fact that there is a war suggests that there is insufficient local capacity to deal with the situation. The number of protracted conflicts could demonstrate this. Even so this cannot be a rule, as the protracted conflict in South Africa, as we just saw, found a solution almost entirely by building on local capacity.

Furthermore, and more challenging to the authors, a victory by one of the warring parties could actually be seen as an expression of local capacity. A victory indicates that there were local actors that were strong enough to prevail on the local scene and impose their particular agenda on the parties. Thus we are coming back to the issue of victory and its role in international attention to a particular situation. The ultimate question is not whether the postwar situation after a victory would be more durable or not, but rather what the quality peace would be. The studies we have looked at have little to say about victory as an alternative to the peacebuilding process. But this outcome has to be part of the picture, as this could be one of the reasons for a breakdown of a peace agreement. Clearly there are parties that believe there is an alternative and pursuing their own hope of victory is the one they may prefer. Achieving victory could be a goal of the government as well as the armed opposition. To this we now turn.

3.3   Civil War and International Attention

A way to approach the issue of the quality of peace after a war is to focus on the outcome of the armed conflict: Does the ending of war by one side defeating the other differ from situations where opposing sides meet and make agreements? Which outcome provides the greatest chance of a lasting peace, and which provides safety and dignity to the population? How does the international community react to either outcome and what is the role of building dignity in the post-conflict situation? Let us expose these questions to a statistical analysis dealing with experiences since 1989, particularly UN peacebuilding missions in this period.[4] Peacebuilding missions are here defined as they are presented in the literature (see chapter 2), focusing in particular on their multidimensional character, which separates them from peacekeeping operations. Furthermore, they are dispatched after the war ends, whereas peacekeeping operations may be in place even during actual combat. The different outcomes, notably victory and peace agreements, are in focus.

The victorious side in a civil war is likely to claim that its victory is a "just" one. It is seen as vindication of its choice to take up arms in the first place, making it a legitimate course of action, and it is also a tribute to the sufferings the war has led to. The war seems "worth it." For the losing side, however, there are no reasons for jubilation. For them there is likely to be fear, flight, or regrouping for a renewed fight. In the case of renewed fight, the next war could be expected to be more vicious than the one just ended. For the victor, in other words, it is important to cement the victory.

The questions that can be asked in the case of a peace agreement are different. This outcome would see more complicated cheers and worries. Most likely all sides will express their satisfaction with the outcome as they have signed on to the deal. They will point to the sacrifices as necessary and significant for the peace agreement. Will they also say that "justice" has been done and dignity restored? Probably this is not as common a statement as in the victory case. A peace agreement involves having to deal with parties that recently were enemies and thus used to be defined by each other as "oppressive," even "criminal," and pursuing an "unjust" cause. They were not seen as reliable partners before the agreement was signed. After successfully concluding an agreement their previous opponents are suddenly portrayed in a different light. On an elite level such deals are probably common, but what about the followers and the populations, whose interests and protection often constitute the justification for the violent struggle? The leaders are likely to benefit from an agreement, but what is in it for the others? Thus the compromises necessary for a peace deal are likely to be more difficult to "sell" to the party's own constituency as "just." A deal is more "justifiable" as a second best outcome: This is what was possible at this time. To many supporters it might be a disappointment or, possibly, acceptable as a tactical change in a continuous struggle now being pursued by unarmed means. Many defenders of an agreement will have to say what the outcome is not: It is not a "defeat." But for those factions focused on victory, they might withdraw their support or turn into spoilers of the accords.

This means that both of the main outcomes, peace agreement and victory, can be related to a return of war. Peacebuilding missions after either type of outcome, therefore, are of interest. Can the elements of quality peace that have been identified, notably dignity and safety, be provided to all inhabitants in both outcomes?

Looking at the outcomes in civil wars since 1989, the clear-cut and lasting victories are few. In 1989 the Romanian communist regime was removed after a short armed conflict. In 1991, there were two outright victories, in Ethiopia and Eritrea, respectively. In 1994, following the genocide, the Rwandan Patriotic Front (RPF) took control over Rwanda. In 1995, the Taliban captured Kabul and large parts of Afghanistan, although only recognized by a few states as the legitimate government (in the UN it was described as a "faction"). In 1997, the rebel troops of Laurent Kabila forced incumbent President Mobutu Sese Seko to flee, turning Zaire into the Democratic Republic of Congo (DRC). That was only the start of a protracted civil war where armed action still continues. Similarly rebel leader Charles Taylor could be said to have won in Liberia, as he became President, albeit through a biased presidential election. However, he was to face a new rebellion and had to leave the country in 2003, when a new regime was installed through negotiations. In 2001 the Northern Alliance (with support of the United States and Russia) removed the Taliban from Kabul and formed a new government (still in place but no longer under Hamid Karzai). In 2003 the United States secured control over Baghdad, Iraq, and, in effect, removed Saddam Hussein from power in an inter-state war, but also unleashed a civil war with the United States as a strong actor.[5] In 2011, the Ghadaffi regime in Libya was overthrown in an internationalized civil war, which started with peaceful demonstrations, as part of the Arab Spring. In a number of cases, in other words, the victories have been short-lived and been followed by refugee flows, formation of new groups, coalitions, new sources of funding, and a restart of wars. The outcome of the conflict in Côte d'Ivoire in 2011 may suggest a different path, and in this case the international community played a major role for the victory of the winner of the presidential elections (Schori 2015).

In a host of cases, civil wars have remained protracted and devastating (e.g., Afghanistan, Burundi, CAR [Central African Republic], Chad, Colombia, Philippines, Somalia, Darfur in Sudan, and Syria). Since 1990 very few rebel movements have achieved their primary goal of taking government power. The 2011 events in Libya are not typical: Most of the time governments are strongly resourced, maintain effective security institutions to protect themselves and their followers, and can rely on international allies to sustain themselves even in the face of popular or military challenges. The rebels are more likely to find themselves in situations of protracted wars or in the unfamiliar game of peace negotiations. When the expected victory is not likely to materialize for either party, negotiations become necessary. Peace agreements, in other words, become logical and, by now, have a reasonable record in actually terminating conflicts.

In case there are no negotiations, the outcome may still not be outright military victory, but a political one. A typical pattern is that the losing top leaders manage to escape before military defeat, and thus never are brought to justice. Sometimes this is part of clandestine deals to end a war; sometimes the losing side has kept options for their own escapes. Ethiopia's Mengistu flew to Zimbabwe; Zaire's Mobutu left for Morocco; Taylor was allowed to leave for Nigeria. A few have been captured and their fates have been quickly sealed, notably Ceausescu of Romania (executed after a videotaped "trial," 1989); Sam Doe in Liberia (tortured to death, on video, 1990); Najibullah in Afghanistan (hanged without due process, 1996); Saddam Hussein captured and executed after a trial in national court (2006); Moammar Ghadaffi killed by militias (2011). The most recent and public case is, no doubt, the killing of al-Qaeda leader Osama Bin Laden (2011).

Neither the escapes nor the summary executions are reassuring outcomes in term of building justice for a post-conflict era. There are alternatives today, notably the international criminal court or legitimate tribunals, which provide both for documentation of crimes that have taken place and a civilized way of dealing with crimes and culprits. It appears that the fear of being brought to trial actually has a stronger impact on leaders than fighting and dying in battles. In the long run, this may have a preventive effect on conflicts escalating into wars.

The followers on the losing side are often paying a higher price than the leaders. Leaders and their families may have used their positions to build up fortunes abroad, partly as a guarantee in case they were to lose power. The ability of the UN Security Council to freeze privately held financial assets might thus be preferable also from the point of view of administering justice against such leaders. Still, the fate of the followers of the losers has certainly been grim in, for instance, Ethiopia and Eritrea after the victory of the revolutionaries, and in Afghanistan after the Taliban victory in 1996.

The future for continued unarmed opposition after a victory by the other side is often bleak. For those associated with the previous regime, the loss of power endangers life and liberty for family, groups, or entire social segments. They are left to the whims of the winner. The winner, furthermore, is often in a situation without counterbalancing forces on the national level. There is a strong temptation to turn laws and institutions to instruments favoring the undisputed powerholders.

However, this may not be the entire picture. There are international measures to prevent gross violations. The international scene since the end of the Cold War has become an arena of humanitarian concerns, with attention to issues of human rights, war crimes, democracy, and rule of law. Thus one might be able to suggest a trend and even formulate a hypothesis: the more international attention and presence in an armed conflict the more likely a more respectful treatment of the losers after the war. To this one could add that this might be beneficial for quality peace; it may provide for more dignity for the losers and thus by implication for all inhabitants in the society.

Some examples can illustrate this. A first case is Liberia. The Hague trial against Charles Taylor is a significant event. After the democratic regime took power in Liberia—with considerable international support and attention—Taylor was transferred to the Special Court on Sierra Leone in 2006. For security reasons this trial was placed in The Hague. He was the first African leader to be tried and his conviction in 2012 sent an important message throughout the continent. The fate of the former President of Côte d'Ivoire, Laurent Gbagbo, captured in April 2011, may also be instructive. The plan was initially to bring him to a national court (Martins 2011), but later he was handed over to the International Criminal Court (ICC) in The Hague.

A further example for reflection is Rwanda. A common lack of post-conflict justice in Africa puts post-victory developments in Rwanda in a special light. It is the only case outside South Africa where there have been reasonable trials, notably an international court dealing with the genocide (placed in Arusha, Tanzania) as well as national procedures. Members of the previous government have been charged, processed properly, and convicted. There is also a reconciliation process, administered through the central government. In the global picture of victories in civil wars, Rwanda may be an exception for internal affairs, not necessarily without its flaws, but definitely different from many other outcomes.[6] It has rested on strong international support, partly building on the guilt felt for inaction during the genocide. However, so far there have not been any trials against members of the leading group, the victors of 1994, for any action relating to the defeat of the previous regime. The heavy Rwandese involvement in the conflicts of neighboring Congo is a further flaw in Rwanda's post-conflict quality peace conditions.[7]

An additional illustration (from an ongoing conflict) is that the ICC also in 2008 charged an incumbent President, Omar Hassan al-Bashir of Sudan, for orchestrating a campaign of genocide in Darfur. The international attention to Darfur has been considerable and led to sanctions and other forms of pressure on Sudan. This serves to demonstrate that sitting presidents are also within the rule of law even while in power, challenging the more common approach of only focusing on the losers.[8] Not only war crimes but also genocide is now on the list of actions for international legal procedures.

In a number of instances, the victims or the losers of civil war can be identified by the outside community and some form of justice can be delivered. Winners of wars, or the holders of power, can be legally challenged. The world is still only at the beginning of this system of accountability, however. It remains to be seen if international attention and reaction can work not only to bring offenders to court but also as a deterrent against war crimes, violence, and war. From the perspective of quality peace, these are important aspects.

In the peace agreement cases, there are probably more stipulations that relate to justice issues: War crimes may be directly addressed, they might be part of the implementation measures, and proposals for truth commission and reconciliation work may be developed (Melander 2010, Joshi and Darby 2013). Truth commissions can serve as an example. They are found in negotiated endings to war and repression (South Africa being the prime example), while they are largely absent in cases of victory consolidation, at least as instruments for scrutinizing the winners. International attention, in other words, might be higher in cases of negotiated outcomes and such outcomes are more likely to have justice-related components.

What will attract international attention and support, the victories or the peace agreements, and why would there be a difference? The basic argument made here is that the international community will have more difficulty in relating to civil war victories. This applies in particular to the post–Cold War period. The Cold War saw more victories than negotiated endings and the outcomes were often derived from support by one or the other of the Cold War contestants. In the post–Cold War period, victories have been more homegrown and thus based on domestic political resources (a form of local capacity, as mentioned above). They are, one could suggest, as a consequence, more likely to demonstrate a lower adherence to international norms. As we have just demonstrated, victors may be reluctant to pursue issues of war crimes, particularly if it could result in a focus on the victors as well. In contrast, such issues are probably addressed in a more even-handed way in peacebuilding outcomes. Peace agreements would thus be closer to the post–Cold War global norms of justice and fairness. This means that the international community would more easily relate to the outcomes building on peace agreements. In addition, this community is assumed to be more involved in such processes—for instance in supporting the processes, assisting in direct negotiations, and in sending mediators.

This means that there will be differences between victories and peace agreements in the content and quality of the outcomes. This, furthermore, will impact on post-conflict involvement. The international community's hesitation may have its mirror image in the reluctance of a victor to participate. To the victor it is the victor that has produced the resulting victory. Why would a victor then involve an unpredictable, unspecified, international community in the operations of its post-conflict administration? Even issues of development aid are likely to be less of an enticement. The victory gives rise to self-righteousness as well as self-reliance. So from both sides there is hesitation. This is how we derive the hypothesis already mentioned: *The international community, in the form of the UN, is more likely to initiate peacebuilding operations in conflicts having ended in peace agreements than victory.*

This also relates to the different scholarly arguments on effective post-conflict peacebuilding, including willingness to negotiate and reach a peaceful agreement. The military victory of one party over the other changes the underlying conditions. It results in the victors' unwillingness to accept or cooperate with a third party attempting to create equitable conditions for the defeated. Peace agreements can, on the one hand, prove a local commitment for peace, and on the other, address some of the UN's hesitation to infringe upon the sovereignty of a state. This observation is also tied to Gilliam and Stedman's finding that the UN is less likely to intervene in states with well-developed armies (Gilliam and Stedman 2003).

The setting up, financing, and operating of a peacebuilding mission is a particularly strong commitment of the international community to a specific society. It means supplying not only physical security (military and police) but also support efforts of, for instance, human rights, democratization, gender equality, and free media. It is a large-scale transfer of resources and knowledge to a formerly war-torn society. It also means a certain transparency: What goes on in a given country is more likely to be observed by the outside world. For political opponents and former elites this may be reassuring; for the incumbents this may be annoying or even threatening. Thus we would expect a difference in the willingness to receive as well as in the willingness to disperse peacebuilding missions depending on the outcome of the war. These arguments can be put to a simple statistical test.

This is done here by using as the information on peace agreements and victory endings of civil wars that can be found in the UCDP datasets. Thus the test uses variables such as peacebuilding missions, victory, peace agreement, and ceasefires (these are the main variables), as well as duration of war, military capabilities of the factions, local commitment, and length of negotiation process, which are additional relevant variables derived from UCDP but also from other sources.

The conflict data consist of fifty-three armed conflicts over government ("civil wars") from 1989 to 2003, where the cutoff point allows for a certain time span, beyond five years, after the war. There are twenty UN peacebuilding operations in the same period (for data, see Appendix 3.2 below). A summary of the results is presented in Table 3.1. See Appendix 3.1, 3.2, and 3.3 for technical details.

From the results displayed in Table 3.1 we can conclude that the UN and international efforts in general are more likely to be initiated if there is a peace agreement. There is a highly significant correlation for peacebuilding (PB) missions and peace agreements (0.557 at the 0.01 level of significance). This is particularly true in conflicts that have continued over a long period of time (0.650 at the 0.01 level). As expected, victorious parties receive (or allow) less such international commitments (there is a negative and nonsignificant correlation of 0.204). It is noteworthy that victories also correlate strongly with conflict years. This can mean that victorious parties are actually less interested in involving international actors, particularly in a peacebuilding mission. We can conclude that the international efforts are geared toward situations that might be more difficult ones for post-conflict development—namely, where the formerly warring parties try to create new relationships under peaceful conditions. It is a demanding situation for the parties as well as for the international missions. It means that such situations could become more transparent and thus exposed to more public scrutiny than situations of victory. In the

Table 3.1

Peacebuilding Missions, War Outcomes, and Democracy

		PB mission	PB years	Peace agreement	Victory score	Intensity	Democracy	Army size
PB mission	Pearson Correlation	1	0.800(**)	0.557(**)	−0.204	0.320(*)	0.276(*)	−0.231
	Sig. (2-tailed)		0.000	0.000	0.147	0.021	0.047	0.103
	N	52	52	52	52	52	52	51
Conflict years	Pearson Correlation	0.650(**)	0.428(**)	0.491(**)	−0.405(**)	0.380(**)	0.325(*)	−0.140
	Sig. (2-tailed)	0.000	0.002	0.000	0.003	0.006	0.020	0.333
	N	51	51	51	51	51	51	50
PB years	Pearson Correlation	0.800(**)	1	0.651(**)	−0.230	0.035	0.145	−0.186
	Sig. (2-tailed)	0.000		0.000	0.101	0.805	0.302	0.192
	N	52	52	52	52	52	52	51
Peace agreement	Pearson Correlation	0.557(**)	0.651(**)	1	−0.211	0.093	0.073	−0.165
	Sig. (2-tailed)	0.000	0.000		0.133	0.511	0.607	0.248
	N	52	52	52	52	52	52	51
Victory score	Pearson Correlation	−0.204	−0.230	−0.211	1	−0.110	−0.134	0.167
	Sig. (2-tailed)	0.147	0.101	0.133		0.437	0.192	0.243
	N	52	52	52	52	52	52	51

continued

Table 3.1 (continued)

		PB mission	PB years	Peace agreement	Victory score	Intensity	Democracy	Army size
Number of victories	Pearson Correlation	0.006	−0.172	−0.234	0.716(**)	0.127	−0.009	0.063
	Sig. (2-tailed)	0.967	0.224	0.095	0.000	0.368	0.951	0.659
	N	52	52	52	52	52	52	51
Intensity	Pearson Correlation	0.320(*)	0.035	0.093	−0.110	1	0.143	−0.103
	Sig. (2-tailed)	0.021	0.805	0.511	0.437		0.313	0.473
	N	52	52	52	52	52	52	51
Region	Pearson Correlation	0.216	0.220	0.290(*)	0.142	0.017	−0.360(**)	−0.374(**)
	Sig. (2-tailed)	0.124	0.116	0.037	0.315	0.903	0.009	0.007
	N	52	52	52	52	52	52	51
Democracy	Pearson Correlation	0.276(*)	0.146	0.073	−0.184	0.143	1	0.031
	Sig. (2-tailed)	0.047	0.300	0.607	0.192	0.313		0.829
	N	52	52	52	52	52	52	51
Army size	Pearson Correlation	−0.231	−0.186	−0.165	0.167	−0.103	0.031	1
	Sig. (2-tailed)	0.103	0.192	0.248	0.243	0.473	0.829	
	N	51	51	51	51	51	51	51

**Correlation is significant at the 0.01 level (2-tailed).
*Correlation is significant at the 0.05 level (2-tailed).

cases of victory the prevailing actors will prefer to initiate their own policies and avoid international examination; examples of victorious situations are those in Ethiopia following the fall of the Mengistu regime and in Eritrea after it gained its independence. Characteristically these two actors only grudgingly agreed even to have a traditional peacekeeping mission on their borders following their disastrous inter-state war in 1998–2000.

Also noteworthy is the correlation with democracy building (there is a significant but not equally strong correlation for peacebuilding missions and democracy: 0.276 at the 0.05 level). We can interpret this to suggest that the presence of a peacebuilding mission does not only mean international attention to the situation, it may also connect to enlarged space for civil society, thus correlating with the presence of democracy. Again victorious parties are likely to be less democratic.[9]

Finally and surprisingly, the significance of the size of the armies of the warring parties does not emerge as a very strong factor. A peace agreement is likely to neutralize the importance of this factor and, in fact, often includes provisions of disarmament. Also in the case of victories the maintenance of the victor's order may not require major armies. Army size might instead, for instance, relate to other conflicts in the region.

3.4 Drawing General Conclusions

Table 3.1 presents robust findings, particularly as they build on a carefully selected and highly comparable group of civil wars (for instance, not incorporating territorial conflicts which could conflate the results). These are conflicts in the post–Cold War period, meaning that the findings concern a limited period of time. Still, it is convincing that international peacebuilding efforts are associated with peace agreements as well as more democratic conditions. It fits well with a general notion of peacebuilding being more connected to quality peace than victory consolidation. However, the results run counter to some other recent findings, notably those reported by Monica Toft in *International Security* (Toft 2010a) and in *Securing the Peace* (Toft 2010b). Thus it is important to relate our new findings to her work as well as integrating some other works, before drawing general conclusions on quality peace in post–civil war settings.

Monica Toft presents data demonstrating not only that victory is more often associated with democratization but also that this is particularly true for rebel victory. Thus, Toft's data (Toft 2010b: 64–65, 173; Toft Appendix 2) are important. As Toft generously makes data available on her website it is possible to look more closely at these findings and attempt to locate the disparity in the results.[10] Toft's Figure 4.1 demonstrates that the difference between the two outcomes (negotiated settlement vs. rebel victory) is most marked twenty years after the ending of the war, when rebel victory makes a sudden jump in improved polity scores, meaning that the outcome is more democratic. Toft is clear about this: "Put simply, following rebel victory, democratization increases. Within ten years, autocracy has decreased markedly by more than one point, and by twenty years that amount has more than doubled" (Toft 2010b: 65). A check in the codebook and the data available on the website (accessed September 29, 2011) show that there are twenty-three cases of rebel victory for which a twenty-year period can be followed. Thus, the most recent rebel victory in Toft's data is the one of Yoweri Museveni in Uganda 1986; the post–Cold War outcomes are not covered. This could be a first explanation for the difference presented here: The quality of negotiated settlements may have improved following the end of the Cold War.

Furthermore, Toft reports changes in democracy scores only for eleven of these rebel victories, thus reducing the relevant number even further and making the findings increasingly dependent on the cases included. In fact, there are only three cases with dramatic increases in polity scores, and this alone explains a large degree of the variance. None of them, however, are reassuring for the thesis of the democratizing effects of rebel victory. Let us quickly review them. They include the short but bloody coup against President Juan Peron in Argentina in 1955 (+15 points registered twenty years later), the coming to power of the Khmer Rouge in Cambodia in 1975 (+10), and the Iranian revolution in 1979 (+13). However, the increased scores following these rebel victories are difficult to attribute to the rebel victory, if we follow the cases more closely.

After the coup that removed Peron in 1955, Argentina went through a period of considerable political instability and remarkably by the twenty-year cut-off point in 1975, Argentina again saw a Peron at the helm, but this time his wife and widow, Isabel Peron, as President. She was removed in another military coup the following year. Moving from one Peron to another, interspersed with military coups and political turbulence, hardly appears to be a major gain in democratization. The second case refers to the events after 1975 in Cambodia. The victorious rebels of the Khmer Rouge led by Pol Pot were deposed by the Vietnamese invasion in 1979, which in turn was ended through international pressure and the Paris peace agreement in 1991. This gave space for elections in 1993. By that time the rebels, who were victorious in 1975, had been marginalized. Thus it is hard to attribute Cambodia's dramatic change in polity scores to this particular rebel victory. If anything, this victory pushed the country deeper into war, repression, politicide, and occupation. It is actually also defined by Toft as a case of war recurrence, but still appears in the column for polity scores after twenty years. In reality, the way out of civil wars and international occupation was through a negotiated settlement among all the parties, resulting in a national unity government and internationally supervised elections. Thus the score in 1995 is more closely attributable to the negotiated outcome than to the rebel victory.

As to the Iranian revolution, the increased score by 1999–2000 is harder to understand, but reflects the coding in Polity IV, where there is an increase recorded for Iran. For the period 1997–2003 a more open, "liberal" President, Ayatollah Mohammad Khatami, was at the helm of the Islamic Republic, although the real power remained with the clergy. It is hard to conclude, however, that there was a dramatic move toward democratization that can be attributed to the rebels-turned-government. The country also had experienced systematic repression of opponents, a series of rebellions (thus this case is also coded as a recurrence), a most severe war with Iraq, protracted tense relations with the United States, etc.

What this overview suggests is that the twenty-year period may be too long for this type of attribution to a particular outcome. As we could see in the case of Cambodia, much can happen that is more conducive to explaining changes. The same is true for some of the other rebel victories. For instance, in the case of Chile 1973, this refers to the coup by General Augusto Pinochet, which is described in the Codebook as a regime which "committed human rights violations, repressed opposing political groups, and suspended democratic processes" (Toft 2011: 39). However, twenty years later, in 1993, the regime had succumbed to domestic pressure and Chile's democracy was restored. This is what is recorded, but the link to the rebel victory actually appears to be the reverse: The peaceful defeat of the Pinochet's rebel-turned-government was a requirement for an open society.

Conducting a similar analysis of the cases for negotiated settlements, they are, as could be expected, very few (as this was typical of the Cold War period) and thus even fewer have passed the twenty-year threshold. In fact, only six have a polity score reported for the twentieth year and only four have a policy change score. From the spreadsheet it is difficult to understand why there is a drop for negotiated settlements at all, as there were very few changes in these scores between year 15 and year 20. The reason is instead that newer cases with higher polity scores still had not reached their twentieth year and thus were dropped from the analysis. This includes Guatemala, El Salvador, Mozambique, Namibia, and Nicaragua, which all were cases with good prospects of surviving their twentieth anniversary. We will return to them below.[11] These observations suggest an important methodological problem of how to relate a particular event to developments decades later.[12] There is a school of thought suggesting path-dependence as an approach where specific events can have large and sustained effects, although it has also been questioned as an approach (Pierson 2000). The point here is, however, that the way a war ends does have profound effects on the postwar conditions, unless overtaken by other violent or dramatic occurrences, such as new war, genocide, economic depression, or regime changes.

These ambiguities in Toft's work and the fact that the computations made here refer to civil wars in a much stricter sense makes the results in Table 3.1 the more convincing. Not the least the fact that the experiences included in the data squarely belong to the post–Cold War period makes it possible to conclude that negotiated settlements are more associated with democratic gains than victories. Furthermore, the results demonstrate that international involvement contributes to this.

Let us now relate this to other scholarship. Doyle and Sambanis (2006) use data for almost the same period as Toft, and also contains a mix of government and territorial conflicts.[13] The authors report that "negotiated settlements are also more likely to reduce the risk of recurrence. . . even when we control for decisive military victory." Furthermore, they state that their notion of positive peacebuilding ("participatory peace") shows no significant statistical association between military victory and peacebuilding success. Rather there is a correlation with negotiated outcomes, UN involvement, and peace in this broader sense (Doyle and Sambanis 2006: 86–88). These findings are more in line with the results here and reinforce the conclusion that negotiated outcomes actually result in a greater chance for positive peacebuilding outcomes.

Similarly Nilsson (2012) finds that negotiated settlements result in more democratic conditions than ceasefires, which in turn have better scores than victories. This study builds on the same data used by Doyle and Sambanis (2006) and argues that the incentive for the victor to democratize is lower. Instead victors are likely to base "their legitimacy on their success on the battlefield rather than through popular support." Furthermore, there is a lower level of war recurrence in the cases of negotiated settlement both two and five years after the end of the war (Nilsson 2012: 360–361). In a related work, building on similar data, Gurses and Mason (2008) arrive at a similar finding, but their argument is that the negotiated settlements result in an internal balance of power situation. Harzell (2009) has investigated the fate of factions, assuming that negotiated settlements would leave more factions in place, but surprisingly finds that more than 40% of the wars with military victory still left other political organizations intact. Thus we can conclude that there is reasonable consensus that civil wars ending in negotiated agreements exhibit more quality peace elements than those ending in military victories, at least for the first few years after the ending of the war. However, the field lacks real long-term studies.

Let us pursue this by relating the data to additional examples and by turning the question around and using the timeline suggested by Toft: Which are the war endings that took place twenty years ago or earlier (after the start year of the UCDP Conflict Encyclopedia) and have lasted to this day—that is, 2014? There are four peace agreements that ended civil wars that meet this criterion. They are all well-known cases in the peacebuilding literature and have been mentioned before in this work: Cambodia from 1991, El Salvador and Mozambique in 1992, and South Africa in 1994. None of these countries has reverted to civil war, but there was an armed conflict in 2013 between the same parties in Mozambique. One of them was involved in an armed conflict with a neighboring country (Cambodia; with Thailand in 2011). Both these instances were quickly contained and led to renewed negotiations along with resorting to established procedures. All of them have seen repeated elections; only in one (El Salvador) did that result in a change of government (FMLN, the former guerrilla group turned political party, won the presidency in 2009 and again in 2014). In Cambodia, political opposition has at times been exiled, while Mozambique has seen the government party, Frelimo, win repeatedly over the challenger and former guerrilla movement, Renamo. The agreement forged in 2014 allowed for Renamo's leader to run in the presidential elections of 2014. The real test would be a Renamo victory in elections, but that has not happened yet. South Africa has seen a series of presidents winning in fair elections since the agreement, but all have represented the same party, ANC. The critique against this party for corruption has been widespread and resulted in the formation of challenging parties, so far without leading to a change in South Africa's power structure.

There are only two civil war victories since the end of the Cold War that had lasted for more than twenty years by the end of 2014: the government conflicts in Ethiopia (ending in 1991 with the rebel victory over the government under Haile Mariam Mengistu), the victor Meles Zenawi being replaced after his death in 2012 by Hailemariam Desalegn from the same party) and Rwanda (the same leader being in place throughout the period, Paul Kagame). Ethiopia has seen continued involvement in state formation conflicts (a host of regional rebellions) and a devastating inter-state war (with Eritrea), as well as interventions in neighboring Somalia. Similarly Rwanda has been party to a host of interventions and uprisings in the Congo. Somewhat surprisingly, in other words, none of the countries with victories in civil wars have found themselves achieving something corresponding to quality peace. Insecurities have remained, partly related to the civil war, partly to other factors.

Thus even if the civil wars ending with negotiated agreements fared somewhat better, the results are not as strong as might have been expected. The picture may change as many of the agreements of the late 1990s and early 2000s continue, assuming that they are not challenged. Thus we can see that all the war endings have been fraught with problems and there is no spectacular story of success. However, three of the four twenty-year peace agreements were achieved through international efforts, while the victories were locally engineered, suggesting that there may be a greater chance of arriving at peaceful conditions with international support. Victories, whether by rebels or governments, do not appear to generate the national or regional stability that many may have wished for. Constructing quality peace after civil wars is obviously a tough challenge to the countries, the actors, and to the international community, but victories do not provide for a shortcut.

3.5   Quality Peace after Civil War

What we have seen is that negotiated endings to civil wars in general are likely to involve more transparency and accountability—that is, lead to more democratic conditions than one-sided victories. Furthermore, international attention is likely to be higher toward such negotiated settlements, and thus also international concerns about post-accord developments will be more quickly translated into policy. On these scores we see a difference between peacebuilding and victory consolidation. There will be more willingness to extend aid, but also to be critical if the record is not what was expected. Victorious parties are not likely to appreciate such transparency and thus may refrain from having international development assistance.

This can be supported by tracking a few particular cases. First there is the victory in Uganda by the National Resistance Movement led by Yoweri Museveni. This was an indigenous victory and initially hailed as the type of rebel victory "the world" would want. However, as time has passed, criticism has increased. The outcomes of the presidential elections in 2006 and 2011, both won by Museveni, were received with skepticism. It appeared that the potential democratic gains were not forthcoming in 2006 (Wallensteen 2008b) and the negative pattern was repeated in the following elections. At the same time, the government found itself involved in a series of internal domestic challenges, some of them stemming from the notorious LRA, the Lord's Resistance Army. Although driven out of the country by 2012, the LRA continued to operate in neighboring countries. The fate of Uganda's political future has become tied to the continued strength and health of one man, Museveni. Looking at a second case, these developments constitute a strong contrast to the parallel developments in Liberia, which took place within the framework of the 2003 comprehensive peace agreement, with heavy international involvement, and saw open elections in 2005 and 2011, respectively. President Ellen Johnson Sirleaf certainly symbolizes this progress, and it remains to be seen whether the institutions are strong enough to manage a transition to a new generation. The peace in Liberia has still not yet been sustained as long as some of the Central American cases. The prognosis, however, seemed promising, until the advent of the Ebola crisis in 2014, injecting fear and unpredictability into a still fragile postwar situation.

Thus there is also an empirical foundation for the conclusions about the benefits of international participation in postwar circumstances when observing particular cases of war-torn countries. As the discussion in the previous sections makes clear, results in quantitative analysis may sometimes depend on coding rules and the cases that are included. Even in a turbulent world there seem to be too few wars for a statistical analysis using too many categories. Thus there is a necessity to test arguments with case analysis or comparative approaches, and so contrasting Uganda and Liberia by the early 2010s, for example, may yield considerable lessons. This also shows that headway can only be made if different methodological approaches are attempted at the same time.

There are additional topics of significance for quality peace and the strategies to be followed after a war. One relates to the criterion of dignity and can be understood from the handling of justice after war. We can postulate that victorious parties (whether governments or rebels) are less likely to be interested in customary justice issues, particularly those that include the protection of life and liberty of their opponents. The domestic politics that follow on peace agreements will, however, have to wrestle with these issues. For instance, in the early 1990s, peace agreements often stipulated amnesty for the warring factions; these agreements have been adhered to. Later agreements, however, have included issues of war crimes and may thus have encountered more difficulties in implementation (Melander 2010). This is part of the transparency that international involvement brings, but may also be an argument for local actors to make deals among themselves, without such provisions. Notably few peace agreements have included items relating to compensation to victims (Joshi and Darby 2013).

Nevertheless the results presented here point to the importance of early democratization, but do not say exactly when and how this should come about. There is considerable concern about finding the "correct" sequence. For instance, Doyle and Sambanis (2006: 341) argue that their results support the conclusion that "elections must usually come after the institutional transformations that establish the foundation of the rule of law." First there is need for internal and subnational democracy, humanitarian deliveries, and rule of law. This leads to the question that is at the heart of a civil war: Who rules? This is the key incompatibility, and the authors leave such issues for later. However, their main message is the importance of local capacity (which also is the argument for international involvement to replace and foster such a capacity). It thus seems important to give priority to building local capacity.

The literature has some suggestions on this, the foremost being power sharing, but also other forms of government coalitions or space for civil society. There have been some recent advances in the study of power sharing, notably by Jarstad and Nilsson (2008), DeRouen et al. (2009), and Gent (2011). The picture emerging is that the political act of sharing national power between the main warring actors occurs when the rebels are increasing in strength, and thus are offered inclusion in the government by the current incumbents. However, only when provisions of military integration between the parties are implemented is there likely to be a lasting postwar situation (Jarstad and Nilsson 2008, DeRouen et al. 2009). Thus when there are no longer two armies confronting each other, the two sides are more likely to work toward continued peace. This conclusion gains support from two recent and contrasting experiences: Côte d'Ivoire and Nepal.

In Côte d'Ivoire, the peace agreements kept the two opposing armies intact, albeit the country was under an international arms embargo. Thus when a dispute arose in December 2010 on the outcome of the elections, the strength of the armies became a decisive factor. It is an important case where a negotiated settlement also led to a military victory; as we observed early on, these two categories are not necessarily exclusive. The outcome was a victory, building on an internationally supported peace deal, and the international attention to the situation has continued in ways not normally the case for victories. One of the new regime's ways of reassuring the international community, following its victory, was the transfer of the arrested former President, Laurent Gbagbo, to the International Criminal Court in The Hague, but also there was the allowing of scrutiny of the human rights situation in the country. Furthermore, there was only one army in the country.

Interestingly in late 2011, a crisis loomed in the stalled peace process in Nepal, where the parties were building their postwar relations on the peace agreement from 2006. It was a peace agreement negotiated between the parties themselves with little significant international involvement, a case deviating from the typical pattern for most of the post–Cold War period, when, as we have seen, peace agreements often were done through international efforts.[14] Nepal invited a peacebuilding mission in 2007 (UNMIN) to assist in the agreed elections and in the military disarmament process (including locating and decommissioning of child soldiers). The UNMIN mission ended in January 2011, leaving the political parties to handle the remaining military issues on their own. When a political impasse was reached in October 2011, the worries increased in Nepal as well as internationally on the fate of the peace process. In the end an agreement was signed on November 1, 2011, by the parties for the integration of the Maoist rebel forces into the national army, thus, making a military pact a crucial aspect of the implementation of the peace agreement. The general and positive reaction to this outcome by the Nepalese public indicates the significance of this particular agreement. The integration of the armed forces made the scenario of Côte d'Ivoire less likely. Thus these two cases confirm the results from the two studies with respect to the implementation, particularly, of military measures (Jarstad and Nilsson 2008 and DeRouen et al. 2009). The treatment of military resources may be crucial for the implementation of peace agreements and for the future of postwar democracy. Certainly, the cases of Côte d'Ivoire and Nepal deserve continued close scrutiny.

Thus power sharing, notably in the form of military integration following civil wars, appears to be very important for the duration of an agreement. In the case of a military victory, of course, a similar state of affairs is arrived at through the power of the victorious army. Even so, the victor faces a choice of how to deal with the losing side. This is the problem that is studied in a novel way by Joshi and Mason (2011) when giving attention to the "governing coalition," which is the size of the politically active components of a society whose "support is necessary to claim political power." They apply a measure building on items such as regime type and executive and participatory competition (Joshi and Mason 2011: 11). The results are interesting also with respect to victory consolidation: The government victories are followed by an expansion of the governing coalition while rebel victories show the reverse patterns. They note that this is contrary to Toft's argument (Toft 2010a) and implies that governments, following a victory, actually may be more favorable to democratization than rebels (Joshi and Mason 2011: 15). Furthermore, for both victory and negotiated settlement democratization seems to result in more durable settlements. Thus the authors conclude that delaying democratic competition after a war, regardless of the outcome, "might allow nondemocratic tendencies to ossify." They go on to argue that "if the new state institutions are not tested early, we cannot know whether they can weather a crisis that risks conflict recurrence" (Joshi and Mason 2011: 21). The authors thus do not find support in their study for the conclusions that seem prevalent, particularly among analysts in the strategic peacebuilding approach (e.g., Paris 2004, Diamond 2005)—namely, that democratization should be delayed.

This is perhaps where the sharpest dividing line can be located between different peacebuilding studies: When should democratic institutions in general, and elections in particular, be introduced? As we have seen, economic arguments have also entered the discussion, warning that early democratic rule can lead to insecurities and thus delay economic recovery. Dilemmas abound in formulating the most optimal strategy for quality peace after a civil war. However, if the quest is not only for duration but also for conditions that require dignity for all segments of a society, the conclusion should be clear. Early construction of democratic institutions and procedures should be preferable. This is also the path seen in the case of Nepal. Once the reformed institutions were in place, with a larger governing coalition, it was also possible to solve a key problem in disarmament. Nepal also illustrates the importance of local capacity in handling the situation. Functioning institutions were in place; there was a civil society as well as independent political parties and academic insights. The international peacebuilding mission was commissioned by the parties to handle particularly sensitive issues, notably elections and cantonment of soldiers. However, the process continued to be led by the Nepalese parties.

What also becomes clear is the importance of international involvement by reasonably unbiased organizations. International peacekeeping can provide security for the period following a civil war. It can provide transparency and serve as a stimulus for local capacity. If, furthermore, local capacity is seen in a larger perspective, including a vibrant civil society and more of gender equality, the prospects for a durable peace of high quality increase.

We can also conclude that the way the victors act is likely to be important for the future, whether they are the same government as before or are made up of the previous rebels. An option is to take an inclusive approach (integrating the former enemy armies into the military, inviting former opponents to take part in a power-sharing arrangement, etc.). Not all victorious actors are likely to share such a perspective, particularly not rebels, as has been seen in Ethiopia since the victory of 1991 (in Ethiopia and in Eritrea, respectively), or in the rebel victory of Cambodia in 1975 (by the Khmer Rouge). Any victor may have a strong feeling of being on an historical mission, rebel victors more than any others. Thus the international community faces a diplomatic and strategic challenge in how to approach victorious regimes in order to make them more amenable to strategies that open up for democratization. The future of the two victories of 2011 in Libya and Côte d'Ivoire may have given the world a test of the future for postrevolutionary changes in the Arab world and Africa. In this case, developments in Côte d'Ivoire have been more encouraging, while Libya increasingly appears as a failed state. The protracted conflict in Syria, furthermore, underlines the difficulties in a path aiming at victory, for the government or the rebels. More than four years of war have only served to increase suffering, literally reduce the economy to rubble, undermine public health (even polio has again been reported), and give space for increasingly extreme groups (the latest being ISIS, challenging Syria, Iraq, and minority populations, as well as powerful states). The outcomes of the four twenty-year peace agreements speak a different language.

Appendix 3.1 Success in Peacebuilding; Revisiting Doyle and Sambanis.

Updating successful cases of peacebuilding, ten and fifteen years after ending. Built on the coding made by Doyle and Sambanis (2000: 784).

10 *years*: no return to war after ten years and minimum democracy level maintained.

15 *years*: no return to war after fifteen years (or by the end of 2008), minimum democracy level maintained.

Yes: Success remained.

No: New war or further reduction in democratic level.

Italics: Territorial conflicts

	War Start	End	After 10 years	After 15 years (or by 2008)
Argentina	1955	1955	No	No
Bangladesh	*1973*	*1994*	*Yes*	*Yes*
Bolivia	1952	1952	No	No
Cambodia	1979	1991	Yes	Yes
CAR	1995	1997	No	No
Chad	1980	1994	No	No
Colombia	1948	1962	Yes (War restarts 1978, D & S)	No (UCDP)
Costa Rica	1948	1948	Yes	Yes
Djibouti	1991	1995	Yes	Yes
Dom.Rep.	1965	1965	Yes	Yes
El Salvador	1979	1992	Yes	Yes
Ethiopia/Eritrea	*1974*	*1991*	*No*	*No*
Ethiopia	1974	1991	No	No
Greece (coup 1967)	1944	1949	Yes	Yes
Guatemala	1954	1954	Yes (war starts 1966, D&S)	No

(*continued*)

	War Start	End	After 10 years	After 15 years (or by 2008)
Guatemala	1974	1994	Yes	Yes
Haiti	1995	1996	No	No
India Partition	1946	1948	Yes (*war in 1965, 1971 ...*)	Yes
India/Sikh	1984	1994	*Yes*	*Yes*
Israel/Palestine	1947	1997	No (*Second intifada*)	*No*
Lebanon	1958	1958	Yes (but war in 1975)	Yes (war 1975)
Malaysia	1948	1959	Yes (separation in 1965)	Yes
Mali	1990	1995	Yes	Yes
Mexico	1992	1994	Yes	Yes
Mozambique	1979	1992	Yes	Yes
Namibia	1965	1989	*Yes*	*Yes*
Nicaragua	1981	1989	Yes	Yes
N. Ireland	1968	1994	*Yes*	*Yes*
Pakistan/ Bangladesh	1971	1971	*Yes*	*Yes*
Paraguay	1947	1947	No (coup?)	No
Philippines	1950	1952	Yes (but military coup 1972 ...)	Yes
Romania	1989	1989	Yes	Yes
Rwanda	1990	1994	No	No
South Africa	1976	1994	Yes	Yes
Sri Lanka JVP	1971	1971	Yes (but restarts 87, D & S)	Yes
Sri Lanka JVP	1987	1989	Yes	Yes
Thailand	1967	1989	Yes (but military coup 1992–93)	Yes
Uganda	1966	1966	No	No
Yemen	1948	1948	Yes	Yes
Yemen	1994	1994	Yes	Yes
Yemen N	1962	1969	Yes	Yes
Yugoslavia/ Croatia	1995	1995	*Yes*	*Yes*
Zimbabwe	1984	1984	Yes (but violence 2002)	Yes

With these data we can distinguish between war endings that take place in 1990 or earlier and compare them to those after 1991. The following table emerges, comparing a total of twenty-three "successful" endings that took place 1990 or earlier to the twenty cases that occurred after 1991.

	Ending 1990 or earlier	Ending after 1991	Total
Failure	45	36	81
Success, two years	23	20	43
Of above cases, "success" also after ten years	19	13	32
Total	68	56	124

Thus the failure rate was 45 out of 68 during the Cold War, which is 66% compared to 64% in the period afterwards and thus not a significant change. Even more remarkable is that the success rate after ten years is 28% for the Cold War period compared to 23% for the period after. That is to say that the record is not going in favor of the post–Cold War efforts at peacebuilding. The numbers, of course, are lower and make statistical methods difficult (which also is noted by Doyle and Sambanis 2000: 787, fn 29). However, they do not make the observation that there is no significant improvement, which is what would be expected in case there was an international learning process. This may even suggest that the Cold War experiences are seen as irrelevant for post–Cold War undertakings. It could be argued that the endings in the Cold War in fact were a result of the superpowers deliberately or in effect "freezing" the outcomes that emerged from the battlefield. To challenge these endings may have invited a nuclear confrontation. Thus the solutions are likely to have been cemented by the opposing global powers providing assistance for "their" party. In the post–Cold War world such solutions are no longer of interest. The parties have had to find solutions with less international support and with less commitment of strategic and other resources to the outcomes. Consequently post–Cold War conflicts fail challenges that are different. The data suggest that, initially, the international community is not strikingly successful in managing the new challenges. Thus the Doyle and Sambanis work strengthens our conclusion that there is now a world order difference that affects the global interest in sustaining solutions. The peacebuilding undertaken since the end of the Cold War can only to a limited extent learn from the experiences of the previous period.

Appendix 3.2 Case Information for Table 3.1.

Intrastate Conflicts—Non-Territorial—1989–2003

1. Afghanistan (1989–2003)
2. Algeria (1991–2003)
3. Angola (1990–1998)
4. Azerbaijan (1993, 1995)
5. Burundi (1991–2003)
6. Cambodia (1989–1998)
7. Central African Republic (2001, 2002, 2006)
8. Chad (1989–2002)
9. Colombia (1989–2003)
10. Comoros (1989)
11. Congo (1993–2002)
12. Djibouti (1991–1999)
13. Egypt (1993–1998)
14. Eritrea (1997, 1999, 2003)
15. Ethiopia (1989, 1990, 1991)
16. El Salvador (1989–1991)
17. Georgia (1991, 1992)
18. Guatemala (1989–1995)
19. Guinea (2000, 2001)
20. Guinea Bissau (1998, 1999)
21. Haiti (1989, 1991, 2004)
22. Iraq (1991–1996)
23. Iran (1991–2001)
24. Ivory Coast/ Côte d'Ivoire (2002–2004)
25. Laos (1989, 1990)
26. Lebanon (1989, 1990)
27. Lesotho (1998)
28. Liberia (1989–2003)
29. Macedonia (2001)
30. Mexico (1994, 1996)
31. Mozambique (1989–1992)
32. Myanmar (1990–1994)
33. Nepal (1996, 2003)
34. Nicaragua (1989)
35. Pakistan (1990)
36. Panama (1989)
37. Paraguay (1989)

38. Peru (1989–1999)
39. Philippines (1989–2003)
40. Romania (1989)
41. Russia (1993)
42. Rwanda (1990–2002)
43. Sierra Leone (1991–2000)
44. Somalia (1989–2002)
45. Sri Lanka (1989, 1990)
46. Sudan (1989–2003)
47. Tajikistan (1992–1998)
48. Togo (1991)
49. Trinidad Tobago (1990)
50. Turkey (1991, 1992)
51. Uganda (1989–2003)
52. Uzbekistan (2000, 2004)
53. Venezuela (1992)

UN Peacebuilding Missions

1. Afghanistan (UNAMA 2002–2003)
2. Angola (UNAVEM 1991–1995)
3. Burundi (ONUB 1996–2006)
4. Cambodia (UNTAG 1991–1993)
5. Central African Republic (BONUCA 2000–2001; MINURCA 1998–2000)
6. Chad (MINURCAT 2007)
7. Congo (MONUC 1999–2006)
8. El Salvador (ONUSAL 1991–1995)
9. Guatemala (MINUGUA 1994–2004)
10. Guinea Bissau (UNOGBIS 1999–2001)
11. Haiti (MINUSTAH 2005–2006)
12. Iraq (UNAMI 2003–2007)
13. Liberia (UNOL 1997–2003 ; UNMIL 2003–2005)
14. Mozambique (UNOMOZ 1992–1994)
15. Nepal (UNMIN 2007)
16. Nicaragua (ONUCA and ONUVEN 1989–1992)
17. Rwanda (UNAMIR 1993–1996)
18. Sierra Leone (UNAMSIL 1999–2005)
19. Sudan (UNMIS 2005–)
20. Tajikistan (UNTOP 2000–2007)

Appendix 3.3 Statistical Information for Table 3.1

Sources for Indicators:

Peace agreement, victories, victory endings of civil wars, duration and intensity of conflict: drawn from UCDP datasets.

Armed conflicts are listed in Appendix 3.2.

Peacebuilding missions: see Appendix 3.2.

Democracy in conflicting country, from Freedom House, Scores 1–10 (where 1 is best/ 10 worst). Situation at time of beginning of the conflict, Yes = 2; No = 1

Region of world—continent numbers given by number of conflicts. Europe = 1; Americas = 2; Middle East = 3; Africa = 4; Asia = 5

Government army size, of conflict country, 1 = small; 2 = medium; 3 = large

See http://www.fas.org/asmp/profiles/wmeat/WMEAT99-00/03-hl-ArmedForces.pdf.

National material capabilities for army—soldiers, supporting industry, military expenditure—from Correlates of War project: http://www.correlatesofwar.org/.

Resources—Economic, special resources/ large quantities, including petroleum, diamonds—from Center for the Study of Civil War, PRIO.

Country has large resources—2; no economically relevant resources—1.

Additional variables, not reported, not significant: GDP, GDP/capita, threat, geographical proximity, magnitude of challenge, contagion effect, P 5 interest such as trade relations, historical relations.

Statistical operations

Correlates: conflict years, peace agreement, intensity, democracy

Regression: r square over 0.5 = > not accidental, plus it's significant for all

Best variables: conflict years and peace agreements

Length: relation between PB years and other variables

Correlates: conflict years, peace agreement

R square close to 0.5, peace agreements as significant variable

-Model Summary

Model	R	R Square	Adjusted R Square	Std. Error of the Estimate
1	0.721(a)	0.520	0.478	0.35631

-a Predictors: (Constant), democracy, peace agreement, intensity, conflict years

-ANOVA(b)

Model		Sum of Squares	df	Mean Square	F	Sig.
1	Regression	6.317	4	1.579	12.439	0.000(a)
	Residual	5.840	46	0.127		
	Total	*12.157*	*50*			

-a Predictors: (Constant), democracy, peace agreement, intensity, conflict years
-b Dependent Variable: PB mission

-Coefficients(a)

Model		Unstandardized Coefficients		Standardized Coefficients	t	Sig.
		B	Std. Error	Beta	B	Std. Error
1	(Constant)	−0.265	0.222		−1.191	0.240
	conflict years	0.020	0.007	0.403	3.030	0.004
	Peace agreement	0.044	0.016	0.334	2.816	0.007
	Intensity	0.154	0.149	0.115	1.030	0.308
	Democracy	*0.037*	*0.032*	*0.122*	*1.125*	*0.266*

-a Dependent Variable: PB mission

CHAPTER 4

Quality Peace and State Formation Conflicts

4.1 Outcomes in State Formation Conflicts

An important point in this book is the significance of the incompatibility for how armed conflicts develop, as well as to how they are solved, and, as a consequence, to how postwar relations are structured (Wallensteen 2015). This is most readily observed when dealing with internal conflicts. Chapter 3 took up the postwar conditions in conflicts over government. Thus chapter 4 focuses on quality peace in internal conflicts over territory. Our definition of quality peace—post-conflict conditions that make the inhabitants of a society (be it an area, a country, a region, a continent, or a planet) secure in life and dignity now and for the foreseeable future—means that the relationship between the former adversaries is crucial. In civil war situations, that entails finding ways to bridge divides within a country. As we have found in chapter 3, a negotiated settlement is more likely to give the previous enemies a stake in peacebuilding after the war. It was also documented that in any postwar peacebuilding efforts early democratization is central, as is the creation of national institutions (local capacity). In state formation conflicts this does not suffice. For instance, the result of a negotiated peace agreement or a military victory could be the creation of two separate states. Thus the relations between the "old" center (also called the former metropolis) and the "new" successor state have to be part of the picture. In fact, quality peace has to be measured both *within* the two entities and *between* them. This task is more complex than dealing with the civil war situations, for political leaders and scholars alike.

In the civil war case, the parties are fighting over the control of the central government, but there is no dispute about the state and its borders. All agree that the state as such should remain the same, even if the rules of governance are changed, notably through a shift of the hands of power, constitutional reform, or different government policies. However, the goals in conflicts over territory are poles apart. At least one set of actors challenges the form of the state. They ask whether all parts of the existing state's territory should be ruled in the same way or even remain in the same country. These are fundamental questions that go beyond the revolution in one country replacing a government with another one. If the territorial demands are met it will result in changes that are observable on a world map. The extent of territorial control for the center will shrink, either through the giving of more autonomy to some areas or agreement to their separation. Thus this is a separate category, with direct effects for conflict resolution and postwar conditions.[1]

The Uppsala Conflict Data Program, UCDP, data demonstrate that the number of armed conflicts in this category since the end of the Cold War is even larger than the "typical" civil wars, as shown in Tables 2.1 and 2.2. In the period 1975–1988 there were thirty-one state formation conflicts while the civil wars were more numerous, forty in all. Since 1989, the numerical relations have been reversed: state formation conflicts have numbered sixty-five and civil wars sixty. During the first period, only four state formation conflicts saw a peace agreement—that is, only one conflict in six (13%). In the twenty-two year period 1989–2010, there were twenty conflicts with thirty-five agreements (31%). Interestingly also the victories increase from the first period to the second from one to eleven cases (17%). At the same time more than half of the state formation conflicts saw neither victory nor a peace agreement (thirty-five out of sixty-five).[2] The ending of state formation conflicts is clearly more difficult, which also means that the experiences in postwar conditions are different. Furthermore, the types of endings can vary. The agreement can be about the creation of an autonomous area within the state (such as for Aceh within Indonesia, in 2005) or an acceptance of independence (such as for East Timor within Indonesia in 1999, now the independent state Timor-Leste, or for the newly independent state of South Sudan in 2011). The victory can also be one of returning to the *status quo ante bellum*, the conditions before the war (notably the government's victory over the Tamil Tigers in Sri Lanka in 2009). In some instances, the rebels may win, forcing not only an acceptance of a new status quo but also the elimination of the previous regime (a notable case is the Eritrean People's Liberation Front, EPLF, defeating the Mengistu regime in Ethiopia in coalition with a "sister movement" and then securing the agreement of the new regime for Eritrea's independence in 1993).

In some situations the distinction between a negotiated settlement and a victory can be blurred. The negotiated agreement may mean that one of the parties withdraws from the disputed territory in a peaceful way, but still in effect gives up its demand. The two cases mentioned by Paris (2004) as successes for peacebuilding, South Africa (Namibia) and Croatia (East Slavonia), have these traits: The former occupier accepts independence (South Africa gives up Namibia) or relinquishes its backing for its ethnic brethren on the other side of the border (Serbia ends its support to the remaining Serb minority in Croatia). In both cases the solutions were achieved through negotiations, but the end result was a new status quo that was closer to the demands of one party. Still the quality of the new arrangement needs to be assessed.

Thus chapter 4 deals with the challenge of postwar peace in state formation conflicts. We are asking how post-conflict conditions are handled and what the possibilities are for creating relations that provide for safety and dignity to the inhabitants in the concerned area for the foreseeable future, whether through peacebuilding or victory consolidation. This is done both by resorting to pertinent theoretical and statistical studies and observations based on relevant cases, such as those of with elements of self-rule within a state—notably Bougainville in Papua New Guinea (a case not often mentioned in the literature, and thus given attention here)—as well as those that resulted in independence (e.g., Eritrea and Namibia).

4.2 Challenges to Peace in State Formation Conflicts

In this book we have separated peacebuilding and victory consolidation outcomes in a postwar period. As we have observed in other studies of postwar experiences, long-term investigations are difficult. To go beyond the twenty-year limit, we have to include conflicts that were active in the Cold War period. As just noted, there was only one victory recorded for the 1975–1988 period in a state formation conflict, the case of the Kurdish region in Iraq. The Cold War was a period when such conflicts were discouraged and subsumed under the major conflagration between the superpowers of the day, as part of the prevailing attitudes and interests of those major powers. "Ethnic" conflicts were generally disregarded in the approaches to the world order at the time. There have been more peace agreements since 1990, notably over Namibia and Mindanao in the Philippines, where the former case has been frequently referred to in the literature on peacebuilding, the other one hardly at all (an exception is the study by Hoodie and Harzell 2005). Namibia has remained a successful case; Mindanao has seen a series of reversals, emergence of new actors, a decline in violence, and a comprehensive agreement in 2014.[3]

Let us take a closer look at the victory case, as it is instructive for understanding the dynamics of state formation conflicts in general, and not the least the problem of the actors credibly committing to peace in these relations. The illustrative historical case is the Iraqi government's victory over Kurdish rebel movements in the north of the country in 1975. The outcome meant the termination of the autonomy that the region previously had been granted by the central government under Saddam Hussein. This victory, furthermore, was a result of the peace agreement between Iraq and Iran dealing with the borders between the two states. As part of the deal Iran withdrew its support for the Kurdish movements, thus tipping the military balance in the direction of the central government. This victory, in other words, was as much a result of the changed policy of the supporting actor as the defeat of the rebel movement itself. As we now know, none of these were lasting outcomes. Five years later, in 1980, Iraq withdrew from the 1975 agreement, attacked the new Islamic Republic in Iran, and an eight-year war followed. It was brutal also for the Kurdish areas, witnessing the use of chemical weapons on the Kurdish population (an example is the attack on Halabja in March 1988). The ceasefire that was in place by August 1988 seemingly cemented the Iraqi government's control over the Kurdish area.

However, the end of this war freed Saddam to start another war, what became the Gulf War of 1990–1991. In the wake of his defeat by the UN-authorized and United States-led counteroffensive, the Kurdish rebels rose again, only to be threatened with a new defeat from Saddam, whose forces had retreated from Kuwait but still were powerful enough to attack in the north. Saddam's victory was ultimately prevented by the Western no-fly zone over the area, effectively barring Saddam from reestablishing control. This intervention created the *de facto* autonomy that the Kurdish region still enjoys, now within the federated structure of post-Saddam Iraq.

This case of repeated experience of warfare and peace demonstrates a number of the distinctive features of state formation conflicts. They are protracted, as government and rebels often are equally unrelenting in their efforts to prevail. Furthermore, the parties need to have access to substantial resources to sustain a conflict; that was the case for both sides in this example. In territorial conflicts rebel organizations are often drawn from particular social groups, which are likely to be supportive and generate the resources necessary. This is one reason for the protracted character of these conflicts. Furthermore, they often have a long history that has formed the identity of the social groups through clashes with the government's approach. The contentions are not necessarily tied to specific leaders or even organizations. Thus the struggle can continue with different actors and conditions. In the same way, the state leaders may change but share a commitment to the central state as it exists.

This has been understood in research projects, such as the Minorities at Risk at University of Maryland (Gurr 2000a, Gurr 2000b), the Ethnic Power Relations at the ETH Zurich (Cederman et al. 2013) and the project on horizontal inequality (Stewart 2002; Deiwiks et al 2012). There are also significant findings based on these and related projects. For instance, Gurses and Rost report that "high levels of discrimination endanger peace in the aftermath of ethnic civil war" and that this is particularly significant if a group is geographically concentrated (Gurses and Rost 2013: 478, 483). It points in the direction of the territorial dimension that is emphasized here. So does the work by Deiwiks et al. (2012) reporting on regional economic differences as well as political exclusion as factors behind secessionist conflict. Similarly Sambanis and Milanovic find a connection between relative regional income and demands for autonomy (Sambanis and Milanovic 2014). These findings support the focus here on territorial conflicts in general, and also the issue of state formation and autonomy in particular.

As the key issue concerns the relationship between the central government and people in a specific region, the possible solutions are different from those in civil wars. Democratic measures, elections, and power sharing do not directly address the territorial issues. Instead, matters of self-rule, autonomy, and local governance are crucial concerns, as well as financial relations between a particular region and the central government. Thus the conditions on which to build a postwar peace include issues other than those in classic civil wars. This does not exclude issues of shared central governance, elections, democracy, and rule of law. The conditions under which such measures operate, however, will be different. What happens to the center—as we saw in the case of the Iraqi government vs. the Kurdish population—affects the subnational region and its autonomy.

Even in the case of a negotiated independence, the former adversaries and their supporters are likely to continue to watch all moves carefully. Suspicion does not go away quickly. The "new" state is likely to closely observe what the "old" state does. There is a remaining security concern as well as a matter of dignity. In the eyes of the rebels, the question lingers whether they "really" are secure and accepted as equals by the "old" metropolis. To some extent also the former metropolis will attend to the developments of its former periphery: Will the "new" state encourage other splinter movements, directly or by inspiration? The treatment of border issues and refugees becomes an indicator for both sides of the "real" intentions of the other. This is so as it normally is the periphery that takes the initiative and demands separation. The war with a center that is reluctant to grant independence will continue in the minds of the separatists, whether there is a victorious or negotiated outcome. Seldom is the center the one that takes the initiative to grant the constituent units independence. In fact, the dissolution of the Soviet Union is unique in this case. Russian President Yeltsin's program—based on the idea that the center, that is Russia, was losing from the Union and thus wanted to "liberate" itself from this burden—is rather remarkable. A number of republics that had not asked for independence suddenly had it, notably in the Central Asian region. Actions by President Putin have given rise to a fear that Russia now aims to reverse this process, reasserting its influence in the former Soviet-held territories. In 2013, Russia's planned Euro-Asian Economic Union clashed with the EU's

Eastern Partnership project in the decision by Ukraine on its membership in one or the other. It escalated quickly to an internal and inter-state confrontation, with battles and many deaths. It involved several state formation issues, notably over Crimea and regions in Eastern Ukraine. From the perspective of separatists, there was a concern over the Ukrainian government's intentions, for instance, with respect to the Russian language. Russia had other considerations, notably the protection of the naval base in Sevastopol, Crimea. Both were concerned about Ukraine's future direction. But the new, more democratic Ukrainian government worried more strongly about the ultimate Russian plans and whether Russia could be a partner to trust.

This makes the notion of credible commitment to an agreed or accepted arrangement significant, and the work of James. D. Fearon from 2004 pertinent (Fearon 2004). Fearon's initial observation that territorial conflicts "have not been noticed in the civil conflict literature as having quite distinct and interesting (if tragic) dynamics" is not fully correct, as this distinction has been part of UCDP for a long period. It deserves to be highlighted (Fearon 2004: 298). There are still good reasons to pursue Fearon's argument on commitments. This yields seven conclusions that are particularly important in analyzing the quality peace problem in state formation conflicts.

First, Fearon demonstrates convincingly that intra-state wars over territory (Fearon calls them "sons of the soil" conflicts) are more protracted than any other type of intra-state conflict. The estimated median and mean durations for these conflicts are reported to be 23.2 and 33.7 years compared to 5.8 and 8.5 for other intra-state conflicts (Fearon 2004: 283). State formation wars are difficult to negotiate, as seen in the statistics and examples above. There are fewer peace agreements in such conflicts. They are also difficult to win, as demonstrated by the information on their average duration. This underlines their difference from civil wars. As we saw in chapter 3, civil wars are often subject to considerable settlement activity. The difficulty in finding solutions to state formation conflicts affects postwar peacebuilding strategies. Reconciliation should not be expected to be on the top of the agenda after such a war, no matter what the outcome.

Second, the origins of territorial conflicts are different from intra-state government conflicts. In this case, the political incompatibility is about a certain identifiable territory to which there is particular attachment for a group that often can be defined in ethnic terms. History is understood in divergent ways and is reflected in how the parties argue about a particular territory. Typically the government will minimize the geographical extent of the area and claim that it is just an "ordinary" part of the present state, an area that wholly or partially constitutes a province or a subregion. In contrast, the rebel movement is likely to point to previous autonomous developments, that the area has a distinct history and a name that may be different from the present "official" nomenclature, and that its geographical extension is much larger than the government claims. In Turkey there is no province called "Kurdistan," but Kurdish movements insist that there is such an area and that it covers a sizable part of what is today's Turkey (and stretches into neighboring states).

A state formation conflict may emerge in different ways that not only stem from geographical marginalization. It may even have started as part of a broader struggle for change of an authoritarian government where national democratic opposition movements were defeated. After the military suppression of the democratic movements in Burma/Myanmar in 1988, students and other opponents joined ethnic movements far away from the capital. Territorially recruited opposition can be more difficult to eliminate by the government, as it may involve sizable ethnic groups. To the opponents the same struggle continues but from territories far away from the central government, where the territorial aspect becomes increasingly salient. The movements may still entertain ideas of reforming the central government but combine this with a concept of autonomy for a particular region. The Sudanese People's Liberation Movement/Army (SPLM/A) for many years was unclear about whether it wanted a share of power in the national government in the capital, Khartoum, or if it wanted a separate state. The peace agreement in 2005 provided for a national government, with SPLM/A participation in a power-sharing arrangement, as well as for a referendum in the South. The vote finally settled the issue and the new state of South Sudan was created in 2011, with recognition by the former capital and the ending of the unity government. It is a speculative question to ask whether a more democratic regime in Khartoum would have made the outcome of the referendum different. In this case, as well as in many other situations, notably in Southeast Asia, authoritarian regimes tend to breed state formation conflicts. When democratic opposition is nonexistent, defeated, or marginalized, territorially based rebel movements may still sustain themselves over longer periods of time (Wallensteen et al. 2009).

Third, the difficult relationship between a central, authoritarian regime and a regional grouping bent on self-rule is illustrated by the Kurdish case, and leads to an important theoretical point. The Kurdish rebels were engaged in a battle within one authoritarian setting (Baathist Iraq), gaining support in the local population, but also becoming of value to an outside authoritarian government (the Shah's Iran). The authoritarian setting determined the fighting, but also made agreements unreliable. The Iraqi government was at the time exposed to severe pressure from inside as well as outside. In Fearon's words, when the central government is weak it can make concessions, "but the more the government has to give away, the more tempted it will be to renege when it is again in a strong position" (Fearon 2004: 295–296). When Iraq's government felt stronger, after having achieved Iran's agreement on borders and on noninterference in Iraqi affairs, it could renege on the previous deal with the Kurds. A peace agreement in one relationship laid the groundwork for a victory in another. Making deals with authoritarian regimes, in other words, is risky for territorially based movements. The more such governments open up the more feasible will other solutions become. Transparency may change the willingness among rebels to make deals with the central government, as there will be more information on what the government is doing. For instance, a stronger parliament will be one of the countervailing factors that can stimulate the government to adhere to agreements, or at least give rebels early warning signs on the possibility of government's reneging.

Fourth, mediation by outside powers may be more rare, as has been observed in the cases of Southeast Asia (Wallensteen et al. 2009), but the global approach we take here may suggest something different. In general, an authoritarian government will perceive any third party involvement as *de facto* recognition of an armed opposition that threatens to break up the country. However, when negotiations actually begin, it may imply that the government has given up its ambition to control the entire territory. Thus the number of agreements is likely to be fewer, but those that are concluded will be more decisive, and also adhered to. The high frequency of overturned peace agreements that we could observe for civil wars is not typical for state formation conflicts. For instance, there is only one agreement on Northern Ireland. Similarly, there is one for Bangladesh (Chittagong Hill Tracts) and for Bosnia (Dayton). They have all been implemented to reasonable degrees. There are also a number of other cases with one agreement where its failure has reduced the interest in renewed negotiations (for instance the cases of the Cabinda enclave in Angola, the Abkhazia territory in Georgia, the Trans-Dniester area in Moldova). Thus either the territorial agreement is implemented and the armed conflict is brought to an end or it fails, resulting in a strongly reduced interest in negotiated outcomes.

There is one case of a state formation conflict with many agreements: Israel–Palestine. This illustrates the commitment problems identified by Fearon. Neither side believes that the other will (or can) adhere to an agreement, as the opponent's goals are seen to be maximalist and thus not fully negotiable. The asymmetry of the situation makes both the superior and inferior actors skeptical about the other side's willingness to commit to an agreement. It also is a case with heavy international involvement. Thus negotiations and new agreements have been made, but none of them comprehensive enough to result in a conclusive settlement of the conflict.

In short, a failure of the first agreement in state formation conflict is not likely to result in a return to negotiations in the near future. It is more probable that the parties pursue their ambitions to win, militarily, politically, and diplomatically. This means that the experiences of a failed negotiation are more devastating than in the case of civil wars, where the parties often are willing to return for further discussions, even to the point that the shifts between war and negotiations appear as "normal politics." It seems that the territorial component makes state formation conflicts more difficult to handle and, as a consequence, that a solution requires a stronger commitment from both sides. If one side reneges on the agreement, it is difficult to rebuild credibility for a new round of talks. It is interesting that the only case where this has happened is the Palestinian issue.[4] This is also a conflict where the actions of both sides are unusually transparent, and thus commitment can be assessed more easily by the opposing sides. If there is no belief of a renewed, credible pledge from the other side, territorial conflicts are less likely to see renewed negotiations after a first failure.

Fifth, a pertinent question then is the rate of war recurrence in state formation conflict. Clearly the cases of failed agreements see a return to armed conflict. The cases where a territorial division actually is carried out and a new state is created on the territory of the older state are interesting from this perspective. Nicholas Sambanis has studied the recurrence of war in cases of "partition."[5] He analyzes 125 civil wars since 1946 where twenty-one are defined as partitions.[6] Sambanis reports that five out of eleven cases of partition saw a restart of war within ten years of the ending (45%), while nonpartition cases had a ratio of return of 34%. Particularly interesting in this context is Sambanis' observation that, if the war ends in a treaty, "the probability of no war recurrence increases" (Sambanis 2000: 465, 474). Agreed, rather than forced, partitions would have a greater likelihood of sustainability.

Sixth, this also means that there are fewer cases of peacebuilding in the territorial conflicts than in others. In that sense, the focus of the literature on peacebuilding in civil war situations is justified. There is more experience to analyze. However, some of the cases that frequently are referred to in this literature do not belong to the discussion on post–civil war conflicts within one and the same state. Cases that are assessed as "successes" actually concern state formation conflicts. This is true for the three cases of Namibia, East Timor, and East Slavonia, which are mentioned by Roland Paris. In chapter 2 it was demonstrated that these and some additional cases today could be seen in a more positive light than when Paris did his work. This is true for those that belong to the category of state formation conflicts, notably Bosnia-Herzegovina and Kosovo. So does the case of Eritrea, but the relations between this new state and the old one, Ethiopia, have been subject to surprisingly scant analysis from a peacebuilding perspective. Indeed the international efforts have also been limited. This makes this case particularly interesting. The devastating war fought from 1998 to 2000 between two states led by movements that were allies in a long fight against the previous regime is also remarkable, and so is their involvement in other conflicts in the region. This should be a particularly pertinent case for the study of limitations in peacebuilding in state formation conflicts.

Seventh, it is reasonable to assume that the resources of the disputed territory are important for both government and rebels: They are a way to find revenue that both may wish to control. For the rebels, furthermore, the key for a sustained battle is not only proceeds from a particular territory, but also that the territory can be a source for recruitment. This suggests that only territories with sufficient population will be able to sustain the battle. This is compatible with the finding that countries with a few large groups are likely to see more of this type of conflict (Collier et al. 2004: 263; Fearon 2004: 286).

There is a common assumption that the territorially based rebel movements mostly emerge in poorer parts of a country; this reflects an expectation that conflict rises from grievances. The reverse may also be true: relatively rich regions may prefer to keep their wealth to themselves and not share with others in the same state. In this way, greed may generate conflict. Also wealthier regions of a country are more able to sustain a rebellion. If such a region is successful in achieving independence, furthermore, this newly created state will face good prospect for economic growth, whereas the "old" state is more likely to confront economic hardships. Thus in this case the opposition to secession would be stronger in the metropolis than in other situations. Sambanis finds that partition often was carried out in countries with a higher level of economic development than other war-torn societies (Sambanis 2000: 458–459). Anecdotal evidence corroborates this observation. Sustained struggles will require access to considerable resources. This will also affect the postwar situation, and provide opportunities for intra-state peacebuilding. However, a sustained battle, waged over many years, may also ruin the territory and make it poorer. The case of Bougainville of Papua New Guinea is instructive, and will get more attention in the following section. Similarly Northern Ireland used to be a welfare state before The Troubles, but by year 2000—after thirty years of conflict—its income may have been closer to that of the Republic of Ireland than to Britain. It is also likely that Eritrea began its new history as an independent country in 1993 on a level of economic development similar to that of the 1950s and 1960s before the liberation struggle intensified.[7]

Even if the will to preserve wealth for oneself may be an incentive for rebellion, state formation conflicts are often triggered by experiences of injustice beyond economics, such as loss of autonomy, police brutality, and flagrant discrimination, for instance, in employment or education opportunities (Gurr 2000a) as well as political exclusion (Cederman et al. 2013). The point is that available economic resources help sustain the struggle, but also may be exhausted. For poor regions, financing a sustained battle will in that situation require other measures that make rebel activity reminiscent of criminal activities, notably drug trafficking (for example, Fearon finds a correlation with "contraband financing"; see Fearon 2004: 281–286). If this is not an option, rebel movements may have to enter alliances with outside actors. As suggested in the example of the Kurdish experience from 1975, dependence on external interests also makes local movements vulnerable to outside calculations where their interest is of marginal significance. Such alliances with outside power may undermine the movement's authenticity in the eyes of the metropolis as well as the outside world. However, armed movements may not have many alternatives. For peacebuilding after the war, there is not only the challenge of restoring what once was, but also developing the area to be on par with what it would have been without the war. If, on top of this, there is an ideological ambition to create a different society, the challenges for the leadership of the "new" state are tremendous.

Thus we ask whether the outcome in the form of a victory or a peace agreement matters for state formation conflicts. In section 4.3 we present an overview of the actual outcomes of state formation conflicts since the end of the Cold War. It will demonstrate that there are solutions along two lines of thought: There is the one most often observed—the division into two states—but there is also a less spectacular but still important way—extending increased autonomy within the existing state. Section 4.4 then proceeds as a comparison of the creation of a new state through victory or negotiation and what that entails for the quality of the future relations between the two entities that were formerly one state. Is there a sufficient element of quality peace through this solution and what is the impact of peacebuilding compared to victory consolidation? In sections 4.5 and 4.6 we ask the same questions, but this time with regard to the quality resulting from autonomy solutions. These three sections will be pursued through a study of pertinent cases derived from the discussion in section 4.3. Section 4.7 summarizes the findings.

4.3 Termination of State Formation Conflicts: An Overview

As we have already made clear, state formation conflicts constitute a large part of the war problem in the post–Cold War period. There is a set of terminated conflicts, which can be analyzed with respect to their ability to provide quality peace in the relations between the warring parties, as well as for general societal development. There are three types of outcome: Victory by the government, victory by the rebels, and negotiated endings where both sides participate and work out an agreement. Victories by government normally mean a return to status quo; victory by the rebels means often the creation of a new state. Negotiated settlements, however, refers to the agreed creation of new states, new autonomies, or other arrangements. If there is a de facto capitulation, that would be referred to as a victory, as it means a return to *status quo ante bellum.* Table 4.1 presents an overview of the outcomes in twenty-five territorial intra-state conflicts since the end of the Cold War. Table 4.1 is the basis for the discussions in this chapter.

Table 4.1 lists intra-state armed conflicts over territory since 1989 where substantial time had passed after the actual war termination, allowing for an assessment of postwar efforts of building quality peace. As a contrast, one case in Ukraine in 2014 has been included although its future is difficult to predict. Some of these conflicts have seen renewed war later, notably Ethiopia–Eritrea and Yemen, but in many there were at least five years without fighting, giving time for developing postwar strategies.

Table 4.1 includes twenty-five cases.[8] This is about half of all conflicts that saw an ending in this period. It is striking that only some of these cases have made it into the mainstream scholarly literature. Typically there is a concern about former Yugoslavia (notably Bosnia and Kosovo), Northern Ireland, Palestine, and to a lesser extent East Timor, Mindanao, and Georgia. These situations all have their particular problems of implementation—for example, tensions over kin that are on the "wrong" side of the border. There is a continuous international concern. The strong international attention to Ukraine during 2014 thus is remarkable, and, from a scholarly perspective, welcome.

Still the most obvious failure in postwar relations is the Ethiopia-Eritrea case and it should be a prominent object of study. The state formation war ended in 1991, the states split formally in 1993, and the inter-state war followed within five years, starting in 1998. It has so far been the most devastating inter-state war in the post–Cold War period. It is pertinent to ask if there were other possible courses of development. The interim period without war did not see any major international involvement.[9] This means that the international community largely was taken by surprise by the outbreak of war, as the separation initially appeared to work out in an amicable way. Another remarkable case of failure that also has been neglected in much conflict analysis is the conflict over Chechnya, with a war ending in 1996, a renewed war in 1999, and since then a continuous low-level armed conflict. Both of these cases have also largely been outside the purview of international organizations. The peacekeeping operation between Eritrea and Ethiopia ended in 2006 and no similar mission has been deployed since then.

Table 4.1 demonstrates that most of the outcomes that have led to a new state (nine cases) or a new autonomous status (eleven cases) have been

Table 4.1

Postwar Situations in State Formation Conflicts since 1989.

Armed conflicts ending with agreement or victory. Status by end of 2014. Excludes some conflicts in Angola, Comoros, India, Mali, Niger, and Senegal. The situation in Crimea in 2014 does not qualify as an armed conflict, but was in fact a Russian victory and resulted in the inclusion of the area into the Russian Federation.

Old State (Center, Metropolis)	New State	New Autonomy	Return to Status Quo Ante Bellum	Present Status Reached by way of	Recurrence of Armed Conflict or War	Inter-national Third Party Presence, 2014
Bangladesh		Chittagong Hill Tracts		Agreement	No	No
Bosnia-Herzegovina (Western Bosnia)			Yes	Victory	No	Yes
Bosnia-Herzegovina		Serb Republic		Agreement	No	Yes
Bosnia-Herzegovina		Croat Republic		Agreement	No	Yes
Croatia		East Slavonia		Agreement	No	No
Ethiopia	Eritrea			Victory/Agreement	Yes	No
Georgia	[Abkhazia]			Victory/No agreement	Yes	No
Georgia	[South Ossetia]			Victory/No agreement	Yes	No
Indonesia	East Timor			Agreement	No	Yes
Indonesia		Aceh		Agreement	No	Yes
Israel		Palestine		Agreement	Yes	Yes
Moldova		Transdniester Republic		Agreement/Not implemented	No	No

Table 4.1 (continued)

Old State (Center, Metropolis)	New State	New Autonomy	Return to Status Quo Ante Bellum	Present Status Reached by way of	Recurrence of Armed Conflict or War	Inter-national Third Party Presence, 2014
Myanmar/Burma (Mon, BMA)			Yes	Victory	No	No
South Africa	Namibia			Agreement	No	No
Papua New Guinea		Bougainville		Agreement	No	No
Philippines		Mindanao		Agreement	Yes	Yes
Russia (Chechnya)			Yes	Victory	Yes	No
Somalia	[Somaliland]			No agreement	No	Yes
Sudan	South Sudan			Agreement	Yes	Yes
Sri Lanka (Tamil Eelam)			Yes	Victory	No	No
Ukraine (East)		Eastern Ukraine (Donetsk and Luhansk)		Ceasefire, Agreement	Yes	Yes
United Kingdom		Northern Ireland		Agreement	No	No
Yemen (S. Yemen)			Yes	Victory	Yes	No
Yugoslavia	Slovenia			Victory/Agreement	No	No
Yugoslavia/Serbia	Kosovo			Agreement/Victory	No	Yes
Total	9	11	5	Agreement:17 Victory: 10	Yes: 9	Yes: 11

achieved through agreements (seventeen cases). All the cases of a return to status quo were the result of government victory (five cases). Rebels in territorial conflicts may have been successful on the military battlefield but in the end their achievements had to be codified through an agreement to have durability. This again is different from the government conflicts of chapter 3. Rebels taking control of the state can continue governmental operations, albeit with new leadership and, presumably, new policies.

Some examples in Table 4.1 point to important complexities. For instance, the two state formation conflicts that Georgia has experienced, Abkhazia and South Ossetia, have seen a victory by what presumably were the rebels. However, the heavy Russian involvement made this disputable. To the Georgian leadership this was an inter-state conflict; to the Russian leadership there is much that says that its actual purpose was to bring down the incumbent Georgian presidency. Whatever the motivation, the Russian hold over the territories is indisputable, and that is also why there is no significant international recognition of the present state of affairs. These two cases, as well as Somaliland, are now in a group of unsolved conflicts without armed conflict at this time (2014). To this we may also add the conflict over Cyprus, which has not seen fighting since 1974 (thus not included in Table 4.1) but is a parallel situation as a large part of the territory of the internationally recognized state is outside that government's control. These are not cases of peacebuilding, as there is no agreement, but still there is a process of consolidation of control by a breakaway actor. These cases demonstrate ambitions to build new state institutions, cementing a military victory (but also keeping a conflict unsolved), most likely with an expectation of achieving recognition in the future.[10]

Among the cases is also Kosovo, where the 1999 UN Security Council Resolution 1244 was a result of an agreement worked through international mediation. It was then interpreted to support the independence of Kosovo and the country made a unilateral declaration of independence in 2008. Serbia's government has still not agreed to this solution, although it is implemented in practice and also recognized by close to half of the membership of the UN. Thus it came about through an agreement but constitutes a de facto victory for those that rebelled against the regime in Serbia. What has followed is a consolidation of this situation in Kosovo itself, whereas the relations to the former metropolis continue to be frosty, but mediated through the EU.

Let us now proceed by studying the cases of state separation (Section 4.4) and autonomy (Sections 4.5, 4.6) in terms of the building of quality peace, whether after negotiated endings or victory. Section 4.7 summarizes the chapter.

4.4. State Separation and Quality Peace

In this section we will study the post–Cold War cases of state separation after war. As Table 4.1 makes clear, there were six armed conflicts that resulted in an agreed secession from one state to form a new one. Our interest is in the transition from the "old" state, the former metropolis, to the creation of the "new" state. These are too few cases for statistical treatment and thus we have to resort to a comparison among the cases. This involves a multi-pronged approach, as we have to analyze the relations between the two sides as well as within each of them. They are the ones that have fought the war and the danger is, of course, that this might recur. In particular, we search for the way the outcomes may meet the criteria of quality peace—that is, dignity for all, security, and the prospect for a peaceful and predictable future in the relations *between* the two entities that were part of the same state before. However, we need also to investigate the postwar strategies of society building *within* each of the two separated entities. Also these policies have to meet the standards for quality peace to be able to make an overall judgment of the new situation.

In addition, our line of inquiry is also concerned about the victory cases and their ability to create lasting conditions. In Table 4.1 there are two government victories that need particular attention: Sri Lanka's government over the LTTE (Liberation Tigers of Tamil Eelam), and Russia's in Chechnya. However, there are also agreements concluded that would, most likely, not have emerged had there not been rebel advances on the battlefield. Rebel victories were translated into reality through agreements with the metropolis.

Let us proceed by following the different types of outcomes, beginning with the rebels and their demand for the creation of a new state. In cases where these demands were denied through a *government victory* the outcome was often a grim one. The most clear-cut case in this period is the victory by the Sri Lankan government over the Tamil Tigers in 2009, including the killing of the leader Velupillai Prabhakaran. The quality of Sri Lanka's consolidation of this victory is a matter of dispute and would require a closer analysis than is possible here.[11] The pertinent questions relate to the criteria for quality peace: Does the outcome respect the dignity of the defeated group and, in particular, the large Tamil population that it claimed to represent? The first years of victory raised doubts about this, as the victory also was associated with authoritarian tendencies in the government vis-à-vis opponents on the government side. The security situation seemed to be more stable and there were, as of 2014, no indications of a restart of the war. This is a case of a decisive victory that only gradually is going to see a challenge, and then probably in a nonviolent or even parliamentary form. Obviously the Tamil population is of such a size that its interests cannot be ignored. The government has largely disregarded international requests for investigations into the fate of former rebel soldiers or the conditions in general in the north of the country. Some changes may follow after the defeat of the incumbent government in January 2015.

Similarly Russia appeared to achieve a victory in the Chechnya conflict in 1996 but saw a return to war within three years. After continued warfare, there was by 2014 a pro-Russia government in place in this region and it had a certain degree of self-rule. However, the armed conflict had not disappeared, but instead spread to adjacent areas, ostensibly in the form of a terrorist campaign rather than traditional warfare. The consolidation of the victory appeared unstable, and questions could be raised as to respect for the dignity of the various population elements in the area. As is the case with Sri Lanka, international access was restricted.

This is rather remarkable as both Russia and Sri Lanka, in the 1990s, were seen as reasonably open societies and many expected a continued move towards a fuller democracy. The experience of encountering determined rebels, and the ensuing intensity of warfare, may have had a negative impact on this trend. The military struggle against separatists contributed to authoritarian tendencies in the metropolis. The brutal victory over the rebels became a setback for democratization in the state as a whole. The war interacted with authoritarian tendencies, which in turn intensified the emphasis on a strong military victory. These victories were hard to win and the resulting government victory did create unfavorable conditions for quality peace in the contested regions, and negatively affected the state as a whole. Under these conditions government victory may lead to territorial control but not necessarily to quality peace.

The cases of rebel victory that actually led to a separation shaped another set of challenges to quality peace in postwar settings. With the creation of a new state, the *difference between victory and peace agreement may seem small.* The new state will act as if the agreement is a victory and will embark on an ambitious program of creating its own state institutions. Many issues are likely to be similar to those advocated in most international peacebuilding programs, such as rule of law, constitutional arrangements, elections, media, transparency, and accountability. The old state faces a host of practical problems if, for instance, important transportation routes are affected. This was the case for Ethiopia following Eritrea's independence, which cut Ethiopia's traditional routes to the sea, and for Sudan after South Sudan's independence, as most of the oil resources were located in the south but the pipelines went through the north.

A peace agreement with the former metropolis renders valuable legitimacy to the "new" state. It provides for a seat in the UN General Assembly. Membership has become a primary symbol of sovereignty. South Sudan and Eritrea embarked on this process immediately following their independence, and with the consent of the "old" states.

This is not always so, as we can see in typical cases of *rebel victory* without a succeeding agreement. For instance, the former metropolis Serbia still has not officially recognized Kosovo's independence. As already mentioned, by 2014 the new state had established diplomatic relations with more than one hundred states, which is a high but far from universal level of recognition. Its international standing rests on cooperation with leading states in the European Union (EU) and, to a lesser extent, the support of the Organization of Islamic Cooperation (OIC). There is a set of other "states" that face even more international opposition, notably North Cyprus (a conflict stemming from the period before 1989), Abkhazia, South Ossetia, and Somaliland, where the "old" states (Cyprus, Georgia, and Somalia, respectively) have refused recognition and so has much of the world. These are frozen conflicts that are becoming even more protracted, as the new entities are not likely to give up their aspirations, nor will the (former) metropolis in their demands for a return to the previous unitary state.

For the former capital, the way the conflict ends might be crucial. If it consents to secession, this is likely to be the result of a prior or simultaneous redefinition of the state. The "old" state will try to define its "loss" of territory as a positive move. It has freed itself of a troubling situation or even a "burden." If it can deal with the new situation in this way, the agreed outcome is not a "loss" but a "gain." The "old" state may, for instance, argue that it now can concentrate its efforts on its own development, rather than be bogged down by the problem of the other. In this way the "old" state also becomes "new." It faces a new beginning, a different purpose, and may, as a result of the division, become more ethnically, religiously, or politically homogeneous.

However, in cases where the separation into two states is the result of a military defeat and a militarily imposed partition, the conditions will be different. There could be a real perception of loss, and the dilemma in the "old" capital is whether to try to regain (even militarily) the lost territory in the future, or to adapt to the new situation. Either way, the outcome creates a legacy that is likely to color relations with the "new" state for the foreseeable future. This could express itself in several ways. Historically we have seen this as fuel for revanchism. Today the expressions may be different, instead even focusing on notions of minority rights or human rights: It may display a concern for ethnic or identity compatriots that end up on the other side of the new border. In the case of an agreed separation, the kin remaining are likely to have to fend for themselves, but an agreement of some quality may involve protection for this particular group. It may, therefore, not necessarily turn into a group that cooperates with the "old" state, but it may be encouraged to move back to keep its old citizenship, thus turning into refugees; or stay and adjust to the new circumstances, with dangers of discrimination, but also opportunities to exert influence.

In the case of an imposed division, however, such population groups may face a more difficult situation. Their fate in the new state may be of primary concern to the old state. It might even be supported and encouraged to press for its "human rights" in the new state. In this way, a group of people can turn into a tool for the old state. Furthermore, this is easily perceived as such by the new state—accurately or not—and thus the new leaders may question the loyalty of this segment to the new conditions. It may become a scapegoat for one side, as well as an excuse for intervention for the other side. The trustworthiness of this group threatens to make it an element in a continued feud, ultimately risking an escalation to a de facto ethnic cleansing. Of course, the situation can be the same the other way around: Kin to the new state may be victimized on the other side of the border, that is, in the old state. The fate of kin in a victorious solution is, therefore, a particularly important indicator of the quality of relations between the new and old states. The flow of refugees and their ability to return indicates the dignity they are awarded.

This means that postwar situations in a state formation conflict have to tackle questions which will not arise in the typical civil war situation. The ability to cooperate across the border is one such issue for the two states to work out and may be central in deciding the fate of the populations that have ended up on the "wrong" side. The skills in managing their shared concerns will be testimony to the two states' ability to build quality peace. It is a matter of meeting both the criterion of "dignity" and the one of "safety" for this particular segment of the population, and for the foreseeable future at that.

A situation that includes *rebel gains*, but where the new situation is *codified in an agreement*, should thus have a better chance of meeting the requirements for quality peace. However, this is not a sufficiently complex conclusion. We can approach this by looking at the cases that fit this category. To these belong the presently independent countries South Sudan and Eritrea with their many similarities, which in turn contrast with Namibia and East Timor with their own important parallels, and finally the situations involving Serbia, Bosnia, and Kosovo as well.

The most remarkable recent failure of peacebuilding after state separation is the case of Ethiopia and Eritrea. The opportunity provided by the agreed solution in 1991 was lost by 1998. This took place at a time when the international community was slowly learning to understand the dynamic of state formation conflicts. In short, the long war against the Mengistu regime in Ethiopia (the Derg) ended in the rebels' victory in 1991. The alliance between the Ethiopian front, EPRDF, and the Eritrean liberation movement, EPLF, was victorious.

The final outcome was diplomatically assisted by the United States. As part of the ending there was an agreement to arrange a referendum in Eritrea on its status. The votes in 1993 made it clear that there was overwhelming support for the de facto existing new state. Thus the bilateral relations seem to have had a reasonable start. An economic agreement was concluded, and to several observers it was mutually beneficial, or even more advantageous, to Eritrea (Lata 2003: 377). Few commentators seem to think that the decisive matter for a breakdown in relations was economic or even territorial. Rather the focus is often on the leaders, their mutual relations, and their perceptions of each other. Eritrea continued to fear Ethiopia's ambitions; Ethiopia may well have hoped for Eritrea's eventual reintegration, albeit on new terms, but may at the same time have worried about Eritrea's potential for weakening Ethiopia (Lata 2003: 373–377, Abbink 2003: 418). Thus post-secession peacebuilding required a conscious approach to affect such perceptions. This is what confidence-building measures aim to do. It may have been an uphill task; there were two rebel leaders who had been victorious, both assuming that they themselves had achieved this historic change. There was little likelihood of them doing anything that they could perceive as undermining their victory and their standing in national history.[12] As Abbink says, with respect to Eritrea and Ethiopia, "one cannot discount the possibility that, with different personal leadership, new forms of cooperation between these two leading parties might indeed be revived" (Abbink 2003: 418). When deepening our understanding we will see that this may not be sufficient. New leaders are likely to have internalized many of the same perceptions as their predecessors. There is a particular need for credible assurances from both sides, most notably for the acceptance of the principles of noninterference. At the same time, this is the common good that is the most difficult to extend in relations which have seen years of tension, violence, and war. Also both sides were probably equally distrustful of neighbors and major powers to accept a role for them in building confidence.

An historical precedent could be found in the tumultuous history of India–Pakistan relations, one of the oldest still ongoing state separation conflicts. It displays many shifts in governments, personalities, political parties, and limited war, suggesting the difficulties in overcoming the obstacles created immediately before or during state separation. Many issues serve to reinforce negative images. A long border may give rise to perceived threats. Ethiopia–Eritrea and India–Pakistan relations give ample evidence of that. Troubles in other neighboring countries may provide further reinforcement. Mutual involvement on opposite sides in Somalia (in the case of Ethiopia and Eritrea) or in Bangladesh and Afghanistan (in the case of Pakistan and India) demonstrate the pervasiveness and persuasiveness of security concerns and threat images.

The 2005 comprehensive peace agreement (CPA) for the North-South conflict in Sudan included a power-sharing arrangement that gave the rebels— Sudanese People's Liberation Movement/Army (SPLA/M)—a prominent role in the national government. The idea clearly was that, if the southern region could be treated with generosity, it would also come to value the state. However, there was little to demonstrate this in the years that followed (Brosché 2009). Instead the provision to have a referendum on a separation was used. Thus by 2011 and with the consent of the North, South Sudan became an independent state. It was quickly recognized internationally and now faces the challenges not only of building the state but also building a lasting peace with the former center. The first years of experience suggest the difficulties of sorting out a number of remaining problems: Borders were undefined, border areas and their statehood were unclear, and prices for oil transportation were disputed. There was considerable crisis diplomacy. Still, an armed conflict occurred in 2012 and tension continued.

It is safe to say that state separation after war encounters particularly complicated relationships. If there is an agreement, there may be some chances of moving toward a degree of quality in the relations. Victories do not have the same standing, whether the victor is the incumbent government or not. In the negotiated outcomes there is at least a common diplomatic recognition to build on. Without that, with a stalemate that is the result of war and a ceasefire, security concerns are likely to remain paramount.

Still we have to note that many cases with more clear-cut *agreements* do not demonstrate different dynamics. For instance the armed conflicts involving Bosnia-Herzegovina and Serbia, as well as Kosovo and Serbia, ended with agreements (Dayton in 1995, the Security Council resolution in 1999). For the new states of Kosovo and Bosnia, the development in the old center, Serbia, remained a central concern. Serbia was slow to communicate a firm commitment to the new status quo. Instead both Kosovo and Bosnia continue to fear Serbian support to Serb groups in the new country (Republika Srpska and Serbs in the North of Kosovo, respectively). Heavy international presence has kept relations at manageable levels. The reduction in armaments in the region may also have contributed to this. The inter-state dignity that diplomatic recognition lends has not been enough to dampen anxiety in the new states.

This is understood more clearly when contrasting this with the two remaining cases of new states in Table 4.1: Namibia and East Timor. These cases are illustrative on this score. In both cases, the former metropolis has given up its aspirations in a credible way. Majority rule in South Africa did not only mean the political end to *apartheid* but also to the policy of supporting white minorities in the region. Similarly the Indonesian self-definition of itself as the continuation of the former Dutch colonies made clear that former Portuguese lands (i.e., Timor-Leste) were not part of the state. In these two cases, peace-building after the agreed separation was helped by the internal developments in the former metropolis. It was a credible development, which may have been somewhat costly to the government at the time, but has definitely been out-weighed by long-term gains.

Such long-term commitment is not likely in a number of the other conflicts mentioned. For instance, there are reasons to fear negative developments for the case of Sudan and South Sudan, although the dissolution in July 2011 was amicable. There were disputes over border areas and issues of economic sig-nificance. Numerous armed movements pursue goals that appeared attractive in the eyes of the two capitals (for strategic, opportunistic, or ethnic reasons). The two Balkan cases also lack such positive developments. In this case, the international concern has contributed to keep the conflicts limited. This may also be required for the Sudanese states. The expenditures for containment in the Balkans have largely been carried by the European Union. A question is if the African continent can do the same for Sudan; at least there were vigorous mediation efforts.

This then leads to an important conclusion: The relationships after state separation are fraught with suspicion, *unless there is a supportive develop-ment in domestic state building* as well. There is a chicken-and-egg problem here. If the internal political discourse of the two new entities after state separation continues to dwell on their inter-state relations, this may in itself generate inter-state tension. If instead the new states largely concentrate on intra-state development, this may be more promising for future inter-state relations. The concepts of security and dignity both play a role in this. For post–civil war peacebuilding, we identified democracy as important for the transformation of conflictual relations into peacebuilding (chapter 3). In the two most recent cases of African separation into two states, we can note that none of them has demonstrated a strong record with respect to democracy or its softer expression: rule of law. There may have been elections, notably in the former capitals, but they have not resulted in an international legitimacy for the elected government or in reassurances to the neighboring states. There were elections in Ethiopia in 2005, 2010 and 2015 respectively and all were questioned, not the least from human rights groups. All returned the same leadership to power. Similarly the elections in Sudan in 2010 were con-ducted so as not to involve a serious challenge to the incumbent president. In the two new states (Eritrea and South Sudan), the democratic procedures have been even more questionable. Thus the formal and legal dignity that has been demanded by these new states has concerned diplomatic recogni-tion, with its concomitant implications of sovereignty, equal rights among states, and noninterference in internal affairs. But the internal developments still remain central in the minds of those on the other side of the border. Suspicion continues to linger in both Ethiopia and Eritrea, as well as in Sudan and South Sudan. The reassurance that would come from an internal policy focusing on treating minorities correctly and reducing armaments has not been forthcoming.

Let us contrast those experiences with the two other dyads of separation where we do not expect renewed conflict: South Africa–Namibia and Indonesia–East Timor. In both cases we are talking about highly asymmetric relations, the old center remaining dominant in the region, but still there is no expectation that it will use its power to retake "lost" territory. Two factors differentiate these cases from the others: shifts to democracy and a change of national identity in the metropolis. South Africa's democratization brought to power a black majority that was not interested in dominating neighboring countries in the way the *apartheid* regime had (which in turn had sprung from its security concerns). Democracy was associated with a redefinition of the country's identity in the region and in the world. It gained a strong international standing by being democratic and nonaggressive. For Indonesia the democratization following the student uprising in 1998 was similar to South Africa: the fall of the previous regime also meant a new approach to solving conflicts through negotiations. This was in turn reinforced by its redefined identity as peaceful state built on the former Dutch possessions (not the Portuguese). This state identity was demonstrated in the solution for the province of Aceh through autonomy, not separation (see section 4.5). Both South Africa and Indonesia could credibly project a new image. Compare this to the developments in Sudan and Ethiopia, where neither country was involved with democratic transparency or with redefining its role in the region. Actions seemed instead to demonstrate a continuation of the past, as could be seen in military movements on border issues and, in the case of Ethiopia, in military incursion into Somalia. This also differentiates these two dyadic cases from the Balkan situations that we have included. Certainly democratization in Serbia has helped to reassure smaller neighbors, but continued support to ethnic kin across borders as well as electoral reversals have not demonstrated a durable commitment to democracy or to nationalistic (rather than chauvinist) policy preferences. A measure that the outside world would apply would, for instance, be the treatment of non-Serb groups in the country (Roma, Albanians, Hungarians) or apologies for atrocities in the wars of the 1990s.

In this analysis much emphasis is put on the former metropolis. Remarkably it has remained the dominant regional actor, in spite of "losing" territory. As the smaller units have demanded independence to reduce their subordination, they have had to remain highly attentive to the actions of the dominant state. To overcome this, the expectation would be for the former metropolis to carry out consistent and costly signals on its acceptance of the new situation. There would also have to be clearly demonstrated acknowledgment of such actions by the new state. There have been some manifestations of such measures, notably exchange of state visits at important occasions. The prosecution of crimes committed during the wars may also belong to such action. Inter-state truth commissions may have a role in jointly confronting the past. Handling new disputes in constructive ways would also be further indications, as would an official policy of not exploiting crises in the new state.[13] Above all, being part of a larger cooperative framework may be the most important. Thus Namibia quickly entered SADC, the Southern African Development Council, and Indonesia pushed for East Timor's inclusion in ASEAN, so far without success.[14] For the other African cases, IGAD would constitute the most obvious joint organization. In 2011, South Sudan was admitted while Eritrea was prevented from taking up its seat, as it had suspended its own membership a couple of years earlier.[15] In the Balkan cases, all countries have stated an interest in closer integration with the European Union.

Bringing this together, we can conclude that government victory in state formation conflicts may often result in, or stimulate, authoritarian tendencies in society, which may harm future peaceful developments in relation to the former opponents. In cases of rebel victory without agreement, a prolonged period of status quo may be the most likely outcome, again far from the criteria for quality peace. The conflicts risk becoming frozen and with little peace-building to report. Also in cases of an agreed separation, the period after the conflict is difficult. Relations remain strained, insecurities continue, and the dignity of having won an equal status as a state may not necessarily translate into tangible gains.

However, we can go one step further, suggesting that democratization of both states, combined with credible respect for the new conditions by the former metropolis and tangible regional integration, would go a long way to reduce the risk of a return to war. In particular, this points to the treatment of minority populations as an important indicator, whether the population segment is directly related to the other state or not. Protection of minority rights and confidence-building measures relating to the war experience may contribute to the creation of quality peace. This means that leadership changes are not the key factor for understanding the postwar chance of peaceful and constructive relations. Such changes are inevitable in the long run, and what matters are the policies pursued and how they are understood, internally as well as in the relations to the former adversary. Let us now move to the less drastic outcomes of an ending of state formation conflicts: autonomy and its quality of peace.

4.5 Autonomy and Quality Peace

There is a considerable literature on the functioning of regional autonomy. Some of this work relates to autonomy as a way of conflict resolution and the construction of long-term relations (Weller and Wolff 2005, Wolff 2013). The solution for the Åland islands in 1921 is a classic case with many lessons for other situations, not the least as it was made by an international organization, the League of Nations (Suksi 2013). Thus regional arrangements within existing states are interesting here: What are the qualities of such an accord that lead to the preservation of identity and security for the foreseeable future? From Table 4.1 we learn that the post–Cold War period witnessed the creation of eleven new autonomy regimes within existing states. This is a unique record and may only have parallels in the first years of the League of Nations.[16] The modern autonomies have aimed at solving protracted armed conflicts and have also largely been implemented.[17]

Two of these solutions reported in Table 4.1 have been defined as "interim" arrangements and will be dealt with in the next section: Palestine and Bougainville. The Palestinian Authority, created by the Oslo process in the 1990s, is an existing autonomy, but its present status is not seen as final by any party. Bougainville is an interesting case as its present status will be the subject of a referendum, at earliest by 2015. In fact the option of a future change in the allegiance of the autonomy is also available in other peace deals, notably the Belfast agreement, which included the possibility of a referendum on the territorial status of Northern Ireland; it can potentially switch from being part of the United Kingdom to joining the Republic of Ireland. It points to a dynamic where autonomies may be seen as temporary measures, and where the possibility of reaching the ultimate goal is retained (independence or shifting sovereignty) but in organized forms and without renewed fighting. It will also be given particular attention in the following section (4.6). Furthermore, the ceasefires in Ukraine have not held, thus making the acceptance of autonomy uncertain for the time being. This leaves us with seven cases to investigate more closely in our search for finding postwar solutions that have a high-quality content.

Theoretically the autonomy solution has an attraction as an optimal way of meeting the contradictory demands for self-determination and territorial integrity. Furthermore, all our cases are the result of negotiated settlements rather than victories. The commitment problems are particularly strong for this category of solutions, as indicated by the Iraqi Kurdish example, and as explained by Fearon (Section 4.2). This example suggests that autonomy is more likely to work under conditions of transparency and trust. Democratic conditions, in other words, would be conducive for longevity of autonomy solutions:

The transparency of democracy makes it possible for the autonomy leaders to assess the commitment of the metropolis to the solution. Attitudes and behavior in the center can be observed. The same, obviously, works the other way around: It gives the center ability to follow what goes on in the autonomous region. For a minority group, however, autonomy may still involve dangers, for instance, in losing its fair share in national resource distribution. Autonomy means that the minority chooses self-rule in its own area over the ability to play a direct role in the metropolis.[18]

The democratic aspect is apparent when consulting Table 4.1: All seven autonomies have been created in open societies. It may be possible to find other cases, notably in ceasefire agreements in Burma/Myanmar, which de facto have recognized the autonomous rule of particular warlords or rebel armies. However, these were expedient measures and have not had the same durability and legitimacy as the solutions included in Table 4.1. If autonomy is to be upheld and reflect popular opinion in an autocratic state, it probably requires a permanent independent armed presence. The experience of the Kurdish autonomy in Iraq illustrates the dynamics. It is difficult for an authoritarian regime to credibly commit to limitations to its authority. There are historical examples of how totalitarian regimes have been willing to grant concessions to national minorities, even building institutions to represent such groups, and then systematically worked to undermine them. The Soviet regime excelled in such "solutions" (Cornell 2002), as have the Communist parties elsewhere in the world. The logic of reneging pointed to by Fearon explains the dynamics.

Thus the solutions in Table 4.1 may have lasting potential. They have been achieved in an era with high regard for democratic norms and increasingly for matters of human rights. These concerns speak directly to the dignity demands of many actors in territorial conflicts. Typically the origins for the rebel demands for self-determination stem from historical legacy (in Aceh there was a traditional sultanate, in Mindanao a key issue has been control over ancestral lands); religious freedoms (use of *sharia* law for Muslims, access to their own language for others); or protection against turning into a minority (rules for rights of residence, for instance).

Even so security concerns linger highly on both sides. A typical worry for the central government is that the autonomy—in spite of what it perceives as its "generosity"—will in the long run not be satisfactory for the (former) rebels (prompting a return instead to the demands for independence), or in the short term inspire other movements in the country or even turn into a base for opposition movements.[19] For both sides, then, the disarmament issues have taken a particularly central role. Disarmament measures were part of the agreements on Chittagong Hill Tracts, East Slavonia, Aceh, Bougainville, and Mindanao.[20]

The implementation of the disarmament measures has been followed with pain-staking detail. An instructive example comes from the case of Aceh, where the rebel movement, GAM, promised to destroy 840 weapons and demobilize 3,000 fighters. The numbers meant that not every fighter had a weapon; GAM's explanation was that troops were needed for transport, but Indonesian officers were suspicious. Even so GAM seemed to have difficulties in presenting the exact number. On the final day of the decommissioning, one weapon still remained. The last one, a pistol, turned out to be used as evidence in a criminal case. Thus it could only be registered and not destroyed as should have been the case. Still GAM met its obligation. Following this, Indonesia completed its military withdrawal from the region, also following the limit of not having more than 14,700 soldiers and 9,100 police in place, thus in effect withdrawing 25,890 soldiers and 5,791 police, all carefully counted by the special Aceh Monitoring Mission (Merikallio 2008: 115, 169–196).

In the Dayton Agreement, however, the two constituent units of Bosnia-Herzegovina were allowed to retain their own military forces, rather than having them integrated into a united framework.[21] Thus this agreement does not achieve as strongly as the others a connection between the autonomous units and the state. The federal construction chosen at Dayton gives more independence to the subunits than any of the other agreements, not only in the field of security. However, a remedy is found in the disarmament measures. It is estimated that the total police forces under the control of the two constituent units at the end of the war was 45,000 and the two armies were about 80,000 each. Ten years later the combined forces of the two armies were 12,000. However, the ambition to integrate the police force had not succeeded (McGrath 2006: 50). Still the limited size of the two armies together with the international presence may provide reasonable reassurance against a restart of the war.

A striking feature of Table 4.1 is that a large number of the autonomies have involved an international presence at the early stages of implementation. The global pattern deviates from the one that could be observed for Southeast Asia (Wallensteen et al. 2009). For instance, the constitutional structure of Bosnia, with two federal units under a central government, was conceived in agreements that were entered into in Washington, D.C. 1994 and in Dayton, Ohio 1995. The arrangement in East Slavonia was negotiated under the auspices of the UN lead mediator Thorvald Stoltenberg, former Minister of Foreign Affairs in Norway. Similarly the negotiations for the Aceh agreement were led by the former President of Finland, Martti Ahtisaari. The negotiations on Bougainville involved considerable international participation, notably by New Zealand. The Northern Ireland negotiations saw the United Kingdom and Ireland together with semiprivate third parties such as former US Senator

George Mitchell and others. Similarly the negotiations on Mindanao engaged neighboring countries. The prime example is, of course, Palestine. The only autonomy agreement that does not exhibit strong international presence is the solution for Chittagong Hill Tracts in Bangladesh. This may be worth some consideration. The autonomy solution is logical for handling a dilemma that may be more obvious to the world as a whole. The local parties may not see it in the same light. To them it is most likely a matter of finding a solution to their problems, not a matter of adhering to international norms or settling norm conflicts. The international contribution thus is to demonstrate the existence of solutions and suggest adaptations to local conditions.

This may raise the question whether these autonomies are in fact novelties in local situations, and thus in some sense foreign to the local culture. As they are accepted and seem to thrive, the local conditions appear to have been conducive for such solutions. It could also be that a more decentralized government structure is more in line with local traditions, and thus would be embraced locally. The international presence may, in that case, be more a way to make the metropolis, the national government, open to such local solutions. It provides reassurance, and helps to improve the center's commitment to new solutions.

Of the various autonomies mentioned in Table 4.1, Aceh is not only the most recent but also the closest application of the principle of self-determination for a regional area within an existing state. It may also be the outcome that meets most of the quality peace criteria: The agreement was largely implemented, local elections were conducted, there were no indications of repression against non-Acehnese inside the autonomy, and disarmament went ahead according to plan. It is also a resource-rich region. It thus is remarkable that the economic issues played such a minor role in the negotiations. The principle of wealth sharing seems to have been agreed upon without much concern. This could otherwise have been a contentious issue. The immediate implementation of the agreement was aided by the huge influx of assistance in the wake of the devastating tsunami that struck Aceh in December 2004 (Wennman and Krause 2009). However, the agreement actually gave Aceh more economic rights than were included in the law on Aceh that the Indonesian parliament passed in 2006 (called LoGA). In an evaluation of the accords and their implementation, CMI (the organization led by Martti Ahtisaari, who conducted the mediation process) pointed to changes that were necessary, notably in transparency around the central government's management of the income from the natural resources in Aceh (CMI 2012). As we have seen in recent history, tensions between the center and the autonomy have threatened the sustainability of the arrangement. Concerns of particular significance have to do with transparency, accountability, and participation. In the perspective of quality peace, this all has to do with dignity and respect for the solution that has been agreed upon. How serious these developments are for the future remains to be seen. It is important that they are highlighted already at this juncture, not the least as the Aceh solution has become a paradigmatic achievement.[22]

This differs from another case in Table 4.1, the UN administration of East Slavonia in 1995–1997. It was a temporary measure to defuse tension in a Serb-populated border area between Yugoslavia/Serbia and Croatia. During the war it had declared itself independent as the Serb Republic of Krajina, with no international recognition. In the Erdut agreement of 1995, it was resolved that the territory was part of Croatia and a transitory regime was created, in fact constituting a government of the area in 1996 and 1997 (Boothby 2004). The aspiration of the Serb population was thus rejected; there was neither independence nor a merger with Serbia. Instead the territory was integrated into Croatia in 1997. As a unit East Slavonia ceased to exist; it did not function as an autonomy in any way reminiscent of the other cases in Table 4.1. However, conditions had been created for the Serb population to participate in local elections and thus exert influence on daily life in the area. In reality, the outcome can be described as a victory for Croatia, but the way the integration was brought about prevented renewed warfare, instead allowing for the return of refugees. It may also have contributed to making the Croat national leadership more sensitive in its policy toward the minorities of the country, even promising special seats in the parliament and other measures (Klemencic and Schofield, ca 1999). The UN mission ended in early 1998. The hopes of the local Serbs for a "soft" border to Serbia and dual citizenship, however, have not (yet) been accomplished. By all accounts the region remains poor, but security and respect are extended to the minorities (which also include other population groups, notably Ruthenians and Hungarians). It is a different story from the one of Aceh, indicating that autonomy solutions sometimes can prove highly successful, at other times only constitute a temporary arrangement for reducing tension and preparing the ground for integration into another state or for the creation of such a new state. In the next session, one such case will be studied, not the least as it still is in the making.

4.6 Autonomy: Solution Versus Step to Separation

State separation may often stem from the failure to create credible and meaningful autonomy. Thus we need to address the stability of this particular solution to state formation conflicts. Obviously negative experience played a role for Eritrea in not wanting to return to an autonomous status within Ethiopia when the Mengistu regime fell in 1991. The solution in 1951—created through the United Nations—gave Eritrea such a status. The former Italian colony of Eritrea merged into a union with Ethiopia. Italy, of course, had invaded Abyssinia and conquered the whole country in 1935–1936. In spite of sanctions by the League of Nations, the world accepted the outcome: Italy was too important in the European balance of power equation. The failure to deal with Italy's aggression also meant the demise of the world organization. After the Second World War, lessons were drawn. One included guilt over Ethiopia and its ruler, Emperor Haile Selassie, which affected the treatment of Eritrea. Still the UN sent out a mission to identify the will of the Eritrean people. Interviews with different traditional leaders and others were claimed to show a preference for joining with Ethiopia, and thus a federation of the two was forged in 1951.[23] This arrangement was undone by Haile Selassie in 1962, when an armed conflict for independence began. Ethiopia's actions raised no international concern. The Eritrean liberation war was to last until 1991. At that time, not surprisingly, proposals for autonomy solutions were rejected by the Eritrean People's Liberation Front (EPLF).

Thus even if the autonomy solution has a theoretical attraction as an optimal way of meeting the contradictory demands of self-determination of peoples and territorial integrity of states, historical experience reduces its credibility. We have already noted that these solutions are few in number (Section 4.4.). Following Fearon, the issue is whether an autonomous region can have sufficient guarantees that the center will honor the agreement. For Eritrea, this belief was shaken by the experience with the Ethiopian Emperor and the thirty-year-long war. A more recent example is the one of South Sudan and Sudan.

In the 2005 Comprehensive Peace Agreement (CPA) for the North–South conflict in Sudan, the movement representing the South, Sudanese People's Liberation Movement/Army (SPLM/A), agreed to form a national unity government with the North. This meant that the regionally based movement would actually have a say in national politics. This would give the region reassurance. The national government would really be committed to the development and well-being of the region, as the region had a strong representation in the center. The CPA rested on the idea that staying with Sudan would be highly attractive to the South and become the preference of the population. However, very little happened in the following years (Brosché 2009). The leader committed to this solution, John Garang, died under mysterious circumstances shortly after CPA went into effect. The North continued its war in Darfur, even to the point that in 2010 President Omar al-Bashir was issued an arrest warrant by the International Criminal Court (ICC) on three charges of war crimes. In the 2011 referendum the SPLM/A movement opted for secession. Sudan was given a rare opportunity with the CPA to keep the country together. However, the actions that were taken did not result in a peacebuilding that gave the South confidence in the present and future protection of its security and dignity.

The experience from Sudan suggests that sharing national power may not be enough for a regionally confined minority to be sufficiently confident about its future.[24] This means that autonomy solutions only work under conditions of transparency and trust.[25] Democratic circumstances, in other words, are conducive for autonomy solutions. This demonstrates to the autonomy leaders that the central state is committed. The attitudes and behavior in the center can be observed. The same, obviously, goes for the state leaders and their ability to follow what goes on in the autonomous region.

However, the Palestinian and Northern Ireland cases may speak against that. Palestinians follow Israeli politics closely but have no illusions about their ability to have an impact on Israeli policy (instead they hope for the support from other democracies, notably the United States and the EU). For the Palestinian leadership the present autonomy is an interim stage and there is a clear international understanding on this score. Thus the application for membership in the UN received wide but not sufficient support. When Sweden in 2014 recognized Palestine as an independent state, it was the 135th state to do this. The lack of progress gives space for more violent approaches and the autonomy is weakened correspondingly. In Northern Ireland, the choice is between being part of one or the other democracy (the United Kingdom or Republic of Ireland). Still the Belfast agreement and the following power sharing has helped to remedy some of the exclusion from politics for the Catholic Republican minority. In this case, the space for violent action has shrunk dramatically since the peace agreement and its implementation, but issues of security and dignity still move the two sides into frictions.

This makes the case of Bougainville interesting as it also has a choice: Is the present autonomy sufficient to remedy the concerns about dignity and security or will the inhabitants vote for independence, when given the chance that is stipulated in the peace agreement?

This conflict took place in a democratic society, Papua New Guinea (PNG), marked by loosely formed political parties, ever-shifting alliances, and considerable expectations of vast incomes from natural resources. The remarkable story is that the conflict was started by a group that did not want to be part of this modern development, and specifically wanted to stop mining on its own island. The valuable copper deposits had made Bougainville the richest part of this diverse and geographically fragmented country. There were roads, schools, health clinics, and job opportunities that made the island attractive. People from other parts of PNG came to work in the mine or in other activities associated with this big Australian investment. The copper sales made up a sizeable share of PNG's total exports and the revenue accounted for close to half the budget of the central government.

A quick overview of the island's recent history is necessary.[26] The guerrilla force, BRA [Bougainville Revolutionary Army], put an end to the flow of money to PNG and Bougainville in 1989 by blowing up the pylons supplying the electricity for the mine operation. BRA followed up by taking control of the mining area. The once booming economy ground to a halt. The government and its armed forces repeatedly tried to retake the area, sealed off the island, and allied itself to other groups on the island. At times it also engaged in negotiations, which early on included the possibility of an autonomy solution.[27] The peace agreement in 2001 finally brought an end to the war and outlined a process for the future (Regan 2002, Regan 2010). It included the creation of a presidency for Bougainville, a parliament (with seats specifically reserved for ex-combatants and for women), elections, and considerable potential control over island resources, where the Bougainville government can request the transfer of functions from the national government.

The autonomy provisions were far-reaching but depended on the ability of the island leaders to develop institutions to handle all matters that formally could be on its agenda (Wolfers 2006). The peace agreement also specified that a referendum could be arranged on the future status of the island, at the earliest ten years after the introduction of the Bougainville government. Thus there were incentives to implement the agreement. UN observers testified to the acceptable performance of the initial measures of weapons disposal. Clearly this was not a complete disarmament and armed violence continued to plague the island. In 2010 it was estimated that fourteen armed militia groups were still in operation. For a considerable period of time, remnants of the BRA continued to control the mining area. However, by 2005 the Autonomous Bougainville Government could begin to function and its first elected leader was the locally well-known Joseph Kabui, who was largely in favor of independence. An attempt on his life increased tensions. When he died of natural causes a year later, Bougainville's second president was James Tanis, a young former BRA operative, elected for the rest of Kabui's term. Regular presidential elections were held in 2010, resulting in a strong victory for the elderly John Mommis, who was opposed to BRA, but wanted a strong autonomy and was seen to be more inclined to keep Bougainville within PNG.

The political programs for all leaders since the peace agreement have emphasized terms that are important in the quality peace discussion, including peacebuilding, reconciliation, and disarmament. The sequence has been clear: first a disarmament process with international support, primarily to make roads safe for all. This then has been followed by creating representative government through elections and, after this, institution building. Parallel to this there were elaborate and island-wide processes of local reconciliation. It has taken place in the villages, and included the return of former combatants into the local society, in spite of their deeds during the war. Reconciliation has followed local traditions. The efforts were slow but that was seen as an advantage by those involved, who argued that it takes time to reconcile. It appears village leaders preferred an inclusive approach; it was seen as a way of building for the future. This, one may say, has been an elaborate approach for healing the conflicts *within* the island. It means reconnecting across the many divides that the conflict had generated; it combined dignity with security on the local level.[28] The prospects appear positive.

The main issue in the relations *between* the metropolis and the autonomy seem no longer to concern dignity, respect, or security. The creation of the autonomy and the withdrawal of PNG police and military early after the agreement served as costly signals of commitment from the center to the island. Reconstruction has gone ahead. Reports pointed out that Bougainville again had a higher life expectancy than other parts of PNG, as well as a higher enrollment in schools (Wolfers 2007). Instead the issue with the center seems largely to be financial. In a way, it suggested a return to normality; this issue is most likely the contention that plagues all centers and their relations to regional authorities. However, the war experience made this extreme. Bougainville used to be a contributor to the national economy, but most estimates suggest that during the new autonomy regime, the island had only been able to finance a minor part of its expenditures.[29] It had to rely on financial arrangements with the central government. Locating other forms of revenue became a concern for all the presidents, so far with little success. Kabui seemed to prefer development of a self-sufficient agricultural economy, but it would be unlikely to generate the revenues that government services require. Thus the leaders were pushed back to restarting the mining operation again. The politics of this was highly complicated, not the least since BRA stalwarts still held physical control over the old mining area.

The Bougainville case adds more to our understanding of quality peace in state formation conflicts. The peace agreement did not specify a clear winner, but appeared to be a genuine compromise. One of the original leaders of BRA objected to the deal, but was not part of the process. The government withdrew from the island as agreed, and the island received a far-reaching autonomy as outlined. At the same time this agreement projected considerable realism into the postwar situation. There had to be practical conditions in place to make the autonomy work (even more so for a new state to function). Thus a sequence was developed with considerable internal cohesion and logic, going from disarmament via elections to institutions, parallel to social healing. Once functioning institutions are in place, it may become meaningful to ask for a referendum on the status of the island. Achieving independence without preparation may only throw the island into renewed chaos.

Comparing Bougainville to the cases of Table 4.1, the autonomy was probably much weaker at the moment of the peace agreement than for any of the others. There were few functioning institutions. Northern Ireland obviously is located on the other extreme: a firmly entrenched bureaucracy with laws, routines, traditions, and well-educated civil servants prepared to carry out the wishes of any legitimate ruler. The cases emerging from the former Yugoslav states met most of these considerations, except for the credibility of civil servants. Aceh's local governance could also build on a functioning Indonesian administration. The autonomy in Mindanao may have many similarities with Bougainville. This is to say that a host of important matters confronting practical peacebuilding are often taken for granted in peacebuilding studies. When raising the issue of quality peace, however, it emerges more profoundly: Will existing structures actually protect the dignity of the minorities and will they provide security for all? And are these institutions capable of delivering such services over a sustained period of time? The last question, in particular, points to the importance of tax revenue, financial flows, and a functioning economy.

As the aspirations of many Bougainvilleans still concern independence, Table 4.1 is again instructive. New states such as Slovenia and Namibia could take over existing institutions and financial systems. East Timor, on the other hand, saw its prospective capital city almost entirely destroyed in the violence that followed the 1999 referendum on independence. The international presence was in fact the administration and ran the country for the following three years in order to prepare for the new state. South Sudan found itself in a similar situation, as the preceding years had not been enough for preparation. In this case, however, the SPLM/A may have functioned as a de facto state. Together with international donors it may have served to keep the country together, despite internal divisions and tensions with the North. The story of Eritrea's state building remains to be understood, but it is likely that the liberation organization, EPLF, in fact became the state institution or filled institutions with its veterans, keeping their allegiance to the liberation front. Bougainville does not have such a party organization or military machinery to support it. It does not have the support of a committed international community either. Bougainville would resent heavy donor involvement, as this very likely would mean a return of Australian interests. Leaders have not forgotten that the copper production was operated by Australians. Thus it faces tougher challenges than many others cases. At the same time, compared to the experiences of South Sudan and Eritrea, it has a greater chance of continuing on a democratic trajectory, whether it chooses independence or continued autonomy. A state (or an autonomy for that matter) built on a liberation organization is not an optimal way to develop a democratic structure. Fighting wars is one thing, operating a state something quite different.

4.7 Quality Peace in State Formation Solutions

Through an analysis of the twenty-five armed conflicts that have been terminated in the post–Cold War period, we can draw ten general conclusions for quality peace.

First, five cases resulted in a strong and clear-cut government victory, where we found reasons to analyze two in particular (Russia in Chechnya and Sri Lanka over the Tamil Tigers). These victories have come at a price associated with increased authoritarian tendencies in the center itself. In addition, respect for the dignity of those losing the conflict was lacking. Security provisions did not appear sufficiently inclusive in the immediate aftermath of the war ending. International reviews of the situation were resented. There may be an element of "peace," but the qualities associated with longevity are lacking.

Second, there are nine cases that resulted in a new situation close to the rebel demands for independence. First, this includes three cases where the outcome was not achieved by the rebels alone but required considerable outside support (Kosovo, Abkhazia, South Ossetia). Then there are the cases of forming a new state where the rebels militarily gained control over the territory on their own: Eritrea, Slovenia, and Somaliland. Extensive fighting took place only in the first case. Finally there are three cases where government forces stayed on the disputed territory at the end of the war. It required an agreement for them to withdraw and for the rebels to achieve their goals (Namibia, East Timor, and South Sudan). Thus rebel advances were seldom complete, and international efforts were required to bring about a status that was acceptable to the parties and to the international community. The negotiations typically resulted in more democratization or international observation of ongoing activities. Rebel victory in itself is no guarantee for a postwar situation that meets the demands of quality peace.

Third, the ten autonomy outcomes, leaving the undecided situation in Ukraine aside, required considerable negotiations and concessions from all sides. Only one led to a complete integration of the territory into the state (East Slavonia). In all the other cases, the agreed units continue to exist and have developed considerable identity of their own. These situations have prospects of turning into permanent arrangements. In some cases this does not preclude the possible development into a state (Palestine, Bougainville) or union with a neighboring state (Northern Ireland), but through procedures that have been agreed beforehand. In the resulting agreements, considerable elements pertaining to the quality peace criteria were covered. In some cases it has been possible to determine to what extent they also have been implemented. The case of Aceh seems most promising as a continued autonomy within Indonesia, although other cases may be more entrenched and provide for more transparency (Northern Ireland in particular).

Fourth, this means that all outcomes that involved the creation of an internationally recognized state or autonomy also required a negotiating process and an agreement. This added something to the outcome beyond the military advances, and what the negotiation process contributed is often associated with the notions incorporated in quality peace.

Fifth, there was a history of return to war in nine of the twenty-five cases, most dramatically and destructively in the Ethiopia–Eritrea relationship. The ceasefire agreements did not hold in Ukraine in 2014. Renewed violence is connected to a declining interest in coming back to the negotiation table. As we have reported in this chapter, negotiations in state formation conflicts are particularly difficult and the failure of one agreement also affects negatively the chances of reopening a diplomatic channel. Furthermore, this is not merely a matter of waiting for future leadership change. What may be needed is a change that leads to rethinking about the role of the state internally and in relations to other states. Shifting policies away from a preoccupation with security and toward civilian development may be one example. Thus women's organizations played a role in East Timor during the UN period, as well as in Bougainville during and after the war. There are also testimonies to the importance of women in the implementation and building of the new state of Namibia. Civil society organizations in general can contribute to such a shift in the national priorities after war, notably a move from national security to human security. This would then increase the possibility of meeting the requirements for quality peace.

Sixth, our investigation has strongly pointed to the importance of democracy for the long-term functioning of any of the outcomes. The solutions build on finding an arrangement for the territorial issue. This is basic, but the democracy aspect adds to the quality of the settlement. The ability to correctly assess the other side is equally significant for all actors, be it the (former) center, the new state, or the autonomy. This is associated with trust and predictability. The state formation conflicts were largely pursued by rebel groups in the hope of gaining respect and dignity for a particular people. An important way such respect can credibly be extended is through open procedures, participation in national and local affairs, and a free debate, all hallmarks for democracy and respect for dignity.

Seventh, we can note that early disarmament measures have been central in scaling down the dangers in the relations. Also for autonomy solutions, international participation in arms control actions has proved significant.

Eighth, the relations between the new state entities, or between the center and the autonomy, seem also to be tied to the treatment of minorities. A new border is likely to generate new minorities on opposite sides of the divide. Their fate in the new situation will also have an impact on the overall relationship. Establishing credible minority protection for all minorities, in other words, serves as a way of extending respect and recognition.

Ninth, in all these cases territory plays a particularly significant role. The size of territory allotted to each of the units in the Bosnia-Herzegovina state was decided a priori: 49% for the Serb entity, 51% for the federation of Bosniaks and Croats. It is probably a unique way to handle a territorial issue. Some territorial issues were left unresolved by Ethiopia and Eritrea, something that was unfortunate and sparked the new war in 1998. The mistake was repeated in the separation of Sudan and South Sudan. Agreeing on the territory to be included has also been cited as significant in the Mindanao conflict (Hoodie and Harzell 2005: 34–35), whereas other borders could follow previously established lines. "Soft borders"—that is, allowing the easy movement of human beings, not only goods and capital, across the borders—may serve to reduce the impact of the dividing lines.

Tenth, a state's approach to international relations will also be an opening for international regional cooperation on issues that may otherwise continue to generate insecurity. The term "security community" is important and will be a topic of chapters 6 and 7, following an analysis of postwar conditions in inter-state relations in chapter 5.

CHAPTER 5

Quality Peace between States: A Challenge

5.1 Inter-State Peacebuilding: A Neglected Field

The most recent and at the same time by now classic case of peacebuilding after an inter-state war undoubtedly is the case of Franco–German relations after 1945. It is, however, rarely seen in these terms. In one sense this is reasonable, as there was no peace agreement on which to build the peace. The post-1945 developments could be regarded as victory consolidation. It was clear who had won and who had lost. However, Western Europe as a whole suffered from the war. There was a need for reconstruction in ways that would provide for a lasting peace. Whether peacebuilding or victory consolidation, it was a matter of creating new conditions that in reality correspond to the notion that we here label quality peace. It is remarkable to observe that ten years after the end of the Second World War, Germany (in the form of the Federal Republic, at the time mostly referred to as West Germany) was again fully participating in international relations. It immediately became involved in the building of the European community and has remained a fully committed partner to this project through decades of shifting governments and significant world changes. It is a dramatic contrast to the period after the First World War, where German regime change, territorial reduction, and economic reparations provided fuel for revanchism, nationalism, and racism.[1]

Normally the aftermath of the world wars has not been conceived in terms of peacebuilding between states. Instead analysts have preferred discussing "world order," which primarily referred to a new way of structuring power between leading states, presumably to prevent a new world war. We will return to this in chapter 6. Our focus here is on the dyadic relations between countries that were in direct conflict, rather than the full system of international relations. This dyadic dimension adds to our understanding of peacebuilding and victory consolidation as well as to world order. In particular, the notion of quality peace—which we throughout this work apply to any outcome of a war (whether achieved through victory or negotiation)—gives us a way to study also the postwar relations between major powers. Let us begin by relating inter-state peace to the analysis of intra-state conditions.

In chapters 3 and 4 we distinguished between intra-state conflicts according to the incompatibility, the key disagreement. Two such incompatibilities were identified from general conflict theory: control over the central government and control over particular territorial areas. We saw that the building of quality peace will confront different challenges depending on the type of disagreement. Thus it should be important also to distinguish between these two incompatibilities between states. It matters if the purpose of the parties in a particular war is to replace or maintain a particular government, or if it is about a wish to keep or take control over a particular piece of territory.

Franco–German relations illustrate this. The Second World War was largely a confrontation over regime type: Which political system was going to be the dominant one in Europe? The Nazi program was to construct a totalitarian system with Germany in its center. The Western allies wanted a system of democratic states with minimal German influence. The end of the war between the Western powers and Germany was not only through victory, but also through providing a program of a future based on democratic constitutions and practice. The reconstruction of West Germany rested on the idea of transforming the country into a democracy, with an internal power structure that would prevent the central government from again becoming totalitarian. It was to be incapable of waging war on its own. In this way the victory was consolidated based on principles which had similarities to those of pre–Nazi Germany and became fundamental after the war. The government issue was removed as a matter of contention between these former belligerents.[2] The relations to the East and the Soviet Union were a different matter, and related to the Cold War more specifically, and will be returned to in chapter 6.

However, it is interesting to note that there were only marginal territorial changes in Western Europe after 1945. Actually the only remaining issue was solved when the Saarland was (re)united with the Federal Republic in 1957, after voters had rejected the innovative idea of making it into a "European" area. Thus freed from difficult territorial concerns, the Franco–German axis that developed during the leadership of Charles de Gaulle and Konrad Adenauer had a profound effect on European affairs. They were, in different ways, pioneers for the new Europe. De Gaulle was an officer and the leader of the French resistance against Nazi Germany and the first President of the Fifth Republic from 1958. Dr. Konrad Adenauer was a democratically elected conservative Mayor of Cologne until the Nazis took control in 1933, and became the Federal Republic's first Chancellor in 1949, staying on until 1963. The two leaders had unprecedented opportunities to mold relations between the two states within new, democratic, and European frameworks. What actually amounted to peacebuilding between these two countries involved a regional approach, initially incorporating Italy and the three countries of the Benelux, eventually leading to an arrangement for twenty-eight members (by 2013) of the European Union. As economic relations today are central to these states and their membership activities, it is important to recall that this cooperation was a result of an ambitious plan for practical integration to make security concerns fade into the background.[3] The European Union is the result of an application of functionalist ideas of integration that emerged after the Second World War, often associated with academic practitioner David Mitrany (Mitrany 1948). Certainly disputes of interest remained, but there was no expectation that these would be processed through the use of weapons. It also demonstrates the relevance of the ideas of a security community that were developed in the mid-1950s by Karl W. Deutsch (Deutsch et al. 1957). This seemed utopian when first presented but found constructive applications in inter-state peacebuilding after the Second World War.

This also shows the importance of a wider application of the concept of quality peace. Inter-state relations can lead to major regional conflagrations and finding ways to build durable peace in such relations is most important. These relations, furthermore, can be assessed in terms of their qualities beyond the pure absence of war. It is actually remarkable that the world community since the end of the Cold War has been focused on intra-state affairs, not the least since such matters previously were entirely off the agenda. Concerns that earlier were impossible to deal with in international settings have now become the norm of action in postwar thinking. However, if this is done without regard for inter-state relations, the international community is likely to commit an error. Inter-state relations are potentially more destructive than civil or state formation wars. The internal conflicts tend to be more localized and confined to particular regions. Only gradually do they develop into major international concerns. Inter-state tensions and war, however, immediately affect neighbors, major powers, and international organizations. If left unattended, such conflicts can turn into highly destructive confrontations, with more human suffering, regional disruptions, and major power friction. Thus these conflicts require at least a chapter of their own.

Furthermore, the definition of quality peace as a way "to provide the post-conflict conditions that make the inhabitants of a society secure in life and dignity now and for the foreseeable future" clearly applies to inter-state relations, not only to intra-state conditions. The three criteria we have developed also can be asked of postwar inter-state relations: Does the pursued course of action provide safe conditions for all? Is this done in a way that enhances dignity? Are these conditions likely to be sustained? The response to these three questions will tell us if life after a war actually has such a strong quality that there will be little reason to restart the armed conflict.

Applying these criteria to the European Union of 2010s, the answers are largely in the affirmative: There is no expectation of another war among France, Germany, or any of the other EU members. Certainly there are strains, not the least as a result of the financial crises that have gripped the world since 2008, even threatening the breakup of the euro zone, but war is not likely. Matters of disagreements also include fiscal issues or population movements within the EU as well as from the outside. But these are not insecurities threatening the physical survival of the states or their inhabitants. Secondly, the EU gives considerable power to the dominant actors, thus safeguarding at least their sense of dignity (since 2004 France, Germany, Italy, Poland, Spain, and the United Kingdom all have the largest shares of votes following the Nice Treaty). Still there may be dissatisfaction, particularly in Great Britain, about the EU project as such. Also nationalistic groups on the continent challenge the EU, but for other reasons. Smaller states may have different perceptions of how they have been treated in Union deliberations, but at least they are at the table and can have an impact also as Chairs of the Union. The democratic framework, furthermore, provides for transparency and a chance for popular influence. Finally the EU is a project with considerable staying power, having ventured through a series of crises without breaking up. Each new crisis is an additional test, and the financial crisis may be the most serious ever faced. For the time being the EU meets the standards of quality peace.

The EU is consequently relevant in this context. It is an innovative case but, we will ask, is it also unique? What have been the peacebuilding experiences after the inter-state wars we have seen since the end of the Cold War, for instance? As a matter of fact, we may also think about the ending of the Cold War. Did it result in the construction of quality peace among the former antagonists? Table 5.1 provides data on the conflicts that saw armed conflicts for the period 1975–2010. These are the conflicts and related peacebuilding efforts that we will take up in the following sections of this chapter. They will also point to the wider international implications of postwar conditions for inter-state relations. This will be pursued in chapter 6.

Table 5.1 shows there have been twenty-four inter-state armed conflicts since 1975. Sixteen of them occurred in the first period 1975–1988—that is, during the Cold War. Only one conflict repeated itself from one period to the next: India–Pakistan. Also Table 5.1 demonstrates that most wars ended with either a victory or a peace agreement and that the latter were more common after the Cold War. To this can be added that most of the inter-state conflicts were over territorial issues rather than over government (fourteen in the first

Table 5.1

Inter-State Armed Conflicts: Outcomes, 1975–2010.

Number of Armed Conflicts with At Least One Victory or One Peace Agreement

Type of Outcome	1975–1988	1989–2010
Victory	5	2
Peace Agreement	3	4
Neither Victory nor Peace Agreement	8	2
Both Victory and Peace Agreement	0	0
Total Conflicts	16	8

Source: Uppsala Conflict Data Program, 2011

period had a significant territorial component, five in the second period). Some conflicts had an element of both (notably the conflicts between Uganda and Tanzania, North and South Yemen, North and South Vietnam, and Cambodia and Vietnam). There were four conflicts which only involved changes of regimes by outside powers (the US interventions in Grenada, Panama, and Iraq; the Soviet Union in Afghanistan).

Studying first the cases in the post–Cold War period, only one of the four peace agreements displays some degree of continued cooperation between the former warring parties: that between Ecuador and Peru. The short but threatening armed conflict in 1995 led to intensive diplomacy to end a conflict that had continued since 1832. A peace agreement was concluded in 1998. Even so, today's relations are far from the standard set by Franco–German integration. This is even more obvious when comparing them to other conflicts, notably the war between Ethiopia and Eritrea, where there also was a peace agreement; the United States–Iraq relations where there was an initial US victory followed by a protracted civil war, US withdrawal, and continued instability; and the protracted India–Pakistan dyad where there have been attempts at a peace process, but with little headway. From Table 5.1 we can conclude that building postwar quality peace between states remains a challenge. Furthermore, this challenge is hardly attended to by the international community. It is definitely not seen as a question of promoting quality peace. Instead relations are treated as matter of security, balance of power, and crisis diplomacy.

The record is equally bleak if we turn to the earlier cases. Theoretically there would have been more time for building new relations after the war as these conflicts were waged in the 1975–1988 period. One of the five victories is North Vietnam and its allies' victory over South Vietnam, the partner of the United States. The defeated South merged with the North a year later.

The dominance of the North has prevailed. Interestingly Vietnam's relations with the United States improved twenty years later. Now Vietnam is seen as a "normal" actor in international affairs, and there is little research interest in what happened to the relations between two former belligerents. Even the community of scholars dealing with Vietnam seems not to have attended to the question of how "peace" was forged in the South.

Table 5.1 also includes the dyad of Argentina and the United Kingdom. For political actors, the focus has been on the restoration of diplomatic relations. In internal affairs, the dispute is kept alive, particularly in Argentina. There is still no agreed approach to building lasting constructive relations. An additional situation is Tanzania's assistance to defeat Uganda's regime under Idi Amin in order to solve a territorial dispute. Tanzania was militarily successful and withdrew within a year, without much warmth remaining for the governments that followed. The territorial issue has not returned to the agenda. A further case is the Soviet invasion of Afghanistan, which led to the installation of a Soviet-sympathetic regime. This action resulted in a continuous internationalized civil war until a negotiated withdrawal could be implemented in 1989. A case that exhibits dynamics reminiscent of the early days of Franco–German relations is the fifth one, Iran and Iraq. This dyad saw a peace agreement in 1975 (which we commented on in chapter 4 with respect to its impact on the Kurdish community), suggesting an opportunity for developing cordial inter-state relations. After the Iranian Islamic Revolution in 1979, however, relations quickly turned hostile and the 1980s were marked by an eight-year-long devastating war. The ceasefire from 1988 technically remains the basis for their relations. It is not a peace agreement, but regulated some of the issues. The territorial concerns were dealt with by reverting back to the treaty of 1975, but the border issue remains unsolved. There were also other matters, which had to do with the dignity aspects, and thus we need to return to this case (Section 5.4 below).

This record leads us to wonder why postwar conditions in inter-state conflicts appear to be so much more difficult to move into a qualitatively new direction compared to intra-state affairs. There are three specific dimensions captured by the concept of quality peace. First, we ask whether the basic disagreement, the incompatibility, has been removed in such a way as to satisfy the formerly warring parties. The focus is on the disagreement that drives the parties' security concerns. If the basic issues, over which the war was fought, have not been dealt with in a sufficiently thorough way, they can always return, in times of internal or international crisis, and have severe impacts on inter-state relations (Section 5.2). The disagreements constitute the underlying security dilemma that has to be faced by the concept of quality peace. Much scholarship on inter-state relations emphasizes this; thus it has to be the first to be dealt with.

Second, related to this, we search specifically for security measures, such as disarmament or other such confidence-building measures that have been undertaken to restore connections and signal a long-term commitment to improved relations (Section 5.3). This has to do with the predictability dimensions of quality peace.

Third, we ask if the outcome has dealt with justice and dignity, notably in the form of compensation, war crime trials, and transparency, and particularly through democratic reforms (Section 5.4). This is often given less prominence in the literature on inter-state relations, although matters such as equality figure at least in a formal sense. Here we venture to apply this more consistently to inter-state relations. Quality peace in inter-state relations would have to include an affirmative response to these three sets of questions. War may not have occurred, but unsettled issues, threatening armaments, and lack of respect together indicate that relations are characterized by limited or negative peace, rather than the qualities associated with lasting peace.

Thus it is important to deal with the disagreement. As just mentioned, most of the inter-state conflicts deal with territorial issues. In addition, we have to consider the incompatibility over government. It is reasonable to expect that relations will take different qualities if the peace is to be built after a protracted but localized territorial conflict (such as between Britain and Argentina over the Falklands/Malvinas Islands), or after a military intervention where a new government has been installed (such as the US interventions in Grenada, Panama, and Iraq). In the latter case, postwar connections would technically be a matter of relations between the intervener and the new government, but in reality it comes down to the connection between the new government and its population. The externally installed government is likely to face domestic problems of legitimacy. This is different from accepting changes on territorial matters; in these cases domestic opposition may instead have to do with the type of concessions, or the conduct of the war, whether victorious or not. The South Atlantic War resulted in a reconquest of the disputed territory; in the case of an intervention, it is a matter of installing a new government in another country. Thus peace agreements can again be contrasted with victory, but the type of incompatibility may be the stronger explanation for the absence or presence of quality peace strategies.

The discussion in this chapter is complicated by the fact that scholars hardly have considered this subject as a peacebuilding challenge. However, the many studies on the causes of inter-state war should generate insights of value. Thus we will work from recent attempts to integrate the findings on the correlates of onset of inter-state war to an understanding of peace conditions. In particular, two results are relevant in this context: the connection between territorial disputes and the escalation to war; and the democratic peace thesis, which deals with the government issue. What will be attempted here is to extrapolate from these findings to matters of quality peace after war.

Chapter 5 thus explores uncharted intellectual territory. This means that we proceed through exemplification rather than building on previous analysis of other researchers. Furthermore, the conflicts are few, making statistical approaches doubtful. Instead, we will proceed by illustrating the arguments with the most typical cases that emerge from the discussion. The focus is on the serious conflicts, thus leaving aside disputes and armed conflicts that did not result in wars or major territorial readjustments.[4]

5.2 Quality Peace and the Settlement of Issues

In this section we will deal first with the territorial conflicts, whether the outcome is in the form of a peace agreement or victory. Then we will proceed to the wars that were over the government, what has been termed "regime change." Situations that are seen as "typical" and that mostly have involved wars will be exposed to closer scrutiny.

Territorial issues have a particular standing in the explanation of war between states. John A. Vasquez has convincingly demonstrated this in a series of studies (for instance, Vasquez 1995, Vasquez and Henehan 2001, and Senese and Vasquez 2008). From this work we can draw the conclusion that quality peace between states having faced a war over territorial issues has to have the settlement of the territorial dispute as a primary concern. We have already noted that Western European cooperation in the post–World War II period could build on the fact that there were no disagreements on the borders in this part of Europe, and this is confirmed in various studies, notably by Mitchell and Prins (1999). Such settlements have, obviously, to be done to the satisfaction of both parties. Senese and Vasquez write in their conclusion on the steps to war that "... once borders are accepted (even if that acceptance comes about violently) neighbors can have long periods of peace, even if other salient issues arise." Furthermore they state that "... the acceptance of borders is central to establishing peaceful relations. Neighbors do not have to be locked into long-term struggle for power punctuated periodically by war" (Senese and Vasquez 2008: 278–279). Dealing with the territorial issues appears to be a necessary first step for changing relations in a durable peaceful direction.

This conclusion is compatible with the history of Franco–German relations that we recounted earlier in this chapter. The remaining territorial issue between France and Germany was settled in 1957. France and Germany negotiated a bilateral agreement that allowed for Saar's integration into the Federal Republic, in return for a project of canalization of River Moselle that was important to France.[5] Having removed this issue in an agreeable way, it changed the climate of cooperation. Following this the relations between France and Germany turned into an engine for European cooperation, resulting in the longest peace spell between these countries for several centuries.

Studying inter-state conflicts since 1975, we can see that there is a lack of settlements of territorial issues in inter-state conflicts. This means that the future of bilateral inter-state relations has been left in limbo: There is an underlying danger that they will arise again. The number of unsettled disputes is remarkable. The inability of the international community to address these issues even long after a war has been terminated must be regarded as a failure in developing inter-state quality peace. It also demonstrates that international concern often is with the management of acute crises rather than long-term development of relations. A quick review of pertinent cases makes this clear.

Since 1975 there have been many large-scale inter-state conflicts involving territorial issues, most of which have created great international concern. Below we list nine conflicts which did not see a full termination. These conflicts demonstrate the range of challenges to building quality peace between states:

- India–Pakistan, primarily fought over Kashmir, and where UCDP records six armed conflict episodes of which two came to the level of war since 1975 (i.e., with more than 1,000 battle-related deaths in a year).
- Ethiopia–Somalia, primarily concerning the Somali-populated Ogaden area, and where the agreed withdrawals after the war in 1978–1979 did not include a final settlement. Somalia has been without a functioning state since 1991; once there is a government in control over the land, this issue might return.
- Cambodia–Vietnam saw a border conflict in 1975–1977, and this issue was dealt with only after the removal of the incumbent regime in 1978, resulting in an agreement in the 1980s, but the border is still not demarcated. The border dispute occasional is used as an argument in political campaigns in Cambodia.
- China's idea of teaching a "lesson" to Vietnam in 1979 stemmed partly from an unsettled border issue, and fighting continued until 1988.
- Cambodia–Thailand involves smaller, contested border areas. A decision by the International Court of Justice concerned only some of the issues. An armed conflict over a temple area flared up in 2011, but was brought back to the ICJ.
- The Iran–Iraq War partly concerned the border areas. The peace agreement from 1975 was abrogated by Iraq in 1980, reinstated in 1988, but is still not fully implemented.

- The United Kingdom and Argentina fought over the Falkland/Malvinas Islands in 1982. There is still no formal Argentinean agreement to the militarily restored *status quo ante bellum*. Instead, the issue appears regularly in political and diplomatic settings.
- Iraq's occupation of Kuwait in 1990–1991 ended and the UN settled the border issue, but there is still no formal treaty and even post-Saddam governments have yet to fulfill the obligations resulting from the Gulf War.
- In the aftermath of the Eritrea–Ethiopia War, neither the border dispute nor the compensation issues have been settled, although the peace agreement was concluded in 2000.

This overview demonstrates that the settlement between Ecuador and Peru in 1998, mentioned in section 5.1, is different and important (Herz and Pontes Nogueir 2002). Unknown to the parties this solution and its implementation make it unique as an example of a recently settled inter-state conflict. It actually includes a solution to a problem that parallels, for instance, the disputed town of Badme in the Eritrean-Ethiopian conflict. The solution consisted of the creation of a "binational park" in the contested area and the granting of a piece of territory to Ecuador as a non-sovereign private property that can hoist the Ecuadorian flag and have an Ecuadorian monument, although formally being on Peruvian territory.[6] This agreement may not have satisfied all demands but fifteen years later we can observe that the arrangement works, that official maps have been adjusted accordingly, and that the tension between the two countries has given way to mutual trade relations. Both countries, furthermore, have had other crises to attend to, both domestically and with other neighbors. It can tentatively be characterized as a successful case of building an element of quality peace after a peace agreement: The dignity of the two states and their territories were respected, the security concerns diminished with the political settlement, and the parties have implemented the agreements, thus providing predictability and reasonably durable conditions. In line with the arguments of Senese and Vasquez, the solution of the key issue, the territorial dispute, was central in this development.

In the territorial conflict between Cambodia and Vietnam, there is an ongoing process of settling the border issues. This dates to agreements between the two countries in the 1980s, when Cambodia was under Vietnamese occupation (Amer 1997). Officially the parties still adhere to the agreements but also find themselves in a protracted process of implementation.[7] In a way this is a case of peacebuilding after an agreed termination of war, but it is heavily intertwined with the previous invasion by Vietnam and the installation of a new regime in Cambodia. For a long time the border conflict was overshadowed by the conflict over government. It is not a typical case. Even though conditions would largely be favorable for peacebuilding, as there are similar regimes on both sides and a close alliance between them, the implementation procedures have been slow.

The relations between Vietnam and China need also to be discussed in this context. There were unsolved border issues among the reasons for China's invasion in 1979. It was also a matter of regional influence, where China objected to Vietnam's invasion of Cambodia in 1978, removing an ally of China. Possibly there were also Chinese expectations of regime change in Vietnam. After a short war on Vietnamese territory, the Chinese forces withdrew and negotiations started. Clashes continued until 1988. The land borders were regulated in a treaty and demarcated ten years later. However, the maritime issues remain to be settled.

Many of the nine listed cases were victories by the initiator, and what followed should then be seen as victory consolidation. There is no convincing record of victory outcomes leading toward quality peace. The clear-cut military and political success by Britain over Argentina in the dispute over the Falkland/Malvinas Islands has not ended the parties' contention. The ownership of the islands is still disputed. Argentina incorporated its sovereignty of the islands into its new constitution of 1994. The islands are again populated by the same British citizens as before, thus consolidating the British hold, but not moving to a quality peace with Argentina. Tension remains and, at best, this is a case of negative peace: the strength of British defense may deter renewed Argentine attempts of conquest.

This type of "peace" characterizes some of the other situations as well, notably Iran–Iraq (a negotiated solution, although Iraq claimed it as victory in 1988) and Iraq–Kuwait (ultimately a victory for the Kuwaiti side) where trade now flourishes. This does not prevent the unsolved issues from emerging time and time again. De facto relations are not the same as peacebuilding; the unsettled issues are likely to continue to generate security concerns. British and Argentinean military budgets include appropriations for the South Atlantic, thus affecting the threat perceptions of the other side. A reminder occurred in February 2010, when the possibility of oil exploration again made the unsettled issues salient. Ethiopia may have pushed Somalia back, even now controlling territory in Somalia, but there is considerable potential for future conflict, unless this territorial issue as well as the one with Eritrea can be settled. Thus military victories in inter-state territorial relations do not translate easily into quality peace relations.

This means that we find only one successful case of building new relationships in a territorial armed conflict in this period, definitely a low turnout. As could be expected this was through a negotiated settlement. Victories have normally not resulted in quality peace between the former enemies. Embedding the unsolved issues in a web of other relations, notably economic exchange and trade, does not deflect the fact that the territorial issues are unsolved. Even small incidents may suddenly threaten to damage otherwise close relations, as could be seen in the armed conflict over a temple between Cambodia and Thailand in early 2011.

Let us move on to the second category: *issues over governance*. The incompatibilities are even more difficult to transcend in the cases of inter-state intervention resulting in the removal of the government. As mentioned in section 5.1 there are seven cases where government issues played an important role since 1975,[8] notably the following:

- North Vietnam's victory over South Vietnam in 1975, where the sudden collapse of the government in South Vietnam may have been as surprising to the North as it was to the South and its allies.
- Vietnam's invasion of Cambodia in 1978, where the border issue was the initial motivation for the invasion, but the incumbent government quickly retreated to peripheral jungle areas, being replaced with a Vietnam-friendly regime.
- Tanzania's intervention in Uganda in 1979, where the border issue triggered the intervention, but the incumbent fled and a new government was installed.
- The Soviet invasion of Afghanistan in 1979, installing a communist government relying on continued Soviet military presence and support. The regime fell in 1992, three years after Soviet withdrawal.
- Three US interventions—notably in Grenada 1983, Panama 1989, and Iraq 2003—all resulting in regime changes and the creation of democratic structures.

These seven conflicts had been militarily terminated by the end of 2014, at least from the invading state's point of view. Troops had been withdrawn and remaining military commitments had been regulated by inter-state agreements. There was little space for negotiations between the invader and the incumbent. Asking questions from the quality peace perspective then is not only a matter of the formerly occupied country's relations to the invader but also—or chiefly—a question of the connection between the population and the new, externally instituted regime. It is safe to say that in these cases the invader has taken deliberate action to protect itself from losing power to, for example, opponents of the invasion, such as parties supporting the ousted leadership. The three cases involving the United States may include more democratic measures than many of the others, but even so the United States acted to make sure that such groups were kept away from power (notably members of the formerly ruling Baathist party, as well as the US-critical Sadrist groups in Iraq). Grenada and Panama are today, however, democratically ruled and maintain largely positive relations with the United States. These were at the same time the most asymmetrical of all the inter-state conflicts.

With regard to the installed regimes, there is little difference among the remaining cases: The successor regimes are all authoritarian. For example, North Vietnam took firm control of the South of the country, and that has remained the state of affairs. The Communist Party has only lately begun to allow several candidates in national elections, but these are not likely to go beyond a set framework. Interestingly in the debate that led to the reforms of the Communist Party's economic policy in the 1980s, experiences from South Vietnam played a role (Elliott 2012). With respect to Cambodia, Vietnamese forces withdrew in 1989. The following elections were won by the regime originally installed by Vietnam. It has managed to maintain control ever since. Tanzania oversaw the installation of a new regime in Uganda and then pulled out its troops, not the least as this military adventure threatened the stability of its own economy. Its preferred political candidate took power somewhat later, only to lead the country into a new civil war. The Soviet invasion in Afghanistan seemed initially successful, but the regime soon found itself in a vicious civil war it could not win even with massive Soviet support.

From these examples it seems safe to conclude that the conditions after ending these invasions have not included measures approaching inter-state quality peace. The popular support for the regimes remaining after the withdrawal has not been reassuring. Several of them were not able to maintain themselves (Uganda, Afghanistan); others gradually became more autocratic (Cambodia, also a possible scenario for Iraq). Again Grenada and Panama show a different pattern. The lessons for long-term quality peace relations in inter-state governmental conflicts are not many. Only in cases of heavy superiority (the United States vs. its three targets; North Vietnam vs. South Vietnam; and Vietnam vs. Cambodia) do the relations today appear at "peace." However, the real test of durability will be when opposition parties become significant. Such challenges have often been connected to new wars, thus demonstrating the lack of success in making these relations more secure (e.g., Afghanistan after the Soviet withdrawal; Iraq's internationalized civil war since 2003).

The conclusion is that efforts to build quality peace after inter-state wars have been minimal with respect to a settlement of the incompatibility. The victorious actors have often held on to the territory they conquered or the regimes they installed. In some cases they have withdrawn completely, leaving inter-state relations that more remind us of cold peace than a quality beyond that.[9] Even in the cases where peace agreements were used to regulate the incompatibility, this was not successful. Among the territorial conflicts, the case of Ecuador and Peru is unique for this period as a case that involved quality dimensions. It does not give guidance for more general conclusions. Similarly drawing inferences from the very asymmetrical cases of Grenada and Panama would be risky. Let us, however, move more systematically to some other aspects of quality peace.

5.3   Quality Peace and Security Building

The Senese-Vasquez notion of the steps to war not only points to the importance of the territorial issues for the escalation to war, but also to alliances and arms races.

Thus we may ask, in cases of territorial and government conflicts alike, whether alliance patterns and military expenditures have been an important aspect in the postwar efforts to prevent future conflicts. In particular, we are interested in actions that warring parties may have undertaken to reduce tension, develop confidence, and thus improve the chances of a solution to the incompatibilities that we analyzed in section 5.2. The idea is that such measures provide the basis on which to build a joint approach to the unsettled territorial issues. One could draw a parallel to the European case: Among the measures worked out in the middle of the 1950s was the democratization of the new West German Army and its integration into NATO, so as to reduce its ability to act independently. These measures helped to reassure the neighboring countries, made agreements on territorial issues possible, and thus improved the prospect of quality peace by reducing insecurity. Do we find similar security-building actions in the terminated conflicts in Table 5.1?

A first measure is the *withdrawal of forces* behind internationally recognized borders. Looking at the first period, 1975–1988, we can observe that such measures were common. For instance, it was part of the tacit agreement between Ethiopia and Somalia in 1979 and was implemented at the time. Similarly we have observed how Tanzania, Vietnam, China, the United States, and the Soviet Union all at some point withdrew their forces from the territory of the invaded country and thus, in some sense, "normalized" the situation. Similarly the ceasefire between Iran and Iraq included a withdrawal to international borders, which was gradually accomplished in the following years, and monitored by UN inspectors. In all these cases, there was an observable return to a military status before the start of the war. For the period after 1989, similar developments can be observed in some cases, notably the separation of forces between Eritrea and Ethiopia with the use of an international peacekeeping operation (UNMEE). The dividing lines have been upheld also since the work of UNMEE was terminated.

As for other situations, we can note that the United States to this day maintains a heavy military presence in the region of the Middle East, following the two wars it was engaged in (the 1991 Gulf War and the Iraq War), although officially having withdrawn its military combat forces from Iraq. It also pulled out its troops from Panama and Grenada, but remains heavily present in the region. Ecuador and Peru undertook mutual demilitarization measures. India and Pakistan display almost the opposite pattern. There have been no withdrawals from the borders. India officially maintains that Pakistan supports terrorist attacks on India as surrogate warfare and thus there can be no further moves toward peacemaking until such action ceases. To most parties, the withdrawal of forces means a clear commitment to a ceasefire or an end to an ongoing intervention. The military measures we observe are limited and probably not seen as sufficiently reassuring by the opposing parties. Again only the Ecuador–Peru relation displays a different pattern.

Even if troops are withdrawn behind the recognized borders it does not mean building of confidence for negotiations. The opposing sides are also likely to study closely the *military doctrines, procurements, and training* of the other side. Reassuring postures, in other words, would have to be observed in the direct relations as well as in the internal dispositions made by either side. The skeptical questions will be what they may reveal about the actual plans and motives. In this respect, the antagonists India and Pakistan demonstrate similar approaches. For both, there is fear as well as an expectation of one side clandestinely striving to undermine the defense capability of the other. Both sides watch technological advances of the other. We would expect the same to be true for the dyads of Ethiopia versus Eritrea, China versus Vietnam, and Iran versus Iraq. Steps to quality peace, in other words, have to begin in the public discussions on defense budgets in each of the conflictual pairs. The publication of such budgets would constitute a confidence-building measure, as it removes some uncertainty about what actions are possible for the other.

The outbreak of war between Eritrea and Ethiopia is puzzling and requires further scrutiny. It fits only partly the path to war described by Senese and Vasquez. Several accounts of the relations before the war broke out in 1998 mention a reduction in armed forces on both sides, rather than an arms race (Omitoogun 2003; Last 2005: 59). Even the disputed territory as such seems not to have been something that engaged the public before the war. Instead most accounts refer to the personal relations between the leaders as crucial. Some, however, also relate it to Eritrea's decision to introduce its own currency, which of course immediately impacted on border areas as well as interstate relations (Jacquin-Berdal 2005: xiii–xiv; Plaut 2005: 17–18). Still there is no agreement on the significance of economic consideration in the origin of the war (Styan 2005: 180–181). Even measures to solve the border issues were taken well before the outbreak of the war (Plaut 2005: 17; Last 2005: 60). This has implications for the possibility of peacebuilding after the war. The way the war started may also affect what can be done after the war to build quality relations. Although arms expenditures were reduced in the years after the war, as documented for instance in World Bank data,[10] tensions remained. After the withdrawal of the UN Peacekeeping Force in 2008,[11] there were no outside observers available on the frontiers between the two countries. Possibly one can argue that the peacekeepers were in place in a crucial period after the war, and thus played a useful role. Since 2008 relations had to be managed by the countries themselves. Both countries remained highly reclusive with respect to military matters. Public information was kept to a minimum and the strategic debate was only conducted within a select circle. Thus none of these countries has made any attempt to signal peaceful intentions by changing military postures. If the leadership issue is key, the unexpected death of the Ethiopian leader, Meles Zenawi, in 2012 would have opened up the possibility for new initiatives, although the ruling group, national institutions, and government policies were not affected. As mentioned in section 4.4, more is probably needed than just a change of leader, and that is amply demonstrated in this case: The new Ethiopian leader, Hailemariam Desalegn, did not deviate from the previous policy.

In the military field, we can see that there has been little movement since the end of the wars. There is no difference between the cases of victory and peace agreement cases, again with the exception of Ecuador and Peru.

A further consideration is that the parties are likely to carefully watch the *alliances* of the opponent. This is clearly in line with the steps to war thesis. Looking at our cases we can observe that Pakistan, for instance, has been continuously concerned about India's influence in Afghanistan, and often points to this as an indicator of India's "real" intentions. Similarly Ethiopia carefully tracks Eritrea's support to groups in Somalia, as does Eritrea with respect to Ethiopia's influence in the neighboring countries. The war between China and Vietnam in 1979 was partially the result of Vietnam's invasion of Cambodia in 1978, where the demoted regime was allied to China. This alliance relationship, in turn, was one of Vietnam's reasons for the invasion. Traditional Realpolitik considerations also afflict postwar conditions. To the formerly warring parties, military alliances indicate access to military deliveries, training, and support. Even if done by one side explicitly for defensive purposes, the other side is likely to be skeptical. Whatever the motives, the other will find it necessary to take countermeasures. Instead of peacebuilding, alliance relationships after a war are likely to contribute to threat building.

This points to an important aspect of the Franco–German relationship: The two states were members of the *same* alliance. This may have been crucial. If one had been outside the same alliance structure, even as a neutral state, this may have affected the confidence between the two sides. Ecuador and Peru did have working relations with the same neighboring states as well as the United States, and both were members of the regional framework of OAS, the Organization of American States. This may have reduced the need to consider hostile scenarios and contributed to the peacebuilding effort. Finding such shared international structures may then be a necessary priority in postwar interstate relations.

However, this may not exclusively be a matter of a military alliance. The 1991 peace treaty for Cambodia suggests some other possibilities. It was agreed that the country should be neutral and not aligned to any other country. The withdrawal of the Vietnamese troops had by that time been completed and reasonably verified. This, no doubt, contributed to a reduction in tension in their mutual relations but also in the region as a whole. Following this, Vietnam and Cambodia were both admitted into ASEAN, the Association of Southeast Asian Nations, a shared regional framework. As mentioned, the efforts to regulate the border disputes have continued, albeit at a slow pace, and, in particular, economic relations have deepened. Key may be the credible commitment to the process; this may have been strengthened by reduced military spending and by the development of defense doctrines emphasizing peaceful uses of the countries' military capabilities.

The withdrawal of forces from the "other" side of the border is theoretically one of the more effective ways in which a new sense of security can be forged between two countries that have been at war. If accompanied by supportive measures, such as a change in military postures (e.g., an agreement on a demilitarized zone) and membership in nonthreatening regional arrangements, this likely to add to positive dynamics. Such measures are particularly useful in territorial disputes, but may also play a role for the cases of interventions to change governments. The United States quickly withdrew from Panama and Grenada, but not from Iraq. The Soviet Union did not leave Afghanistan until after a protracted war. Possibly this suggests that cases of swift withdrawal will be those where the postwar relations develop in a more peaceful direction. However, in cases where such marked changes of military posture are not visible, moves to new postwar conditions will be impeded. Thus for an intervening power to maintain strong presence in the region of a dyadic conflict may make peacebuilding more difficult. This points in particular to the difficulties in changing conflict dynamics between neighboring states which, of course, legitimately belong to the area. Taking these matters together, they suggest that building quality peace among states after a war faces challenges not seen in other types of conflict.

5.4 Quality Peace and Dignity

The third aspect of quality peace is whether the postwar conditions provide for justice in the inter-state relations, notably in the form of recognition of pain and creation of transparent structures. This means, for instance, recognition of aggression, to be followed by compensation or punishment of perpetrators. As seen in chapters 3 and 4, democratic rule may be a first step toward recognition of the dignity of those involved in the war.

A challenge to postwar situations is the issue of justice and dignity. There could be relevant stipulations if the war ends through a peace agreement. During the war the parties often brand the other as the originator of the conflict; it is common that each side sees itself as a victim of aggression. Both sides may have compelling stories of the injustices committed against them. In several conflicts the determination of the origin of the conflict is a central issue, and some peace agreements have provisions for this. Thus there is a demand for justice between the two states. It is a matter of restoring dignity in a relationship. Seasoned mediators understand the dynamics of such demands and tend to avoid them until other agreements are in place (Svensson and Wallensteen 2010: 120–122).

However, in situations of victory consolidation, concerns about justice and dignity take a different route. It may more likely be a matter of capturing the leadership and punishing the perpetrators of alleged crimes. Issues of truth may be less important to the victors.

The question of justice is a delicate matter. For instance, to define the origins of a conflict may sound reasonable. In international affairs, however, it may not be the full story. Leaders realize the potential implication of such demands. If one side can get the leaders of the other side to admit guilt, it may undermine their domestic standing. It becomes a form of victory. Obviously few leaders are willing to agree to this and they are likely to find ways to prevent "justice." In practice, we can observe that "justice" is applicable only after the leader has fallen from power.[12] In other words, this form of justice is more difficult to administer in inter-state relations, not the least as leaders mostly are protected from being captured by the opponent. This may be a reason for why monetary compensation has become a typical measure for acknowledging past sufferings. It may, in effect, be the only traditional way in which punishment could be dispensed by one actor to the other. Compensatory schemes could be described as a form of restorative justice, instead of the retributive justice of trials and punishments.

This "model" has many applications in the history of European wars, most recently in the Versailles Treaty of 1919 (MacMillan 2003). Defeated states were defined as being the aggressors in the outbreak of the war in 1914. In particular, Germany was singled out and forced to pay compensation. The war reparations became a focus in the critique against this particular peace agreement. The objections came from very different quarters. Nationalist Germans argued that this was unfair, and had destructive effects on the German economy. This line of argument was picked up by Adolf Hitler and was used in subsequent Nazi propaganda against the agreement. The other critique became the origin of Keynesianism, as it argued that the reparations would result in unemployment and economic stagnation, rather than the infusion of capital into the economy that the postwar situation required (Keynes 1920). The 1920s saw depressions and economic swings, gaining international adherents to Keynes' analysis, while the Nazi party managed to take control in Germany.

These experiences led the victorious Western powers after the Second World War to conclude that the previous approach should not be repeated.[13] Still there was a need to brand the losers. For instance, the UN Charter mentions "enemy states" as a separate category of states, thus treating the losers differently than the winners (see for instance UN Charter Art. 53). However, this was not the starting point for a reparations scheme. On the contrary, the Western leaders perceived a danger of another Great Depression as the industrial production for military needs was drawing down. They also feared that unemployment would benefit extreme groups, particularly the Communist parties, but potentially also a resurfaced German nationalism. Thus a grand injection of capital was the preferred solution. The post–World War II period saw the massive Marshall Plan program, instead of traditional reparations.[14] The issue of possible compensation was defined as a matter of economics rather than justice to the victims. It was in all likelihood important for the later emergence of the European community. The regional framework of the Organization for European Economic Cooperation (OEEC), today the Organization for Economic Cooperation and Development (OECD), was set up to handle development aid, and Germany soon became a member.[15] Germany (and Japan) may have been described as "enemy states," but without punitive economic consequences. Post–World War II inter-state relations were given a different direction than after the previous world war.

Let us thus see how matters of compensation and economic relations have been treated in the major inter-state conflicts of the past thirty-five years. From a quality peace perspective, the picture is far from encouraging. The ending of the Iran–Iraq war has still not been settled to the satisfaction of both parties. There is no peace treaty, although many of the provisions in the ceasefire agreement from 1988 (UNSCR 598) have been implemented, notably the return of prisoners-of-war. The border seems to function in practice, but there have also been a number of Iranian violations, notably in the pursuit of Kurdish rebel groups, or in shelling across the border. In addition, the UN ceasefire resolution stated that the responsibility for the war should be determined, leading to compensation to the victims. In 1991, the Secretary General concluded that Iraq was responsible, but also ruled out any form of compensation (Svensson and Wallensteen 2010: 64–65). The matter has still not gone away. For instance, in 2010 an Iranian official questioned the Iraqi war reparations, even suggesting a way in which they could come about, through the joint exploitation of shared oil fields. Clearly, he was not alone in taking this up.[16]

Remarkably even the clear-cut outcome of the Gulf War 1990–1991 has not led to a full settlement, although the regime in Iraq has changed and more than twenty years have passed since the UN Security Council resolutions in 1991 ended the war. Frost (2010) points out that this includes a series of matters, notably "paying war reparations to Kuwait, settling Saddam's debts, repatriating the human remains of Kuwaiti nationals missing since 1990, dismantling Iraq's capacity to build weapons of mass destruction (WMDs), and officially recognizing the land border between Iraq and Kuwait." This is a long list of unfulfilled obligations, including a demand for reparations, and there is no international body pursuing them at this time.

The peace agreement between Ethiopia and Eritrea had a compensation mechanism where the legitimate claims of one side were to be counted against the corresponding claims of the other sides. This Claims Commission first had to establish the responsibility for the war and then moved on to the compensation issue. In 2005 it stated that Eritrea's claims that it acted in self-defense could not be substantiated. In essence, it made Eritrea responsible for the war. However, as the parallel Boundary Commission had found that the contested territory of Badme belonged to Eritrea and consequently should be returned to the country by Ethiopia (which continued to hold on to the territory), both sides achieved something through this process. In 2009, furthermore, the Claims Commission made its final award giving USD 174 million to Ethiopia and USD 163.5 million to Eritrea. As this was a state-to-state arrangement it would mean that Eritrea should pay the difference—that is, around USD 10 million to Ethiopia (Matheson 2009). Again this is a measure that remains to be settled.

This overview is testimony to the fact that imposition of war reparations is a difficult way to achieve justice in inter-state relations. However, if a country is interested in building peace with another, certainly such stipulations could become appropriate measures of confidence building. Offering to pay the amounts, or at least initiating a discussion on them, could be a way to break a deadlock and lead to further moves. It fits with the ideas of costly signaling. Bringing these issues to the table could be expensive for the one doing it, thus demonstrating serious intent (Fearon 1995).

These matters of compensation, however, are mostly seen when there is an agreement between the parties, whether an agreed capitulation, or a more equal treaty. In the clear-cut victories where there is no such document to resort to (as in the case of asymmetrical interventions—notably the US in Grenada, Panama and Iraq; the Soviet Union in Afghanistan; or North Vietnam's victory over South Vietnam), it is a question of finding other appropriate measures.[17] Interestingly it is the victor or the intervener that could be expected to support the loser. It is in the tradition of the Marshall Plan rather than the Versailles approach. There has been an expectation of the victor or stronger party to extend development assistance or training of reconstructed military forces. The damages inflicted prior to the conflict, for example, on US interests in Grenada and Panama may hardly be comparable to the damages caused by the US intervention itself. Nowhere is this more obvious than in the case of Iraq, where the destruction caused by the US forces is difficult to compare to the destruction Iraq may have caused to US interests. However, the traditional approach was, of course, that the victor had the "right" to the resources of the loser. The moral argument was that the loser had inflicted damage on the winner. For instance, when Iraqi forces entered Kuwait in 1990, they also shipped a lot of valuable equipment and other assets to Iraq. The spoils of war belonged to the victor. In the intervention cases, however, this has not been the typical approach. As the interventions have been made "for the good" of the invaded country by "freeing it" from a previous regime, they have also resulted in schemes of reconstruction, or development assistance.

An alternative to agreed reparations for meting out justice after a war is, of course, the abdication or collapse of the opponent's regime, including the capture of the former regime's leadership by the victorious side. Again, making a parallel to the Franco–German case, this was an important element at the end of the Second World War. A number of the key German perpetrators of war crimes were detained and brought to the first international tribunal, what became known as the Nuremberg Trials. Personalities that cooperated with the German occupation, notably Marshal Pétain of France and Vidkun Quisling of Norway, were tried in national courts. During the Cold War, however, trials were remarkably rare in inter-state relations. For instance, the capitulation of South Vietnam to the North Vietnamese forces in 1975 included the capture of a great number of the regime's leaders. Even if some officials managed to escape to the United States, many remained and gave up voluntarily. They were imprisoned for an indefinite period of time in "reeducation camps," as many were considered war criminals. However, there are no reports of mass executions, or of official trials.[18]

The resort to trials against leaders has become more common after the Cold War, as can be seen in several of our cases. Interesting examples concern the

US capture of strongman Manuel Noriega in Panama and Saddam Hussein in Iraq. Both were brought to trials. Noriega was first tried in the United States, served his sentence, and then was sent to France for another crime. Only in 2011 was he, at the age of 77, returned to Panama to serve a national sentence in the country he controlled in the 1980s. Saddam Hussein was brought to an Iraqi trial, convicted for crimes against Shiites, and then executed, without other issues being brought up, notably his role in the wars against Iran and Kuwait or on the Kurdish population. Other members of the Saddam regime have also been tried and convicted. National trials by the new regime seem to be the most likely scenario. In addition to the Iraq case we can note that Argentina's defeat in the war against Britain also resulted in the fall of the military junta that initiated the war. Members were later tried in Argentine courts. Members of the Khmer Rouge government that was deposed by Vietnam's invasion were brought to court in the capital of Cambodia, Phnom Penh, although only thirty years later. The International Criminal Court is an alternative in inter-state conflicts, but so far all the crimes that have been taken up in the ICC have concerned intra-state issues.

It can be asked to what degree the trials and the compensation schemes actually are measures of justice. They involve a few, although responsible, persons; compensatory monetary transactions are made between states; largely the local population is not participating or benefiting directly. Giving a role to the population in the decision making seems much more likely to generate justice to all. This brings us to an additional aspect of quality peace: the impact of democratic rule.

A credible democratic arrangement has more of the elements we would need in building quality peace between states. The heavily discussed democratic peace hypothesis suggests that two democratic states do not fight wars with one another (for instance see Russett 1993, Maoz and Russett 1993, Russett and Oneal 2001, Gleditsch 2008). Based on this finding, long-term peacebuilding would have to include the development of democratic structures on both sides of a divide.

Using this as an indicator of quality peace for the cases we are studying yields a disappointing record. The experience of the Ecuador–Peru relation is an example of two more open societies finding a resolution. The final agreement was subject to discussion in the elected assemblies on both sides. It fits with the democratic peace hypothesis. However, several other dyads with such features have had no particular success in developing quality peace. The dyad of Britain and Argentina is a prime example, both being stable democracies after the war. Perhaps it can be argued that the democratic structures on both sides have prevented renewed escalation to war, but it has not helped in moving forward to a closer relationship or an ending of the incompatibility.

Similarly India and Pakistan is a protracted relationship where the democratic credentials on both sides have varied. For the past decade there have been several spells where both have been democratic on a level approaching what could be observed for Ecuador and Peru. Still peace initiatives have encountered serious difficulties. The same applies to the Iraq–Kuwait relations where both societies are more open today. Instead we may note that several of the most autocratic dyads have seen more achievements in dealing with outstanding issues, as could be witnessed in the Cambodia–Vietnam and Vietnam–China dyads. The integration of South Vietnam into North Vietnam may, however, tell a different story, once it is available for serious research.

The most asymmetric cases—notably United States–Grenada, United States–Panama and United States–Iraq—also involved deliberate democracy promotion by the stronger party. In the first two cases, such institutions were already in place and the intervention resulted in their reactivation. In the case of Iraq, the democratic program encountered serious difficulties, as there was a particular ethnic composition that played a role. For instance, for Kurds and Shiites, together forming the vast majority of the country's population, the end of Saddam's rule meant an end to Sunni domination. The debates on the constitution have since then involved issues of the strength of the central government versus the constituent units, as well as control over the oil resources. At times these discussions have led to considerable violence. It is difficult to describe this as a process of developing quality peace.

Thus we can see that inter-state relations lack concerted efforts by the parties to move toward quality peace in matters that pertain to justice and dignity. This is a definite contrast to the patterns we observed for intra-state conflicts, and even for state formation conflicts. There are particular features to inter-state relations that may make them less susceptible to quality peace. This is the theme of the following section.

5.5 Challenges to Inter-state Quality Peace

The focus in this chapter has been on the ability of two antagonistic states to forge peace after war. This turns out to be a challenge to the research community and policymakers alike. There are, simply, very few examples of such peacebuilding in the past three decades. The two cases that have been presented throughout this chapter appear special and hard to generalize from: The Franco–German relations since the 1950s and the Ecuador–Peru relations since the mid-1990s. Both stand out as exceptional. The solution to the territorial issues removed a potential trigger for conflict escalation. The open societies provided for transparency. The conflicts had gone on for a considerable period of time and by now ceased to generate nationalist fervor. There were shared memberships in a regional organization and a degree of military integration into a larger framework. All this seems to have contributed to a favorable building of durable conditions for peace. The scale of integration in the France–Germany relations goes much deeper, however, with economic integration, shared currency, and joint leadership of the regional body, the EU. Still, on the quality peace score, these two cases contrast with the other dyads such as India–Pakistan, Ethiopia–Eritrea, and China–Vietnam, or the asymmetrical cases of occupation of one state by another, notably Vietnam–Cambodia, North Vietnam–South Vietnam, and the United States versus Grenada, Panama, and Iraq, respectively. In all these cases we have seen measures aiming at consolidation of victory or the status quo, combined with preparation for meeting dangers of a new confrontation. In some cases war is very recent, which may explain the concern with security measures. However, so was the Second World War for Germany and France when they started their new relations, and the same is true for Ecuador and Peru. It was the recent war experience that sparked the efforts of changing the relations.

If there are any general lessons that can be generated from this overview, they converge on two issues: the importance of solving territorial issues as a first necessary step for building a quality peace and, less strongly, the importance of democratic institutions on both sides of the warring dyad. These observations clearly contrast peacebuilding from victory consolidation. If territorial issues are resolved to a reasonable mutual satisfaction, there is a basis for new relations. This can only be done through negotiations. If these solutions are created between two (reasonably) democratic societies, the dangers of war are reduced and the conditions for quality peace are laid. However, the numbers of cases for this conclusion for this period (chiefly post-1975) are few, thus, suggesting the need for more study.

The picture is blurred by the fact that relations can develop even though territorial issues have not been removed from the agenda. This is so no matter what type of regime rules the country. The relations between the United Kingdom and Argentina have continued and include economic exchanges, although the territorial issue has not been settled, at least not as both sides see it. There may be a low risk of another armed conflict between the two, but the relations are not characterized by quality peace; the territorial issue stands in the way of confidence building. The same can be said for the China–Vietnam and Vietnam–Cambodia pairs. Trade and other forms of cooperation prosper, but there is an underlying fear that the unsettled territorial issues can emerge if there is a crisis or a change of government in any of these states. It becomes an uneasy peace, rather than the quality peace we are looking for.

There are, however, also cases where there were no territorial issues of importance in the incompatibility. This is particularly true for the asymmetric relations involving one major power versus a weaker independent state. This dynamic follows another logic, where neither peacebuilding nor victory consolidation is the correct term for describing postwar relations. It appears more as integration on conditions set by the superior actor. If the weaker state and its population accept the situation, there is likely to be a period of sustained peace (Grenada and Panama fit this picture, as does former South Vietnam); if this is not the case, then conflicts are likely to continue, initially perhaps remaining localized (as we saw in immediate post–Soviet Afghanistan, or after the US withdrawal from Iraq in 2010), but eventually turning into global concerns (as exemplified with the challenges from the Taliban, al-Qaeda, and ISIS arising from asymmetric situations).

The reasons for a major power to be involved in interventions may not necessarily have to do only with a bilateral dispute. In a major power's perspective, a state can take on significance in a larger strategic equation. The weaker state's choice of governance, for example, may suggest the possibility of a closer alliance with one major power rather another, thus affecting major power relations. This means we also have to consider issues of global affairs and how they relate to postwar conditions between states. Chapter 6 discusses the relevant global context.

In this chapter we also asked why postwar conditions in inter-state conflicts appear to be more difficult to move toward quality peace than intra-state conflicts. There seems to be more urgency in overcoming *all* the effects of war in civil and state formation situations. Popular expectations and international demands push governments in this direction, in ways that do not occur between states. Inter-state relations, furthermore, appear to function even if war effects linger. Half-baked arrangements, such as a ceasefire, a fait accompli, or a nondemarcated border, seem to be sufficient for the resumption of international trade and investment. However, it also means that there are remaining dangers, and thus these terminations are far from the notion of quality peace.

The issues of inter-state peacebuilding are a lacuna in research as well as in policy. A first step is to fill this area with more research. The ideas of a project on the Correlates of Peace would have a first topic to venture into (Wallensteen 2012). The Correlates of War data can be useful but has to be complemented with data also on the relations between the warring actors during the years after the war. Different dimensions would have to be included where quality indicators are introduced. The length of a situation of nonwar does not provide an indication of the inherent dangers in an unsolved territorial dispute, for instance. There are indeed many challenges for researchers and in this field the researchers may have to take the lead by pointing to these dangers, hopefully stimulating concrete action to remedy the situation.

CHAPTER 6

Quality Peace and World Order: Uncharted Terrain

6.1 Bringing in World Order

The most challenging question for building quality peace is clearly major power relations. Thus we will approach this problem in this chapter, with the use of the notion of "world order" as a way to describe relations between particular major powers after major wars. This is also a challenge for peacebuilding: How do such wars end and what are the possibilities of building quality peace on this often global level? Major wars may end in peace agreement as well as in victory, making the key questions we have addressed in this book pertinent. In fact, the general notions of peacebuilding that we have encountered in previous chapters should also be operative on this level, if they are of general value. However, we also meet a particular methodological problem. There are not that many world orders to examine. There is only one world. The only possible comparisons are to see how global relations change over time. The continuous unfolding of history makes such comparisons difficult. There are many reflections about turning points in history, delimiting one period (or "order") from another. The farther away the point in time, the more complicated is the assessment. The number of noncomparable elements increases dramatically. Thus contrasting two recent periods makes the most sense. There are two recent turning points in major power relations that should be particularly comparable: the endings of the Second World War and the Cold War, respectively. We have seen differences before and after 1989 throughout this book. Here these differences are related to the way major power relations are structured. This chapter thus is more discursive and essayistic in style, without losing track of the key questions of quality peace: How does a world order meet the challenges of dignity, security, and predictability? In responding to this we also need discuss whether "world order" is the appropriate term and, if so, raise the question of naming such "world orders."

We have seen in chapters 3 and 4 that the notion of quality peace is easily applicable to conflicts within states, be they over government or territory. In chapter 5 we noted that inter-state relations seldom are analyzed in such terms, but also that they add value to the analysis, not the least by illustrating important deficiencies in international relations. Against this background, we would expect the unfamiliarity of the notion of quality peace might be even more pronounced for the relations among dominant powers. The rivalry between them is often taken for granted (Diehl and Goertz 2001, Chan 2013). These actors are seen to constantly compete for status, influence, resources–in short, for preeminence. Sometimes one or the other succeeds in dominating world affairs, at least for a period of time. Mostly they find that they will have to deal with one another in ways that are often described by the concept of "world order," seemingly a loosely structured set of connections that indicate a shared understanding of the limits of their individual power. The term, furthermore, has often been used to capture the restructuring of power that follows world war outcomes, or other endings of major power conflagrations. Thus the end of the Cold War was described by US President George Bush, Sr. as the beginning of a new world order—for example, at the moment when the United States had attacked Iraq forces in Kuwait: "What is at stake is more than one small country; it is a big idea: a new world order, where diverse nations are drawn together in common cause to achieve the universal aspirations of mankind—peace and security, freedom, and the rule of law" (George H.W. Bush, January 29, 1991). The "new" world order was built on cooperation between the major powers, but there was also a value basis for this new order. Certainly, the United States would have a crucial role in this. It was implied by Bush and has been very specific in the writings of Henry Kissinger, for example (2014).

However, there is something more implied in the notion of "order": that there are certain (explicit or implicit) principles by which these "orders" operate (Goldstein and Pevehouse 2013). These could be seen as rules, and sometimes have been enshrined in key agreements between the major powers or in institutions they dominate. The comprehensive agreements in Vienna 1815 after the Napoleonic Wars were seen as the beginning of a new world order in a cooperative framework described as the Concert of Europe. The Versailles Treaty of 1919 became the starting point of a new world organization, the League of Nations, with explicit policies, for instance, on national self-determination. The Second World War was not followed by an agreed, comprehensive arrangement, but is nevertheless seen as the start of a new order (Ikenberry 2001, Bull and Hurrell 2002). The UN Charter of 1945 could be seen as a shared understanding of how a global framework ideally was to function. The end of the Cold War did not result in a settlement either, but President Bush, Sr. had no problem in defining it as the start of a new world order. In fact, the UN Charter was being used in a new way. Looking for founding documents, one could point to the Paris Charter of 1990 and the Istanbul Charter for European Security of 1999. Turning points in relations among major powers do not go unnoticed. Not all of them qualify as the creation of a new "order" or even a new "era." The world order notion relates not only to a change in relations among the powerful, but also the application over a stretch of time of separate, and somewhat coherent, principles for dealing with conflicts.

This means that the concept of world order has elements of what Anne-Marie Slaughter describes as "a system of global governance that institutionalizes cooperation and contains conflict sufficiently to allow all nations and their peoples to achieve greater peace, prosperity, stewardship of the earth, and minimum standards of human dignity" (Slaughter 2004: 15, 166). Such orders can be "effective" and "just," Slaughter writes. This definition contains many of the desirables of humankind. It also points to what such an order should achieve. However, if the first part is treated as the definition of an order ("a system of global governances that institutionalizes cooperation and contains conflict") and the remainder as dependent variables, then it comes closer to the approach in this book, where world order is treated as an independent variable. The key question is: Will a particular configuration of world power achieve quality peace? If the answer is in the affirmative, it would be a quality peace order that is both "effective" and "just."

There are also other conceptions, the most significant being the extent and quality of change in the international system. From a more materialistic perspective, the changes that are in focus may be other than those we have in mind here. For instance, Timothy Sinclair, when introducing Robert Cox's thinking, notes the importance of turning points. In this perspective, the end of the Cold War is actually "a change *in* the Cold War, not a change *from* the Cold War," as key structures remain the same, notably "the national security state, the ideology of national security itself, intelligence and surveillance systems, and the cooptation of the political leadership in subordinate states, amongst other things" (Sinclair 1996: 4). In this perspective, the end of the Cold War does not amount to such a fundamental transformation as many others would like to say, particularly those who "only" focus on major power relations. Nevertheless, the end of the Cold War is a major transformation, and there is sufficient evidence to suggest that it not only meant an end to a particular global major power confrontation; it also implied the emergence of new forms and centers of power. For example, it unleashed or freed forces such as nongovernmental actors, nonstate actors, new economic centers, new forms of international cooperation, new types of enterprises, and new global forms of production, as well as Internet and social media with instant connections between powers and people alike. This seems to be more than just a minor change within a Cold War world order. Obviously it did not change everything. The importance of power vested in particular actors remained a constant but the global distribution of power turned in a new direction.

Particularly important for our undertaking is that the concept of world order points to a significant global framework, which is likely to have an impact on most other relationships. The major powers—variously described as "superpowers," "great powers," or just "leading states"—are seen as the holders of paramount levers of influence. It is easily understood that they have an impact on other inter-state relations, through alliances and enmities, but the world order concept—as used by Slaughter, Cox, and others —stretches further. It suggests that the world order affects the *way* armed conflicts are solved in, for example, the principles applied. One could postulate that if the major states are democracies, democratic solutions will be preferred; when a major power is autocratic that may also be its solution for internal conflicts around the world. This is where it connects to quality peace: Does a particular world order encourage the factors that constitute the elements of quality peace—that is, security, dignity, and predictability?

To meet such criteria, the concept of world order has to include matters of international law, moral principles, and mechanisms for governance. As expected, this makes the notion of world order not only interesting to academics, but also to religious personalities (notably Pope John XXIII) and political leaders, as could be seen in the world order discussions already in the mid-1960s (a prime example is Falk and Mendlovitz 1966). Here it is sufficient to say that a world order is a particular power configuration with global implications and which rests on identifiable principles for dealing with armed conflicts and related social concerns.

As mentioned, the concept suggests a degree of permanency. What is set up is a system of relations that are expected to last and thus provide predictability. Otherwise, we would not be able to talk about "order"; established world orders do not change easily. The status quo (in terms of power distribution) has considerable inbuilt strength: Those states which control the most military power, geographical positions, economic resources, and ideological sources make up a structure with rewards, punishments, and internalization that is not easy to change. These are long-term entrenched relations among major states, building on – in the end also binding them to – the political principles they have favored. The "order" also is an order for the powerful. If they break out of this understanding, the "order" is threatened, and may be replaced. A world war is one way in which such changes are created. Often they draw more attention since they are so dramatic. Typically historical writers point to the world orders that followed the end of the Thirty Years' War in 1648 or the Napoleonic

Wars in 1815. These were great wars, not so say disasters, which were followed by longer periods of cooperative relations among the major powers. Particular labels were developed, the most known being the Concert of Europe for the order following after 1815, but there are several others important shifts (Wallensteen 1981, Wallensteen 2011a).

However, there are also long-term developments that are quiet or not readily observed but nevertheless result in significant changes. Such transformations are to a lesser degree driven by particular decision makers and special decisions. Long-term change is a matter of collective decisions within at least one unit going in the same direction over a considerable period of time. The rise of the United States during the 1800s is an interesting example of a transformation in global affairs that took place without a military confrontation with the leading states at that time. The rise of China during the past twenty-five years has many parallels. In 2010 China's economy replaced Japan's as the second largest in the world, without one single shot being exchanged between the two for sixty-five years. However, it is not certain that this will result in a G-2 world order of the United States and China.

There seems to be utility in the concept of world order for capturing lasting characteristics of a global system. "Order" of course has a conservative ring to it, as seen is terms such as "law and order." However, the question raised here is if a given "order" contributes to quality peace or not. We could imagine a number of "orders" that do not. The "orders" of the 1800s, for example, included major power agreements supporting colonialism and the division of Africa. This certainly violated the meaning of quality peace.

At the same time there are few alternative terms. Candidates such as "global order" appear bland, while "global community" exaggerates the degree of shared values.[1] Here, world order will do as a way describing the type of relationships existing between major powers and having an impact of how wars are ended and peace restored.

Thus this chapter deals with postwar conditions in a different setting from the dyadic concerns we have demonstrated in the previous chapters. Chapter 6 deals with the challenges of postwar conditions to the collectivity of states, international governmental and nongovernmental organizations, and civil society at large. Can such a world order contribute to quality peace? Can a world order in itself be quality peace? Does it affect the particularly dyadic relations that previous chapters have studied?

This means we need to consider in some depth the two recent endings of world confrontations. The first is the Second World War, and how major power relations were structured following this. It was a matter of the victors relating to the losers as well as to each other. This leads us logically into a discussion of the Cold War as a form of "order" that was neither desired nor planned by any of the leading actors. It was a result of major power confrontations, clashes of interest, and failure of collective action (Section 6.2). Secondly, we have to evaluate the end of the Cold War and the period in which we find ourselves today. It is a world order still without a name, other than what it is *not*: It is the *post*–Cold War period (Section 6.3). In both cases we are interested in how, if at all, the leading actors considered matters of constructing quality peace among themselves or in dealing with other conflicts. From this some conclusions emerge (Section 6.4).

6.2 After World War II: The Consolidation of Victory

In chapter 5 it was observed that the postwar relations between states seldom exhibit the traits associated with quality peace. However, we could point to exceptions suggesting that it is not inconceivable. Dealing with inter-state relations is, undoubtedly, a necessity to reduce the likelihood of war in the international system as a whole. This of course applies even more to the major powers and the type of world order they create among themselves. The essence of being a major power is to be independent and not tied to other actors. To act according to one's own agenda in crises or for long-term benefit is often seen as the ultimate purpose and rationale for major powers. From this perspective measures aimed at peacebuilding could mean a reduction of autonomy in exchange for the gains of a more stable and secure future relationship. According to Realpolitik considerations, such trade-offs are only to be done when they serve the "national" interest of a particular state. The major powers, in other words, are not expected to be reliable in their pursuit of peace policies toward other major powers. Their commitment to such a policy is less credible than for any other actors.

However, in a world order perspective this may not necessarily be so. The behavior of a major power in one conflict will be judged by other major powers with regard to its implications for other conflicts. The other powers are looking for consistency in order to assess the direction of a particular actor. Inconsistencies will increase unpredictability and thus lead to insecurity among major powers. This speaks to the fact that major powers prefer to act consistently so as to communicate their "true" intentions to all other actors. It may be costly to be inconsistent. In that sense, a world order is conservative: The actors are likely to change goals and actions slowly so as not to upset significant relations. World orders may gradually be reformed, while "revolution" means the end of one particular order. Elsewhere this has been described as universalism versus particularism and that there are fluctuations between universalist and particularist relationships with different impact on onset of wars, confrontations, and internal wars (Wallensteen 1984, Schahczenski 1991, Valeriano and Theo 2009, Wallensteen 2011a, Travlos 2013).

The prime example in chapter 5 concerned the post–World War II relations between France and Germany. They definitely were major powers, still wielding strong influence in Europe and elsewhere, although no longer the superpowers of the era. Their new relationships changed European affairs in a dramatic way. In terms of power, each one today probably has more influence over the other and over their neighbors than they did as military powers. The European financial crisis in the years after 2008 demonstrated this with great clarity. So why would it be impossible also to imagine that other major power relations could change? Particularly if peacebuilding provides for new types of influence at the same time as it increases the well-being of the citizens—for instance as a result of reduced fears of war and the possibility of allocating national resources for welfare expenditures?

A most important world order argument against this analysis is that the Franco–German relationship since 1945 was dependent on the dominance of the United States and the Soviet Union. It could be that there was democracy, economic integration, a mutually developed regional framework, and a successful ending of territorial issues between the two formerly warring parties. More fundamentally, it could be argued that both were members of the same alliance and the same bloc in the Cold War: the United States-led North Atlantic Treaty Organization (NATO). Furthermore, the shared threat that the two were exposed to came from the Soviet Union. It was evident: Soviet forces were standing in Berlin and holding eastern Germany with an offense-oriented military doctrine. This external threat and joint membership served to cement the integration of many Western European nations. The European Union owed its existence to US presence and commitment to Western Europe in the face of a common existential danger. The Cold War may have been a necessary factor for the emergence of Franco–German reconciliation. It may not have been a sufficient condition or the full story—many of the elements were built by the two states in their mutual relations—but the systemic factor added necessary incentives.

Still, it should be noted that the Cold War was not a time of consistent tensions, while the process of building new Franco–German relations was one of continuous and deepening cooperation. The building of a new European system was a persistent enterprise, in spite of fluctuations in global relations. Thus, although related to the Cold War, it gained a momentum of its own, with its own tensions, setbacks, and crises. It was dependent on the Cold War, but not dominated by it. It grew deeper after the Cold War, with stronger institutions and a shared currency.

This means it is important to recall that the Cold War took place in the shadow of the Second World War. We cannot just "begin" the history of contemporary inter-state relations by the second half of 1945. The "order" that developed was a result of the "disorder" that preceded it. This puts victory consolidation after the Second World War in a special light. It was associated with the allies' military occupation of Germany, Austria, Italy, Korea, and Japan. This made the situation different from many other cases of victory consolidation that we have discussed in this book.[2] The possibility of a withdrawal of the occupation forces created incentives of compliance for the new political leadership in these countries. It also made it possible for the occupiers to exert an extraordinary influence on the political scene in the emerging postwar societies. A remarkable feature is that these foreign forces gradually were redefined to become an allied presence in the new conflicts that emerged.

Nevertheless, we can note that there were two separate forms of victory consolidation taking place. There was one on the Western, United States-led side, another on the Eastern, Soviet-dominated side of the military dividing lines drawn through Europe, Korea, and elsewhere. It is noteworthy that both processes stemmed from the negative encounters with Adolf Hitler. On the Western side the agreement in Munich in 1938 became an experience that colored the chances of negotiations between the major powers for the coming years. Hitler had not abided by the very favorable deal he was given by Britain and France at the expense of Czechoslovakia. It turned out he simply wanted more, and thus was not a reliable partner for peacemaking. "Appeasement" became the negative word associated with this deal. For the West there was a continuous fear of repeating the same mistake with other major foes. Remarkably the Soviet Union had a similar experience. The nonaggression pact it concluded in August 1939 with Nazi Germany, which involved the partitioning of Poland among other matters, lasted only until June 1941, when the Soviet Union was attacked. Thus negotiating with any opponent was seen with skepticism by the Soviet leadership. When tension arose between the victors after 1945, it was no longer possible to settle matters through negotiations. The post-1945 "world order" was built in a different way.

One element in this was the consolidation of the victory, where the two sides chose very different paths. As a result, the Western consolidation was closer to the quality peace notions than the Eastern one. It is also the consolidation that lasted the longest. In Europe it included the measures we have mentioned in chapter 5, particularly with respect to Germany: democratization, military integration, economic recovery, and territorial settlements. In addition, we should add important measures of reconciliation (as defined, for example, in Brounéus 2008). This includes the unprecedented German acknowledgment of the atrocities during the Second World War which was needed if the state would be regarded as a continuation of previous German states (particularly this refers to the Holocaust and reparations to Israel, but as of late also the memorials to other victims of persecution, notably gays and Roma). There was also an initial policy of denazification and prosecution of Nazi war crimes. This contrasts with the Eastern policy, which was one of extracting resources from Germany (including the dismantling of factories), the introduction of a Soviet-style Communist system, strict Soviet control over the military, and no recognition of guilt over the past (the argument was that being a "revolutionary" state the German Democratic Republic bore no responsibility for what had been done in the name of Germany before its existence). Thus only West Germany demonstrated measures that accorded dignity to the victims of German repression. It also reassured its neighbors in the West of its peaceful intentions by being involved in different integration projects on the Western side, thus contributing to a sense of security and predictability.[3] On the Eastern side, such reassurance was not achieved except in one instance: East Germany's recognition of the new borders with Poland (the Oder-Neisse line, in German), something West Germany could not accept for several decades. However, East German troops participated in the Soviet invasion of Czechoslovakia in 1968, thus contributing to insecurity and unpredictability. The East German state was entirely dependent on Soviet support to maintain itself, and thus it became one of Moscow's most loyal allies.

The policy of Western victory consolidation in Europe also is a contrast to the other battlefront of the Second World War: East Asia. Japan capitulated and the United States largely by itself took control over the territory. A peace agreement was made with the United States, but not with the Soviet Union (nor with its successor, Russia). The Emperor was allowed to remain in place. The reformation of Japan did not go as deep as in Germany. In Germany there were old traditions of democracy to resort to, and there was more willingness to acknowledge the past (the lack of which continues to plague Japan's relations with all its neighbors). The democracy of Japan was, in fact, monopolized by one political party for the entire period of the Cold War, again a contrast to West Germany, where the opposition had an impact on German policy in a peace-promoting direction and in government coalitions.[4] The consolidation of the US victory in East Asia, consequently, did not move equally strongly in the direction of quality peace, as was the case in Western Europe.

Thus there were contrasting polices in different arenas, as well as between the two main victors, the United States and the Soviet Union. Their understanding of what the victory meant and who had contributed the most diverged. In the immediate postwar period there was little urge to sort this out. The summit conference in Potsdam in 1945 was not followed by more encounters at the top level until the meeting in Geneva in 1955. This in turn followed on the peace agreement with Austria that led to the country's reunification.[5] For ten years, the top leadership did not engage in personal contact across the divide.

This points to the importance of the relationship between the major powers, the victors of the Second World War. Their divergent policies also reflected their contrasting ambitions. The confrontation between the two major powers, the United States and the Soviet Union, made up the Cold War. A lasting victory also required consolidation of major power relations. That turned out to be more difficult and directs us to one of the complexities of the Cold War: There were considerable variations in superpower relations between periods of cooperation and confrontation. The periods of relaxed tensions have often had labels; thus there were periods variously described as the Spirit of Geneva (1955), Spirit of Camp David (1959), as well as détente (after the Cuban missile crisis in the period of the early to mid-1960s, during the Nixon–Ford presidencies in the early 1970s, and during the Gorbachev period from the mid-1980s to early 1990s). Generalizing from this, it is obvious that major power relations cannot be described as consisting of just one type of relationship (for instance, constant rivalry). It is important to note that there are fluctuations, even to the point that one can ask: Which one is actually the most basic for long-term relations? Is rivalry the chief condition and only interrupted by spells of relaxed tension, orchestrated by well-meaning leaders? Or could relaxed relations be the default position, the one to be expected, only interrupted by conflict events and aggressive actions, pursued by adventurist political principals? There are arguments in both directions. The data are fairly clear: Particularist periods are more likely to result in inter-state wars between major powers than universalist ones, demonstrating the dangers that might be involved (Wallensteen 1984, Wallensteen 2011a).

Let us now assess the direct relations between the superpowers of the Cold War in terms of the criteria of quality peace. The absence of war among the two major protagonists and their allies rested, according to Realpolitik analysts, on deterrence. In the Western version, the overwhelming Soviet conventional superiority in Europe had to be deterred by a threat of rapid escalation to a nuclear confrontation, where major population centers of the Soviet Union would be destroyed. In the Eastern version, the threat of nuclear annihilation from the West could only be deterred by a strong and immediate threat to unleash a full conventional military invasion of Western Europe. As matters developed, both sides acquired increasingly aggressive nuclear postures. The result was a nonwar situation built on fear, referred to as "a balance of terror," or MAD: mutually assured destruction. It was a form of security resting on extreme insecurity. It deliberately reduced the predictability, of course: There was to be uncertainty whether these forces would be set in motion now or in the near future. Each crisis involved heightened insecurity. There was no respect for the dignity of the other: The populations were not excluded from the threat. There was a gradual move away from exclusively targeting population centers toward aiming at military installations as precision in weapons development increased, but this was hardly done out of respect for the civilians on the other side. It was a "peace" of the negative type, far from our notion of quality peace. This situation, in fact, underscores the importance of introducing quality elements into the peace definition. The only redeeming aspect of the Cold War is that it did *not* result in a hot war between the major powers and it was possible to extricate the world from this confrontation in the late 1980s. What may have explained this? There are a host of possible explanations, and the full story remains to be told.[6] Here one aspect is particularly important and it emerges from a comparison with the previously dominant rivalry.

In the case of Franco–German relations, we noted that the removal of territorial disputes was significant in making for peacebuilding. For the American–Soviet relations this was also an important, but often overlooked, factor: There were no such direct territorial disputes between the parties. There was in fact a notable lack of a history of repeated wars and unsolved territorial disputes (Wallensteen 1981, Wallensteen 2011a).[7] The concerns the two had were related to territory belonging to other actors. Thus, there was no classical *Geopolitik* confrontation. Furthermore, there were no direct memories of wars between the two. They had, remarkably, been on the same side in the two World Wars that preceded the Cold War.[8] There was no need to complicate relations by a resort to revanchism, or to become emotional about what happened to relatives or earlier leaders. Each crisis could be dealt with in a remarkably rational manner. The Realpolitik considerations that took place were all building on the fear of the other acquiring leverage, for instance, by moving ahead in weapons technology. The confrontation fueled an unprecedented arms race, but not a race of arrogance and adventurism. The armament issues became central throughout the history of these relations (and remained so after the Cold War). In particular nuclear weapons, weapon carriers that could reach the other (missiles, airplanes, submarines), and nuclear defense systems have set their marks on their mutual dealings.

There was, however, an *Idealpolitik* confrontation. One side had a "better" solution to the way a country should be run than the other: Democracy, liberalism and capitalism were posited against socialism, state control, and one-party politics. These principles were reflected in their respective policies of victory consolidation in Europe and on the Korean peninsula. Their divergent perspectives of governance, furthermore, collided in countries far away from the two main protagonists. But each side saw them as fundamental for how conflicts locally could be solved. It also made places distant from Washington, D.C. and Moscow strategically important. A victory by a group or regime supported by the other was axiomatically a negative. It was seen to affect the balance of global power.

On one score, the Cold War period is quite clear. It was not a period for solving armed conflicts, and thus the notion of peacebuilding was not present in the evaluation of the outcomes. As we noted in chapter 1, peacebuilding became a political concept at the end of the Cold War. Correctly it is seen as a new development in international relations. Thus what we could see during the Cold War was a focus on winning wars and, if that was not possible, continuing them (at least to prevent the other from winning). The local postwar situation in this period was one characterized by victory consolidation, not peacebuilding. This was, in fact, part of the victory consolidation that marked the entire Cold War. The two victors from the Second World War tried to cement their power positions globally. As they saw it, that meant that local conflicts also had to be won. A local, victorious actor would do whatever it could to make its victory as entrenched as possible. Thus on all levels the notion of victory was the paramount principle for ending conflicts.

The variations in détente and confrontation had more to do with direct relations between the major powers. They were willing to take action that reduced the danger of war directly between the two, but at the same time kept supporting "their" side in local confrontations. Thus there were attempts at arms control, confidence-building measures, and disarmament of particular strategic nuclear weapons directly between the two. At the same time there were very few peace agreements. The agreements that were entered into aimed at regulating particular issues, rather than solving entire problems. On the whole, however, there were few agreements. The examples of unsolved issues are many:

- The Soviet Union established control over Eastern and Central Europe in the years 1944–1948, sometimes with force (Baltic countries, Ukraine), sometimes with the help of local communist parties, remaining Soviet armed forces, and intelligence services (Poland, East Germany, Czechoslovakia, Hungary, Romania, Bulgaria). Only in 1988 did this control begin to break up in an escalating process that ended the Soviet bloc by 1991.
- When China was taken over by the Communist forces in 1949, the Nationalists escaped to Taiwan and each side was supported by its allies in the Cold War. The war was stopped, but there is still no peace agreement. Although there is much trade and even democratization (on one side), the issue remains volatile and prevents peacebuilding in East Asia.
- The 1953 armistice agreement ended the fighting in the Korean War, dividing the peninsula approximately along the 38th parallel into two countries, supported by each side of the Cold War. Both have consolidated their hold,

and the situation has continued until today, but with increasing risks, as North Korea has developed nuclear weapons.

- The 1950s also saw the 1954 Geneva Accords on Indochina, temporarily dividing Vietnam into two states along the 17th parallel, to be reunited within two years in a nationwide election. South Vietnam refused to follow through on this, supported by the United States. That led to a new war and a new agreement, this time in Paris 1973, which divided the South into areas under two different governments, allowing the United States to withdraw its troops. This agreement, in turn, was undone by the defeat of one of the governments in 1975. The postwar period was characterized by reunification under the new rulers, in effect consolidation of the victory. These conditions remain today.

- Neighboring Laos saw repeated attempts at keeping the country out of the Vietnam war, basically by forming coalition governments (e.g., in 1957, 1961, 1973) but in 1975 the communist forces took all power and consolidated their victory. This remains the situation today.

- The revolution in Cuba in 1959 saw the consolidation of the Castro regime that remains today, and there is still no agreement with the United States or with the opposition in Cuba. In the period that followed, military regimes were instituted throughout Latin America, United States-supported based on their anticommunist deeds (rather than their democratic credentials). Democratization as well as negotiated settlements did not follow until the winding down of the Cold War (for example in Chile, Brazil, and Central America).

- Decolonization conflicts in Asia and Africa led to the end of the British, French, Belgian, Dutch, Spanish, and Portuguese empires from the 1950s to the 1970s, thus terminating classical colonialism. Those that involved the military victory of a liberation front often saw the same leadership or organization in control for decades (e.g., Algeria, Angola, Indonesia, Zimbabwe—see chapters 2 and 3), whereas those that ended in agreements, were pursued with limited violence, and saw little support from the Cold War parties have had qualitatively different trajectories (India, Ghana, Kenya, Malaysia). In protracted conflicts agreements did not come until the end of the Cold War (Mozambique, Namibia, South Africa).

From this we can conclude that the principles approaching those included in quality peace were lacking throughout this period. The victory consolidation applied during the Cold War built on the might of one side over the other, resulting in persecution of dissenters, extrajudicial killings, refugees escaping repression, etc., in both of the two blocs (e.g., from Eastern Europe since the late 1940s; from China and Cuba in the 1950s; from Vietnam after 1975; and from dictatorships in South America, particularly after the coup in Chile, in 1973). The respect for the dignity of the opponent, a central element in quality peace, was lacking, not the least as there was no resort to openness that would allow free expression of grievances.

Furthermore, there was little security. The military victories involved confrontations with domestic groups as well as outside actors, which continued to strengthen insecurity and military expenditures, even involving the victorious regimes in conflicts in the region (e.g., Vietnam and China in Indochina, and one Central American country providing bases for action in another). The illusionary strength and nationalist appeal of the victorious regimes may, however, have led to an impression of their sustainability. It seemed certain that the regimes would remain in power for a foreseeable future, at least long enough to allow for international capital to get a return on its investment.

However, the term *Cold* War is fitting, as there was no hot war directly between the major powers. Their policies in Europe were more cautious in relation to each other. At the same time, there was concern over what could happen in South America, Africa, the Middle East, and Asia, and how that could potentially also make the situation in Europe and East Asia explosive. There were deliberate attempts to prevent this from happening. Indeed, the UN Secretary-General Dag Hammarskjöld (1953–1961) developed the notion of "preventive diplomacy," referring to the importance of preventing minor disputes from escalating to global confrontation (Lund 1996: 3). Still, there was a series of confrontations outside Europe and East Asia that threatened exactly such a development (the Cuban Missile Crisis of 1962 and the October War of 1973 in the Middle East are two examples).

From this perspective it is remarkable to note that the direct US–Soviet relations were often dominated by armament issues. In particular, nuclear weapons, weapon carriers that could reach the other side (missiles, airplanes, submarines), and nuclear defense systems have set their marks on their mutual dealings. Thus we find a number of arms control agreements emerging from contentious but competent negotiations directly between the two, seldom involving other states or third parties. In a notable way the two antagonists could also develop constructive relations. The aim was to reduce the dangers of inadvertent nuclear war, but not to solve the main *Idealpolitik* disagreement between the two, or even dampen the confrontations that went on elsewhere in the world. The many confrontations around the world created insecurity between the two, which they tried to manage. The defeat of the supporters of the other side was expected to result in a semblance of stability and predictability, and thus the winning strategies were pursued without regard for key aspects of dignity and safety for people and states alike. The major states protected themselves from being engulfed by the confrontations they fueled. The ultimate purpose, in our terms, was the consolidation of their victory from the Second World War, where each side found that it had contributed the most and wanted the other's recognition. The pursuit of global victory, in other words, did not lead to the peace they aspired. On the contrary, it generated further conflict. Thus the Cold War was a world order that negated quality peace.

This makes the West European experience even more notable, as it built on different principles. The framework of cooperation that was developed involving early settlement of disputes, economic integration, democratic rule, and shared memberships was not threatened by the insecurities of the Cold War. The alliance membership might have involved the European countries in a new world war or in interventions outside Europe but, on the whole, diplomacy and caution prevailed. The European actors often had their own relations to the Soviet bloc and could act to dampen down tensions as well as to make a united Western stand more credible. The European developments were seen more as a semi-independent approach to regional, but not global, order. The end of the Cold War opened opportunities for similar approaches elsewhere. The Cold War represented a paradoxical coexistence of global and local confrontation and a European deliberate construction of regional quality peace. Even if the ending of the Cold War demonstrated a fundamental change in the distribution of power in the world, the European project was not affected negatively—which would have been logical if it had been entirely dependent on the tensions of the Cold War —but instead continued to grow under the new conditions.

The Cold War then began as a matter of consolidating the victory over Nazi Germany and Imperial Japan. The two main victors also became the two main foes. In a way, the Cold War was a major confrontation over who actually won the Second World War and thus had the "right" to create its particular form of world order. The West built its consolidation of victory on principles that contain many of the ideas of quality peace in its relationships to Germany. However, the same principles were not applied in its confrontation with the Soviet Union in a host of local conflicts. Victory at almost any price was preferred, thus precluding the development of lasting relationships. The Soviet policy of victory consolidation used in Eastern Europe was traditional and had none of the traits of quality peace. Thus the entire construction in the form of the Warsaw Pact, Communist party control, and Soviet domination faltered. It led to the almost simultaneous dissolution of the Soviet bloc and the Soviet Union itself. It is not surprising that the consolidation of Soviet-supported victories in the Third World displayed similar elements of brutality, neglect of popular participation, and thus lack of predictability. The end of the Cold War, therefore, was a major transformation, not only affecting the major powers themselves, but virtually all governments and countries around the globe. To put it dramatically: The end of the Cold War was also the actual end of the Second World War.[9]

6.3 After the Cold War: A "New World Order"

The most dramatic major power relationship to study in postwar relationships is the one between the United States and Russia after the end of the Cold War. The two had been involved in a deadly confrontation for more than forty years and now found themselves in a novel situation. However, the period since the end of the Cold War also involves other changes, notably the rise of China. Thus when focusing on conflict resolution and the building of postwar peace we need to view these relationships in particular and ask if their development points to an increased chance for a world order contributing to quality peace in all other relations. Let us begin with the relationships between the West and Russia, and then turn to the relations with China.

It is interesting to see that the new period starts with a positive note. The US President at the time of ending the Cold War, George H.W. Bush, did not proclaim the outcome as a "victory" but rather as the beginning of a "New World Order" as we saw earlier in this chapter. The first challenge to this new order, he said in September 1990, was Iraq's invasion of Kuwait in August 1990: "The crisis in the Persian Gulf, as grave as it is, also offers a rare opportunity to move toward an historic period of cooperation. Out of these troubled times, . . . a new world order . . . can emerge: a new era . . . freer from the threat of terror, stronger in the pursuit of justice, and more secure in the quest for peace. . . . A world where the strong respect the rights of the weak . . . " (President George H.W. Bush to the US Congress, September 11, 1990).[10] With the help of the three categories used for quality peace (security, dignity, and predictability), we can now try to gauge this relationship for the past twenty-five years with respect to the territorial and governmental incompatibilities that dominate violent relations.

We have already in section 6.2 noted a remarkable trait in US–Soviet relations: the lack of a previous history of repeated wars and unsolved territorial disputes. This stands in sharp contrast to the France–Germany dyad or many other major power relations (Germany–Russia, China–Japan, to name two), where territory and geographical proximity are factors which impact both sides. Thus for the US–Soviet/Russia dyad, it was not necessary for diplomacy and politics to deal with a legacy of mutual land disputes or wars. Instead, as we noted, armament issues have been central throughout the history of these relations. Nuclear weapons, whether deployed in offensive or defense systems, set their marks. This has been a continuous concern also after the Cold War.

The stockpiles on both sides have been substantially reduced with the help of mutual agreements, but both retain sufficient capacity to destroy the other. This means that new weapons that may influence this balance affect the overall Russo–American dyad. It is unique that changes in armaments among major powers are almost the sole indicators of threat and fear. Thus Russia's relations with the United States soured when President George W. Bush pursued the idea of a missile defense system in Europe, and the Obama administration did not change this position. In theory the reverse is true: Disarmament measures may signal confidence-building and generate reassurance. During the Cold War, the United States embarked on technological projects to protect its mainland by constructing missile shields. Similar ambitions in the post–Cold War era have drawn the same type of criticism from the counterpart, today's Russian leaders. Like their Soviet predecessors, they worry about the maintenance of their own deterrence capacity. Matters of procurement, technological development, and trade in strategic military equipment continue to be closely watched on both sides. Tensions are not as relaxed as they could be, in view of the fact that there are no unsolved territorial disputes and very few clashes of rival interest elsewhere in the world. The steps-to-war thesis that we discussed in chapter 5 runs into a problem. In this major power dyad armaments themselves seem to be a first step, rather than the territorial concerns. However, one could turn this the other way: As there were no territorial concerns historically and still are none, the likelihood of the mutual tensions escalating to war remains low.

This does not exclude the possibility that other issues may enter, having some of the characteristics that make analysts concerned. During the Cold War, the Soviet Union was vigilant about possible or actual "moves" by NATO in nearby areas; Russia seems to have inherited the same worries. The countries in the outer perimeter of the Soviet Union became independent states in 1991, as part of the dissolution of the union. These areas are still of interest to Russia. Some of the countries are now members of NATO (the Baltic countries) as are some former Soviet allies of the Warsaw Pact (Poland, Hungary, Czech Republic, Slovakia, Romania, Bulgaria). This may heighten Russian leaders' anxiety about the direction of former Soviet republics remaining outside this framework (Belarus, Ukraine, Moldova, and Caucasian and Central Asian states). For instance, the politics in Georgia gained significance for both sides: The United States wanted to protect Georgia's democratic system and economic links to the West, Russia saw this as US interference in a region outside traditional American spheres of influence and within a customary "Russian" area. The short armed conflict in 2008 thus was seen differently by the two sides, but largely in a way that confirms existing suspicions of the other.

Thus as was the case during the Cold War "distant" areas become important for the relations between the West and Russia. But the picture is less polarized than was the case in earlier times. Then agreement was rare, today it is more common. There was agreement on UN Security Council measures against the Ghadaffi regime in Libya in March 2011 (UN Resolutions 1970 and 1973, for instance). The civil war in the country, however, strained the major power relations. NATO's application of the agreed no-fly zone led to apprehension in Russia. Thus no direct UN Security Council actions, such as sanctions or military measures, were allowed for the parallel situation in Syria. The Council issued warnings and dispatched mediators and monitors, but with limited mandates.

Relations between Russia and the West in the early 2010s are quite different from what was typical in the early 1990s, when an era of globalization was on the rise and old conflicts were rapidly disappearing. There was a period of vigorous peacemaking, ending conflicts in Angola, Horn of Africa, Central America, and Indochina. The democratization that took place in Russia at the time provided for increased transparency and confidence in the West; the lack of US and Western interference in Russian affairs and in many of the former Soviet member states provided assurance for Russia. It was a period of remarkable openness, confidence, and agreement. It was a typical example of universalist policies: Both sides were eager to prevent renewed tension and thus acted so as to incorporate the legitimate interest of the other in the formulation of their foreign policy. As NATO was considering including a number of former Warsaw Pact or Soviet states, the question was raised whether Russia would also be eligible. It joined the Partnership for Peace that was created in the mid-1990s. There was also a separate agreement between NATO and Russia. All this amounted to a remarkable development with considerable prospect for developing quality peace in the major power relations with largely positive implications for other countries in the concerned regions.

The early 2000s saw a change in this regard. The United States' heavy focus on terrorism as a result of the attacks on September 11, 2001, was supported by the Russian leadership, as was the action on Afghanistan. However, US unilateralism in Iraq in 2003 made Russia's leaders fear a US return to particularism. Relations became cooler. At the same time, the increasingly autocratic reign of Vladimir Putin in Russia made the West concerned about the fate of the promising democratic developments in that country. Certainly, Putin's close ally Dmitry Medvedev was more attractive to the West, but also less powerful. The ideas of cooperation remain but not the closeness in political and personal relations. In an interview in 2009, at the time Medvedev was Russia's President, the Russian ambassador to NATO summarized the discussion on Russia–NATO relations: "Great powers don't join coalitions, they create coalitions. Russia considers itself a great power."[11] Mutual relations moved away from a continuation of joint projects that might have led to a more positive peace. The Obama administration's attempt to "reset" relations was an undertaking that required considerable follow-up to change this dynamic.

As was the case during the Cold War years, Russia was again anxious to be treated as equal power. It was sensitive not to being listened to. There was a similar complaint at the time of the Soviet Union: The West and the United States had a tendency to deal with the opponent as a second-tier power. For a period after the Cold War, the West took Russia for granted, for instance, in cooperation in the Security Council. Thus, Russia again had to use its veto to block decisions and demonstrate its presence. This became a pattern. American diplomacy and policymaking would have to consider the role and interests of Russia in a new way, if the relations were again to approach the conscious building of peace. The dignity Russia wants is recognition as an equal partner, whereas the West looks for deeper democracy. The security to which both sides aspired was connected to nuclear developments, as well as actions in areas close to Russia and its interest (Georgia, Syria). The predictability that both desired required closer consultation on exactly these issues. The 1990s saw more of this than the 2000s, which saw more than the 2010s.

The Ukrainian crisis of 2013–2014 was testimony to these increasingly different perceptions. President Putin, fearing further advances by NATO, bolstered nationalist arguments (protecting Russians in Ukraine) and emphasized strategic considerations (shield the naval basis in Sevastopol on Crimea). The West's support for Ukraine's sovereignty was equally predictable, emphasizing democracy, free elections, and the country's right to choose its own foreign policy, while expecting a correct treatment of the Russian population. As the crisis escalated with inclusion of Crimea into the Russian Federation, Ukraine moving close to EU as well as NATO, and the separatist war in Eastern Ukraine, there was also a clash of several principles that have been taken for granted since the end of the Cold War: respect for territorial integrity, the importance of democratic procedures, the resort to national and international legal approaches. The Ukraine crisis has repercussions on inter-state relations in the period to follow, potentially leading to a rupture in the world order that has lasted for twenty-five years.

The other major power relationship with implications for the future is the one between the United States and China. Much has been written on the changing economic landscape. The continuous high growth rates of China that were kept up for more than two decades have dramatically changed this relationship. The China that US President Nixon visited forty years ago was remarkably different from the one now receiving Western guests. It coincides with an equally remarkable transformation of the regional security situation. East Asia has been at "peace" since the late 1970s. There have been no inter-state wars and only some intra-state conflicts in the whole region stretching from North Korea to Timor-Leste (Tønnesson et al. 2013). It is largely in a postwar phase, after the end of the Korean and Vietnam wars. Consolidating these outcomes has been the main concern of all the actors. It is also notable that none of these wars ended in peace agreements, as outlined above. The 1973 Paris agreement that was supposed to end the Vietnam War unraveled in 1975. The North and its allies prevailed, and gradually rebuilt relations with the region and the former enemies, except China, with whom it saw a war in 1979, also without a peace agreement. Similarly the Korean War is at a standstill along an agreed demilitarized zone, and the two sides have consolidated this division. Thus it is not remarkable to observe that the post-1979 period has been one without armed conflict. It is more difficult to assess if it is also a period of deliberate building of a regional security community that approaches a quality peace arrangement.

A field of cooperation would then be to start to promote quality peace activities in the many frozen conflicts in the region mentioned in section 6.2. The lack of headway in inter-state efforts reflects on the responsibility of the major powers. It does not bode well for a transformation of major power relations. The elements pointed to by the steps-to-war thesis are highly relevant in this context. There are a remarkably large number of unsettled territorial issues to which China is a party, but so are its close or distant neighbors—notably Korea, Japan, Vietnam, Philippines, and Malaysia. Most of the disputes concern islands, barely inhabitable, but still giving the owner access to areas under the ocean with potential for oil or other valuable resources. In a post-terrorism era, the United States under President Obama hoped to increase its presence in the region. This was exemplified by the 2011 agreement with Australia, providing America facilities for land, air, and sea forces in Darwin in the north of Australia. The concern is that one of the variables Senese and Vasquez point to begins to fall into place: There is a rival present in the region and it is seen by some of the smaller states as an actual or potential ally. In view of such possibilities, the need for developing quality peace options becomes significant. Major power peacebuilding could, in this case, be seen as preventive action to stem a turn away from the relative peacefulness that has mark the region for several decades (Tønnesson 2012). Most likely the lack of war is a fundamental aspect for sustained growth for China and other growing economies in the region.[12] However, history tells us that security arguments sometimes win over economic considerations.

Summarizing this we can observe that two significant actors have undergone dramatic changes largely since the end of the Cold War. There has been a redefinition of Russia's role in the world as a result of *Geo-, Real- and Idealpolitik* changes. China's standing has shifted, as a result of its economic growth and its strong emphasis on *Kapitalpolitik*. However, the United States remains the preeminent actor. It was actually the victor in all three global confrontations of the 20th century. Its engagement in relations with other major powers is likely to be colored by this fact. The United States finds it difficult to extend to Russia as well as to China the degree of equality they expect, although it would not cost much for the United States to demonstrate that. The fact is that these relationships are central for global development, although they concern separate regions. The United States has not been at direct war with Russia ever, and has been militarily engaged with China only in the Korean War. The US has many recent experiences of solving conflicts with Russia, as demonstrated by the many peace processes that marked the 1990s and also resulted in an impressive set of negotiated solutions that we studied in chapters 3 and 4. The 2000s saw such cooperation in some situations, notably in crises with al-Qaeda over Afghanistan and Libya. But there has also been a record of failed cooperation: the 2003 Iraq War, Georgia in 2008, and Syria since 2011. There is not the same record of cooperation with China in conflict resolution. Lately there have been joint efforts on matters such as North Korea, Myanmar, and Sudan. But there are at the same time disagreements over, for instance, Iran and Syria.

The relations between China and Russia require a particular comment. On many of the global issues, China's policy has been closer to Russia's, something that may have implications for the long-term development of peaceful relations. The countries have formed a shared security organization, the Shanghai Cooperation Council, which now also includes other states in Central and South Asia. They have voted together in the UN Security Council, vetoing Westerns proposals that they saw as interfering in domestic affairs. However, Russia's actions on Ukraine in 2014 did not gain the approval of China. In contrast to predictions of an alliance between Russia and China, China may well find it more valuable to be neutral in the tensions between the West and Russia. This squares with the leadership's repeated emphasis on China's need for peaceful conditions to foster its own economic growth. Perhaps the business approach is what would be expected from China, rather than alliance making in either direction.

6.4 World Order and Quality Peace

As this overview makes clear, there is utility in the use of the concept of world order. There seems to be a consistent pattern of behavior among major powers that warrants such a label. There are also notable changes in such patterns, basically occurring around the year 1989, thus providing us with two different world orders for the past seventy years. We can also observe strains in the relationships, foreshadowing a different turn of events.

We also see that developing quality peace among major states after wars or confrontations is rare, but there are considerable experiences of alliances. Some of them may be no more than matters of convenience and opportunity, but others actually have resulted in lasting relations providing for security, equality, and stability. On the whole this is to be applauded, at least at the dyadic level. Furthermore, this underscores the close connection of many of the outcomes that we have seen in conflicts in chapters 3, 4, and 5: The priorities of the major powers and their rivalries have created different approaches to postwar conditions around the world. The post–World War II period focused on victory as the only solution. Some of these victories were instituted in ways which are closer to quality peace considerations (notably in Western Europe). However, in other conflicts, postwar conditions were pursued as a traditional consolidation of victory. The important aspect was the rivalry, not the creation of reasonable durable conditions based on local concerns. Thus the post–Cold War period turned out in a different way. As there was less of a rivalry, other concerns got a chance to be heard. Postwar conditions, therefore, have been shaped more through peace agreements than victory, and thus more as peacebuilding than victory consolidation. As we have seen in chapters 3, 4 and 5, this yielded more space for postwar conditions corresponding to the notions of quality peace. The world order dimension, in other words, turns out to be an important explanation for the choice of strategies also in seemingly peripheral postwar conditions. Thus peacebuilding strategies emphasizing elements such as democracy, equality, disarmament, integration, and cooperation have been consensual during the post–Cold War world order. It has built on an ability of major powers to cooperate, also using components of quality peace: extending diplomatic and political respect, pursuing nonprovocative military actions, and doing this in a consistent way over a period of time, including changes in government.

However, we could also see that this was particularly true for areas where the Cold War major powers, the West and the Soviet Union/Russia, were particularly strongly involved. Soviet/Russian withdrawal from situations in Africa, South America, and Europe also opened the way for solutions building on quality peace elements. This was not equally true for situations in the Middle East, and, as we have seen, strained relations in Eastern Europe, notably around Ukraine. Furthermore, East Asia saw even less of such applications. In fact, many situations remained politically as "frozen" as they had been during the Cold War. They exhibited traits that had less to do with the West's relations to the Soviet Union/Russia, and thus were less affected by changes in these dyads. The emergence of China as an economic power also will have an impact on these conditions.

Thus we can conclude that the concept and reality of world order discussed in sections 6.2 and 6.3 have not encompassed the entire "world"; it has been an "order" built from centers in Europe and North America. East Asia diverges from this pattern, and an important focus for the future of world developments will have to be the relations between the United States and China.

The fact that there are, as of yet, no new major power rivalries of global proportions thus creates a window of opportunity for more local building of quality peace in the parts of the world that have been affected most by the Cold War. The specter of a breakdown in relations between the West and Russia, may, however, shut this window. This is most likely with respect to countries close to Russia, geographically (Moldova, Belarus, Central Asia, Caucasus) or politically (Cuba, Venezuela, Nicaragua). It would replace the search for peacebuilding with a competition for allies in a new confrontation, moving the world order away from the construction of quality peace. It remains for us to consider the implications of this for regional peace as well as for international organizations. This is what we will do in chapter 7.

CHAPTER 7

Quality Peace and International Organizations

7.1 World Order and Global Institutions

The postwar strategies we can observe have a link to the principles of a world order, which in turn are formed by the participating states and other actors. However, implementation requires institutionalized responses, either by the same actors or the institutions they can create. The outbreak of the First World War demonstrated that coordination among major powers through occasional meetings and ad hoc diplomacy was insufficient. Thus the war was followed by the creation of the first worldwide governmental organization for peace and security, The League of Nations, as an institutional expression of the need for contact and cooperation, and the simultaneous requirement to build postwar conditions through concerted action. The demise of the League provided other lessons, particularly the need to include all major powers. Thus emerged the United Nations with its layered structure of a General Assembly, a Security Council with veto rights and mandatory powers, and a Secretariat with its own mandate. The UN Charter contains the provisions for their use and remains essentially unchanged since it was signed in June 1945.[1] The UN came about as a result of shared learning of the use of collective action to deal with threats to the security of states and peoples (Kelsen 1948, Franck 2002).

At about the same time, however, another project emerged specifically dealing with one of the most historically war-torn regions, Western Europe. The ideas were originally promoted by two French personalities, Jean Monnet and Robert Schuman. A policy statement by the French Government in 1950 proposed to integrate the production of coal and steel of the Western European states in order to avoid a new war between them.[2] An even more complex organizational framework developed, what is today the European Union. The UN and EU were both created to deal with postwar conditions to ensure that war would not recur. Thus these two entities have to be assessed in terms of their actual or potential contribution to quality peace. We begin by considering regional organizations in general, noting their development, and especially the increasing outreach into the global arena of one of them, the EU (Section 7.2). Then we turn to the truly global one, the UN (Section 7.3). In the final section (7.4), some ideas for international organizations and quality peace are outlined.

7.2 Regional Orders and Their Limits

The idea of regional cooperation has been seen in different lights, notably as a way of protecting a particular part of the world from global competition, or as a way of finding a territorial barrier against major power rivalry, preventing it from escalating. Also, regional organizations have been seen as complements to the international order. For instance, the UN Charter Chapter VIII is entirely devoted to regional arrangements (Wallensteen and Bjurner 2015). So far, regional dynamics have been highly dependent on the major powers and their concerns. Regional efforts have often been tied to the interest of a dominant actor in a region, reminiscent of traditional spheres of influence. In much of Latin America, the United States had a determining role, as did France and Britain in many conflicts in Africa and Asia. Soviet control over Eastern Europe was total and its influence extended to other areas. Thus the chances of developing more independent, regional initiatives toward conflict resolution and peacebuilding were limited.

Important ideas emerged, however, focusing on the possibilities of developing regional security communities. A powerful representation of this was found in the work of Karl W. Deutsch (1957), where he included two types: the pluralistic security community consisting of independent states still cooperating with each other, and the amalgamated community where the states actually integrate into a shared framework. Cooperation among the Nordic states is an example of the former; today's European integration approaches the latter. Such communities were marked by willingness to solve conflicts peacefully and the use of war among its members was basically unthinkable. The concept has been applied to a number of situations, notably the Baltic Sea and even the Black Sea (Wallensteen et al. 1994, Weaver 2011). It is also argued that the creation of ASEAN, the Association of South East Asian states, was inspired by Nordic cooperation and its pluralism. For Deutsch an important point was to demonstrate that such security communities could be possible as an alternative to the Cold War dynamics, not only as a particular form of regional cooperation, but also with a potential application to relations between major powers.

To many, however, withdrawal and protection from major power rivalry may have been a stronger impetus, also suggesting that regional cooperation would lead to locally more acceptable solutions to conflicts. Thus during the Cold War some states programmatically wanted to remove themselves from the Cold War, notably the members of the nonaligned movement. Their role in the United Nations was important, but its impact on ending wars and building regional peace was limited. In chapter 6 we pointed to the European project and its relationship to major power rivalry. Occasionally we have also highlighted the Central American initiatives that led to a solution more fitting to the region than what the Cold War parties could offer (Wehr and Lederach 1991). The strength of major power rivalry seemed overwhelming, however; this suggests that the end of the Cold War would potentially allow for regional or local initiatives. The hope of such developments sparked the idea of a "new regionalism," often associated with Björn Hettne (Hettne 1999), but other writers also pointed to the new conditions and the possibility of more independent initiatives on a regional basis (Morgan 1997, Väyrynen 2003).

Furthermore, as the Cold War ended, there was considerable energy in some regional bodies, both in reforming old ones and in creating entirely new organizations. The Helsinki Conference became the Organization for Security and Cooperation in Europe (OSCE). The Organization for African Unity became the African Union (AU). In both cases, internal affairs became new items on the agenda, in the form of human rights, electoral monitoring, and adherence to constitutional practices. ECOWAS, the Economic Community for Western African States, deployed military missions to West African countries. The Association of Southeast Asian Nations (ASEAN) was enlarged to include communist as well as militarily ruled states. In the same vein, OIC renamed itself the Organization for Islamic Cooperation, with a new emphasis on peace and security.[3] All of these initiatives were significant in stimulating action on regional peace and security.

However, there were also setbacks, most markedly seen in the many new crises that sparked in 2014: Ukraine (four different conflicts: over the government, the peninsula of Crimea, and two Russian-dominated areas of Luhansk and Donetsk); the renewed crisis over Gaza; and the advances of ISIS in the civil wars of Syria and Iraq. In none of these were the regional organizations able to be as present as their mandates would demand. EU became party to the complicated Ukrainian situation, as did the League of Arab States in the Middle Eastern conflicts. OSCE managed to get a monitoring role for the ceasefires in Eastern Ukraine. However, in all these conflicts, the major powers preferred to keep the initiatives, not giving space to the regional organizations (or to the UN, but that is the topic for the next section).

The neighborhood is important for building peace after war. Vulnerable states are likely to be highly dependent on what happens in the region as a whole. Data demonstrate that external actors often are involved in internal wars, and that neighbors make up a large share (Wallensteen and Sollenberg 1998, Harbom and Wallensteen 2005). At the same time they do have an interest in ending wars and, consequently, are also engaged in peacemaking attempts. Thus there is a potential for action on the regional level.

We now need to ask if these organizations contribute in practice, and not only in theory, to settlement of conflicts that have regional dimensions. Furthermore, does this contribute to a regional order that is independent or semi-independent of the global order we discussed in chapter 6? What can these organizations contribute to the settlement of territorial and governmental issues? What is the outcome if we apply the criteria of quality peace to their work?

As to territorial issues, an innovative example was mentioned in the potential settlement of the Saarland questions (Section 5.2), where the idea of a European—that is, a regional—solution was mentioned. If a particular and contested piece of territory could be handled in forms that were distinct and separate from the two parties, that could be a particular regional contribution to quality peace. In reality, it may mean extending a form of regionally guaranteed autonomy to a particular area. This approach was rejected by the people in Saarland. Similar notions have not materialized elsewhere. There is a logical attraction to such a regional settlement, but it may have severe difficulties in meeting the aspirations of local inhabitants.

A further example is the attraction of membership in a regional body. In the EU enlargement process, membership in the organization was made conditional on the settlement of disputes with other countries, particularly with regard to borders. Some successes were recorded, as membership was highly appealing to governments. However, Cyprus was admitted in 2004 without first having settled the conflict over the Turkish-ruled north of the island. It left the conflict lingering, also having a negative effect on the chances of incorporating Turkey into the Union. With regard to the Balkan disputes, the EU has used this incentive more effectively, for instance, in the relations between Serbia and Kosovo.

Ideas of regional settlement of disputed territorial waters in the South China Sea or in East Asia have concentrated on finding regionally agreed formulas for dividing the waters along state lines, rather than thinking of them as regionally shared resources. As we have seen in chapter 5 and in section 6.3, there are a number of inter-state territorial disputes that have not been solved. They could very well constitute the first step in a chain of events that lead to major conflagrations between heavily armed actors. Regional approaches should be encouraged but do not seem to be frequent, easily accepted, or more successful.

Remarkably, disputes over government may be more promising for regional action. In the practice of the African Union (AU), adherence to existing national constitutions has become an important tenet. It has led to the use of sanctions by the AU against coup regimes, albeit with mixed result, but it's nevertheless an important sign of the times (Eriksson 2010). Also in Western Africa there have been cases of outside intervention to prevent unconstitutional changes, notably by ECOWAS. ASEAN has tried, through diplomacy and the use of what has been termed "the ASEAN way,"[4] for example, to get the military government of Myanmar to open up for democratic governance. However, the process that was initiated in that country in 2011 was more tied to the change in government in the country than to regional efforts. The AU may have more recent experiences in regional action for "good governance" than ASEAN. In many parts of the world, the noninterference principle is still strong, and it may be particularly entrenched in Asia.

Regional quality peace remains a challenge to the international community. In a regional setting it might be easier to respect the dignity of other states and populations. The fact that the actors are close in geography, history, and culture could mean that they also understand each other. Sharing in building security would ideally also contribute to enhancing security through principles of noninterference combined with constructive engagement. However, these are all theoretical possibilities. The practice is less convincing. As we noted above, most internationalized conflicts involve neighbors. The artificial nature of frontiers makes for cross-border interests that undermine legal principles of noninterference. On the positive side a regional body is smaller and has a formally more equal standing for all members (than, for example, a global body like the UN Security Council) thus extending diplomatic dignity to all. Its action can be based on close insights into particular conflicts, not the least on the history of a conflict. It may also be more attentive to arms flows and other matters that create insecurity for all. It is not difficult to argue that the neighbors may have more to gain from building a peaceful neighborhood, rather than fueling conflicts that eventually may engulf them through refugee flows, arms smuggling, cross-border raids, and alliances with states and nonstate actors alike. Regional organizations are also there to stay, and thus should be able to provide predictability that is important to quality peace.

However, we have also seen partisan involvement in many conflicts by neighboring states—notably in Central Africa, the Horn of Africa, and West Asia, to mention just a few recent examples. Neighbors often believe they support the winners and thus help to shorten the war, but may in fact contribute to a protracted conflict that ultimately threatens the region as a whole. The lack of peacebuilding in one state is not only a failure of the warring actors; it may also be a regional failure. These observations do not yield high expectations that regional orders actually will develop and grow to be somewhat independent of global developments. Their present contribution to quality peace is more theoretical than practical.

A novel topic is that regional bodies can play a role outside their own original area of operation. As was mentioned, the possibility of membership has been used as a tool for peacemaking by the European Union (e.g., in the Balkans). Similarly there are ideas for expanding ASEAN into a body for all of East Asia and perhaps South Asia (e.g., ARF, the ASEAN Regional Forum). Inclusion of new members could be made conditional on the settlement of particular conflicts. Thus the EU approach to Ukraine and other former Soviet republics was to invite them into a partnership, rather than directly into a union as such. The attraction to join the EU can be used for promoting quality peace.

There is also the possibility of regional organizations participating in peace missions outside their own areas. This has been a tendency particularly for the EU. The organization has engaged in sanctions on Zimbabwe and Burma/Myanmar, and sent its own peacekeepers to the Democratic Republic of Congo. It has a whole set of special representatives for different conflicts around the globe. This is unusual for a regional body. It suggests that EU sees itself as different from customary regional organizations. With its own foreign service, it reaches beyond its regional confines. It has also raised the expectations of what an organization can do (Johansson et al. 2010). In 2014 nine European states created the European Institute of Peace to enhance such initiatives, although formally outside the EU framework. As the EU has applied principles of quality peace to its inner operations, the question emerges whether it also can do that in its international relations. Its increasingly global reach may make it into a global organization, potentially in competition with the United Nations. We will return to this in section 7.4.

We should also note that there is one area where regional (as well as other international) organizations can contribute more effectively even if counterintuitively: by removing problems from political contention. This is done by managing particular issues without making them arenas of political contestation. This could be seen as part of structural conflict prevention: creating institutions that prevent issues from becoming contentious. An example is the oldest still-functioning international organization, the Rhine Commission in Western Europe (Huisman et al. 2000). It has existed since the Congress of Vienna (actually there was also a predecessor, established already in 1804). It was created as part of the postwar arrangements intended to preserve peace in Europe. It certainly has not prevented wars in Western Europe, but issues over this river and its management have not been part of the wars. It is an old functionalist dream, that practical matters could be dealt with by practical organizations and thus managed, more or less, as technical problems (Mitrany 1948).

This approach could potentially be applied to other internationally shared rivers, such as the Nile, Congo, Zambezi, Mekong, Ganges, or Amazon, or even to other public goods. It would remove some issues from potential postwar contention and thus serve to prevent them from becoming conflict topics. From a quality peace perspective, this may be an important benefit. Such organizations provide equal treatment for all participants, equal access to common goods and, by being outside the main lines of contention, credible predictability.

In the same manner, one might envisage practical cooperation around major lakes, archipelagos, or oceans, which in turn may stimulate cooperation in other fields. Examples can be found in the Baltic Sea, the South Pacific, and in the Caribbean. Finding international ways to deal with seemingly "new" issues, such as lack of access to fresh water and reliable transportation; or common criminal concerns, such as smuggling and trafficking; or facing collective threats such as drought and climate change may suggest new ways for cooperation. To a lesser extent these issues may be part of existing patterns of conflict. Perhaps this would be an approach to regions that do not yet have any form of regional cooperation. In the words of Hettne, these are areas that lack "regionness," an awareness of themselves as a "region" (Hettne 1999). This refers particularly to Northeast Asia, where the security interests of China, Japan, North Korea, South Korea, Taiwan, Russia, and the United States intersect. Could one imagine regional cooperation on matters of fisheries, transportation routes, and climate issues as a starting point for building practical cooperation that eventually may contribute to quality peace? There is reason to be skeptical, as the security concerns often are paramount and need a first solution. Beyond this, however, such questions make the regional dimension important. A region involving fewer countries may be a method for demonstrating constructive intent that also contributes to confidence building.

Regional organizations complement global bodies, rather than replace them (Wallensteen and Bjurner 2015). They have some advantages in terms of quality peace criteria, notably the formal equality among the members. However, when disputes turn into wars, their role diminishes and the states become the central actors, as seen in a series of crises in 2014. Would then a global organization fare better? Let us turn to the role of the UN in the building of quality peace.

7.3 The United Nations in the Post–Cold War Period

Chapters 5 and 6 have largely demonstrated that deliberate attempts to build quality peace in inter-state relations, among major power relations, and in regional matters have been remarkably rare. It contrasts the intensive international commitment to peacebuilding after civil wars (Chapter 3) and in some of the state formation wars (Chapter 4). However, by focusing on the notion of world order, it may be possible to understand major power rivalries and inter-state tensions as part of a global agenda for quality peace. This naturally leads to a focus on the UN. In chapter 1 we pointed out that the notion of peacebuilding stems from the UN Secretary-General at the time, Boutros Boutros-Ghali. Thus we would expect the world organization to take a leading position in shaping a world order building on the elements of quality peace. The following graph gives pertinent information on the way the work of the UN Security Council has changed.

Graph 7.1 demonstrates clearly the significance of the end of the Cold War for the United Nations. It became activated in a new way, more in line with original expectations when the organization was created. The number of decisions increased, the number of blocked draft decisions ("vetoes") declined, and thus a more cooperative pattern emerged. From other information we know that decisions were more often taken under Chapter VII, meaning that the Security Council required mandatory actions from its membership (Wallensteen and Johansson 2014). The UN became actively engaged in a number of conflict issues. Some of them concerned conflict prevention and mediation during ongoing conflicts. Some, however, also dealt with postwar conditions. As we saw in chapters 2 and 3, the organization played an important role in

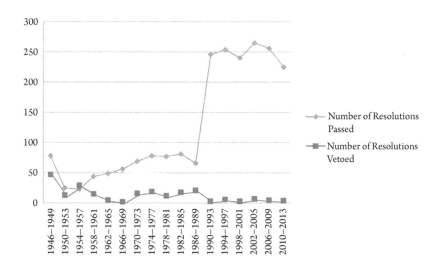

Graph 7.1 UN SECURITY COUNCIL RESOLUTIONS, 1946–2013 Number of resolutions passed and vetoed, four-year periods, absolute numbers. Source: United Nations Documentation: Research Guide. http://www.un.org/Depts/dhl/resguide/scact.htm, accessed on November 20 2014, compiled by Audrey Ann Faber.

most of the peace processes dealing with internal conflicts. It took many and varied forms. It went from providing technical expertise in negotiations and implementation to actually being involved in making deals and enforcing agreements. This is what gave the UN an unprecedented role in internal conflicts, in humanitarian issues and also—as a consequence—in peacebuilding and in preventing backsliding into renewed conflict.

However, in the inter-state and major power relations, we saw less mention of the UN. In a way this is to be expected. In the post–Cold War world inter-state conflicts have been rare. Solutions have sometimes been found directly between the states, by resorting to regional bodies or using international instruments such as courts of arbitration and justice. In some instances, the UN played an instrumental role in negotiations and implementation of such conflicts (e.g., Ethiopia–Eritrea 2000). In the postwar periods, however, we found little of UN activity in inter-state conflicts. Also, in major power relations, the UN did not have a direct role. The lines of communication were directly between the capitals. The major process in Europe involved little UN action. In the formation of EU the UN is mentioned but policies were largely pursued outside the UN framework. The same is true both for the consolidation of Soviet victory in Eastern Europe and for its ending of that control. Critical issues were dealt with between the majors directly, in summit meetings or bilateral contacts. For big power relationships, the UN may only acquire a significant role in conflicts, where the UN legal and universal frameworks are needed (again, as determined by the leading actors, for instance in the Iran–Iraq war or Gulf War of 1991, or the application of R 2 P in Libya in 2011). The Security Council can act only when the five permanent members do not disagree. This means that the United Nations is a forum for some crisis management, possibly preventing some wars from becoming too destructive and unsettling for regional and global relations. Certainly this is an improvement compared to the Cold War era, when the organization had almost no role to play and when crisis management was entirely in the hands of the major powers operating outside its framework (Wallensteen and Johansson 2004, Wallensteen and Johansson 2015). However, in many recent crises where the major powers have been highly active, it was difficult for UN agencies to find a role beyond the humanitarian one. Whether the UN will have a role in postwar conditions, of course, will depend on the outcomes of theses crises. In the new issues confronting the world the record has been far from positive. For Ukraine, OSCE may be the organization agreed upon; for the Syria/Iraq crises all sides aim for victory, although there is a UN mediator in place (Staffan de Mistura); and in the Gaza crisis neighbors were more important, in addition to the United States. Remarkably, in conflicts in Africa, the UN has an important role in conflict termination and in post-agreement periods. Major power contentions have been more limited in this region, almost to the point of not observing its significance.

As we have observed, there are a number of territorial disputes that have not been resolved, and thus could constitute the first step in a chain of events that leads to major conflagration between heavily armed actors. Approaching them through an international framework could be a way to prevent such as sequence of events. This points to a possible role for the world organization.

The UN does have a series of instruments at its disposal that not only can be used for prevention, but also for postwar developments. The use of sanctions for peacebuilding after civil war is a new feature. It has been applied in some West African cases, where the Security Council made the lifting of sanctions contingent on progress in national peacebuilding. Thus sanctions on certain Liberian export products were not raised until the government was able to control the trade and had secured its share of revenue (Wallensteen 2011a: 206–228). In this way, the implementation of the peace agreements was supported, as well as the ability of the government to reassert itself vis-à-vis other interests. It contributed to peacebuilding in Liberia through a novel use of a classical method. The same may be true of other situations as well, but there have been few such cases reported.[5]

Similarly, one could argue that involvement in mediation in order to reach an agreement would provide for a continued commitment in the implementation phase. In traditional mediation, the assignment ends with an agreement, if possible. In practice, it has now become more common that international mediators are also called in later in the process. Mediators provide insights into the provisions of an accord, for example. It underscores that mediation is a commitment for an organization, not just for a particular mediator. It points to the importance of mediation teams that can stay focused on a conflict in the postwar phase (Svensson and Wallensteen 2010).

The focus on peace agreements is natural, as the UN system often was involved in the processes. It is more difficult to find a role for the UN in cases of victory consolidation. As the leading organs of the UN deal with threats to international peace and security, a victory means the end to an acute threat. What follows after the war will be seen as internal affairs for the involved countries; thus there is no expectation of action by the international community. The experience from the post–Second World War period demonstrated this. The UN had no role in the politics of the defeated countries. This was entirely the prerogative of the victorious states. In theory, the post–Cold War situation might offer the possibility for more UN engagement in victory situations. However, there is little evidence of this. The Security Council was seen as— and remains—basically a crisis management institution. As long as there is a sequence of events going from peace negotiations to agreements, possible victories, and war termination, the UN may be involved all the way throughout a peace process. However, in the clear-cut victories without prior internationalized negotiations, neither the Security Council nor the Secretariat is likely to be heavily engaged.[6]

This means that other UN institutions have to take up concerns about victory consolidation. For example, Sri Lanka has protested against international criticism of its record on civilian deaths in the ending of the war against the LTTE in 2009. Such critiques stemmed from human rights organizations but were also raised by the UN Human Rights Council in 2012. Sri Lanka had considerable support in this, notably from China and Russia, but still lost the vote, and was subject to sharp disapproval.[7]

Another pertinent body in this context is the International Criminal Court, which is free to indict any individual who has committed war crimes. It appears that the Court has been able to do this without regard to the outcome of a conflict. Thus victorious leaders also have been investigated and indicted. It is often difficult for national actors to deal with war crimes in postwar conditions. The existence of an international alternative reduces that pressure at the same time that it enhances the chances for a fair trial of the accused. In this way international courts can contribute to a national process of acknowledgment as a part of reconciliation.

Thus the UN system as a whole does have important resources for dealing with postwar conditions. In this work we have set out three criteria for assessing if particular solutions or postwar conditions actually lead toward quality peace. Also UN action could be exposed to scrutiny. It helps to demonstrate the strengths and weaknesses of this particular body.

First of all, quality peace requires *respect for the dignity* of the involved actors. Being a state-to-state organization means that all member-states are formally treated equally. This equality of the member-states is the basis for the organization. It is a major reason why states aspire to become members. It seems to provide them with respect for their independence, territorial integrity, and form of internal governance. Equality is expressed in the fact that each state, no matter what size or power, has one vote in the General Assembly. More complicated is that there is no further requirement for membership. The Charter (Art. 4) mentions "peace-loving" states, but the meaning of this has not been discussed since the 1950s. Whether regimes are democratic or act properly on human rights does not matter for membership. The recent principle of responsibility to protect (R2P) includes support for the notion of national sovereignty, but adds that such sovereignty can be undermined if a government does not deal with issues of genocide, ethnic cleansing, and mass human rights violations. It suggests that there has to be a particular level of quality to sovereignty. However, membership has never been denied on this score, not even since the end of the Cold War. The equality of the states is firmly entrenched in the UN system. An important question for the future is if the organization will change as the number of democratic member-states increases. The UN is already involved in internal affairs, such as in electoral monitoring. With increasing democratic membership the organization may also come to embrace deeper meanings of quality peace.

In stark contrast to the General Assembly, the Security Council is a body for cooperation among the major powers. The Security Council consists of only fifteen of the 193 members (i.e., now less than 8% of the membership). Five members have permanent seats, giving them distinct advantages over the others, both in voting rights and historical memory. This, of course, reflects a real distribution of global power. The five have most of the world's nuclear weapons and military resources. For instance, their joint share of world military expenditures is around sixty per cent (SIPRI Yearbook 2012). Their combined share of world trade and world production is remarkable. Depending on the measure their combined share is between 40% and 60% of total world trade or world GDP. The composition of the Security Council is a reflection of the inequalities in the world. As could be expected, this state of affairs is continuously debated. Most proposals from other states go in the direction of adding more states to the Council, both as permanent and elected members, so as to improve the Council's reflection of the full UN membership. As of yet no proposal has gained necessary support.

However, the strength of the major powers in the organization also serves a purpose. In particular for the major powers, it means that their interests are protected. There is no way in which the organization can be used against them. This is the meaning, of course, of the voting rules and the veto. If the organization would side with one party in a major power dispute, it becomes an instrument for that party. The veto prevents that from happening and protects the dignity of the major powers. This makes them interested in remaining part of the organization, even if it does not always act exactly as a particular power may want. For less powerful states, this still is not satisfactory. Their interests are not protected in the same way. They will have to build considerable regional or international support for themselves or take their own unilateral measures for security. How to accommodate middle-range and smaller states remains a significant challenge to the present UN structure.

Thus there are several flaws in the way the UN organization respects the dignity of all involved. Still the actual UN approach to conflicts, particularly if undertaken by the UN Secretariat, is often balanced, dealing with parties in an evenhanded way. This is the way the culture of the organization operates. It is built to solve conflicts, and thus willing to listen to all sides. Mediation missions are likely to present proposals that meet the demand of opposing forces.

As the purpose is to find a way out of particular conflicts, this makes sense. It also leads to a balanced approach with respect to peacebuilding. However, it may not work equally well with respect to the wars that have ended in victory, unless the victory is based on a Security Council decision.

Thus the UN approach becomes more complicated when strong actors want determined action and can base this on UN principles, such as countering aggression, terrorism and nuclear proliferation, or upholding of the norms of responsibility to protect (R 2 P). In a number of situations, it has been possible to muster the necessary support for such deliberate UN action (notably on Kuwait in 1990; al Qaeda in 1999 and 2001; sanctions on North Korea and Iran since 2006; and Libya and Côte d'Ivoire in 2011). However, there have also been repeated experiences of stalemate, ineffective action, or inaction during the crisis as such (Bosnia 1992–1995, Rwanda 1994, Syria since 2011) only in some circumstances resulting in UN postwar involvement.

The UN contribution becomes even more complicated when major actors operate outside the UN framework (as was done by NATO in the Kosovo crisis of 1999 and the Anglo-American coalition on Iraq in 2003). Former Secretary-General Kofi Annan describes this in some detail (Annan 2012: 114–119, 357). Russia's opposition to having the 2014 Ukrainian crisis in the Security Council is a further example of this, following on a similar stand on Georgia in 2008. Smaller states may have benefited from the protection of the UN Charter in some of these instances, and may also have had a stronger standing in the international community if the UN had been involved.

The second aspect of UN and the quality peace criteria it its ability to *provide security* for the populations that are exposed to the dangers of wars, repressive regimes, and terroristic nonstate actors, as well as lack of the rule of law, breakdown of health services, and other phenomena associated with the concept of state failure. Again this is where the experiences just cited affect the appeal of the organization. Few states have drawn the conclusion that they can reduce their own military expenditures while expecting that their sovereignty will be protected by the world organization. The few times such protection has been forthcoming, notably to Kuwait in 1990–1991, are too exceptional for a state to make such a drastic decision. The UN is more a complementary resource. The states will have to find other solutions, notably investing in their own security, identifying allies that can make firm and credible commitments, or working at creating a secure environment in the state's own neighborhood.

This does not exclude an approach to the UN and to the world community at large. Certainly the UN system is involved in a great number of conflicts around the world—for instance, in its capacity as a third party, external monitor, or donor. This is useful, but much of the basic structure for a state or population's security will have to come from other sources. A different way to say this is that the ambitious reform agenda initiated at the General Assembly session of the period of 2005–2006 was a start that may have to be revisited and reinvigorated.[8] It resulted in the creation of the Human Rights Council, as well as the Peacebuilding Commission (PBC), to support the work that goes in the direction of quality peace initiatives. However, the latter commission has suffered from a weak position in the organization as well as a lack of resources and clear-cut definition of what its actual contribution should be.

Thirdly, these observations affect the *predictability* of the UN in working for quality peace. It is difficult to predict which conflicts the Security Council will react to, or what resources an active Secretary-General will be able to generate. Thus the question of long-term commitment becomes crucial. The Peacebuilding Commission (PBC) and its affiliated organizations were created for a durable engagement in postwar situations. The international community through its peacebuilding institutions made a commitment. The Commission was careful in its selection of cases and use of resources. This means that only a handful of countries have been the focus of the organization. By 2014 it included Burundi, Central African Republic (CAR), Guinea, Guinea-Bissau, Liberia, and Sierra Leone, all of which had been on the PBC list for a number of years. All these situations concerned postwar conditions in civil wars—that is, the type of conflicts we discussed in chapter 3. None was a case of victory consolidation. Mostly these states had peace agreements and the PBC aim was to support the implementation of such agreements or other arrangements. All cases were from Africa and could all be classified as weak states with a danger not only of a return to war but also of state collapse.

The record illustrates some of the problems. Armed conflict recurred repeatedly in CAR. Guinea-Bissau saw a coup in 2012 but also a transition to elections. Similarly Guinea (Conakry) faced severe demonstrations in 2013, but the results from the elections later in the year were accepted. Burundi, Liberia, and Sierra Leone were, from this perspective, cases without a return to the use of political violence. By the autumn of 2014 three of the six countries faced a severe Ebola outbreak that was difficult to control, due to a lack of state capacity and health services. The resources from the international community and the UN for preventing a recurrence may have been limited and the strategies used can be discussed. This discussion brings us full circle to section 2.3 in this book. Have the strategies improved since Roland Paris wrote his critical evaluation?

Analyzing the projects financed by the associated Peacebuilding Fund, we could find that building democracy and security was prioritized.[9] The agenda for peacebuilding as well as quality peace is obviously much larger and needs to be addressed more fully. In a new UN reform process, the mandate, decision making, and resources of the Peacebuilding Commission should be of central concern. In fact, the wording of the General Assembly resolution in September 2005 makes that clear, saying that "the main purpose of the Peacebuilding Commission is to bring together all relevant actors to marshal resources and to advise on and propose integrated strategies for post-conflict peacebuilding and recovery. . . [and] extend the period of attention by the international community to post-conflict recovery." (World Summit Outcome 2005, paragraphs 97–98). The marshaling of resources was a key concern in 2005. By 2014 it was clear that the Commission and the Fund operated on highly limited resources and thus only had a limited impact to report. Thus the significance of a UN commitment to peacebuilding is restrained by lack of significant resources and therefore is difficult for states to rely on. This will also affect its ability to "bring together all relevant actors," as stated in the founding document. The PBC dealt only with a few states, in order to establish a record for the future, but also to scale down expectations.

Thus we see that there is an increased role for the UN in international peacemaking since the end of the Cold War. It has led to the creation of new institutions, notably the Human Rights Council and the Peacebuilding Commission. Separately, but related, there is the International Criminal Court, which can play a role no matter what the outcome is of a particular conflict. However, there are also considerable challenges to the UN system. We can note that it is not involved in situations of victory consolidation. It is not involved where major power interests drive conflicts as well as peace efforts. There is a problem of organization priority for peacebuilding efforts as well as difficulties with adequate resources. There is a need to reform the organization in crucial respects in order to make it an actor in the consistent building of quality peace. Some ideas are suggested in the following section.

7.4 International Organizations and the Future of Quality Peace

The world order that has dominated international actions since the end of the Cold War has also led to a paradigmatic shift for international organizations. For the United Nations it has meant involvement in conflict prevention, conflict resolution, and postwar conditions. It has affected the political doctrine from which the UN (as well as other international organizations) operates. It is also possible to see elements of a challenge to the UN as the leading international peacemaking institution. Let us briefly explore this and how it relates to the notion of quality peace.

The original basis for UN action was the theory of collective security. All states were expected to unite against a country committing aggression, and thus deter any state from doing that, as it would know that it faced global isolation and possible intervention (Wallensteen 2015: 228–233). In practice, the Cold War undermined the classical collective security idea, as major powers could prevent the UN system from acting in situations which actually were within its realm, according to the specifications of Article 39, Chapter VII. To these belonged the Soviet invasions of Hungary (1956), Czechoslovakia (1968), and Afghanistan (1979), as well as US actions in Guatemala (1954), and Vietnam (1954–1975). The veto in the Security Council limited the scope of collective action. Collective security became selective security. Sometimes collective action was even narrower and entirely outside the UN system: collective defense by major power alliances.

The post–Cold War period provided for a broader perspective and avoided some of the prior barriers. A result was the impressive UN engagement in conflicts around the globe. This went further than originally thought, as it actually challenged national sovereignty by authorizing humanitarian action, giving peacekeeping forces mandates to use force under certain circumstances, involving the UN in peace processes also in internal conflicts, and, following September 11, 2001, pursuing sanctions strategies that asked for new legislation in member-states (Ahrnens 2008). Thus the scope of international action has been enlarged, although the UN does not have *all* the world's armed conflicts on its agenda. It still means that the postwar situations receive less attention. There is more effort going into the early phases of conflict and in alleviating humanitarian suffering during the conflict than into the conditions after the end to war. The latter is largely seen as a matter of development assistance following humanitarian aid. The resources and the mandate of the Peacebuilding Commission are, as we saw in section 7.3, limited. This is where the notion of quality peace comes in. It specifies that the conditions after a war should not only be seen as a matter of implementing a peace deal or stabilizing a victory, but as a strategy for fostering quality peace. It requires considerable thought in order to actually and simultaneously improve dignity, security, and predictability. As was noted in Chapters 2–6, this is a long-term engagement. Collective security then does not end at negative peace; it is also a concern for developing conditions that mean a particular situation will not again become a concern for Security Council crisis action.

This is where the EU approach becomes interesting. It is also a collective body, concerned about security among its members. Its approach is one of enhancing common values such as democracy and human rights, as well as knitting the members so closely together that an armed conflict is no longer conceivable. All this is done with the perspective of long-term commitments. The history of the EU so far testifies to a reasonable application of this program, with some failures as mentioned in section 7.2 (Cyprus, Ukraine). This is where EU may have a distinct advantage over the UN. It is not an organ for handling the type of crises that the UN has to deal with. It has its own internal crises on budget matters, financial issues, or admission of new members. However, it is often sufficiently united on international issues to have its own strategy, not the least involving long-term commitment. An example is the EU's massive contribution to building up the Palestinian Authority to make it a properly functioning governmental body. This is an essential element in finding a solution to the Israeli-Palestinian problem.

Does this suggest that the EU is a competitor to the UN? The organization definitely has the ambition of becoming globally relevant, and is projecting an image that differs from the UN as it emphasizes democracy, human rights, and economic opportunities. However, it cannot seriously compete with the UN. One way to demonstrate this is to note the difference with respect to peace operations. In August 2012, the UN had deployed 108,000 men and women in twenty-two peace operations around the world, while there were seventeen EU missions that at the same time supplying 4,000. The EU missions were smaller, and more expensive.[10] We may add that they were normally better equipped, had more mobility, and were more specifically trained for international missions. Still, EU was definitely involved in smaller missions that seldom had as much local impact as the UN (Johansson et al. 2010).

This suggests instead the value of closer cooperation between the UN and EU, both in peace operations and in postwar reconstruction. The EU may be able to raise troops, which can carry out rapid deployment functions, for example, by having more armored vehicles and heavier weapons in place and thus projecting stronger deterrent functions. The UN forces, however, could supply the local presence that is also necessary. In a cooperative enterprise the two organizations would be able to deal effectively with local threats or violations of ceasefire agreements. As to postwar situations, the EU has considerable resources and experience, not the least from the Palestinian situation. Rather than the UN building up its own resources, an arrangement between these two bodies would provide for a more optimal international engagement in the conflicts of the post–Cold War era, particularly for postwar conditions. Cooperation between these two leading international peace projects would have a chance of making quality peace not just a shared doctrine but also a reality on the ground.

It is interesting that such global regional cooperation was visualized already at the inception of the two organizations. The UN Charter includes Chapter VIII for regional arrangements, written long before the EU existed. The Schuman Declaration, which is regarded as the starting point for the EU, said explicitly that "a Representative of the United Nations will be accredited to the Authority, and will be instructed to make a public report to the United

Nations twice yearly, giving an account of the working of the new organization."[11] The founders wanted to make clear that the EU was not to develop into a competitor to the world organization but a complement. The postwar conditions in the post–Cold War world may demand more of such cooperation to provide for quality peace.

Even if this would be an ideal situation, there are of course obstacles. The crises in Ukraine during 2014 led to confrontations between Russia and the West where the EU and its member states were part of the conflagration. If an effect of this is an increased difficulty in coordinating UN and EU peacebuilding measures in a number of postwar situations, that is a tragedy.

CHAPTER 8

Paths to Quality Peace

8.1 Twenty-Five Conclusions

The motivation for this book was a shortcoming in the approaches by academics and practitioners alike to the issue of peacebuilding. There was a debate positing different peacebuilding approaches against each other. Thus authors neglected the importance of the alternative: victory outcome and victory consolidation. Those also had to be part of the conversation, as they do take place, often are what the parties strive for, and thus have to be compared to negotiated outcomes. In fact the argument in favor of a negotiated settlement—for the warring parties, the society as a whole, and the international community—is that it provides more lasting and positive conditions than victory, and thus reduces danger of recurrence of war. That was a hypothesis that required considerable elaboration. This book has taken on that task.

Venturing into this question, it was not sufficient to compare two different types of outcomes of a war and the resulting postwar conditions. There was also a need to develop criteria for how to evaluate these conditions. That led to the notion of quality peace, elaborating on different understandings of "peace" and "peacebuilding." The result is that quality peace is defined as postwar conditions that make the inhabitants of a society (be it an area, a country, a region, a continent, or a planet) secure in life and dignity now and for the foreseeable future. This provides for a crude yardstick, enough for a first attempt at the problem of peace-generating postwar conditions.

Furthermore, we then had to observe that there are differences among armed conflicts. One such difference concerns the parties that are in conflict with one another; another the purpose of their struggle. Combining this, it was optimal to apply the trichotomy of the Uppsala Conflict Data Program. This meant distinguishing among three types of conflicts: internal conflicts over government, internal conflicts over territory (state formation conflicts), and inter-state conflicts (which also can be over government or territory).

Typically peacebuilding studies have focused only on the first type, but still included some cases of the second type, thus diluting their findings.

Finally, as has often been pointed out, there is a difference between the Cold War and the post–Cold War period. In this book, we have found that this reflects a world order difference that relates to victory consolidation and peacebuilding in an important way. Thus the relationships between major powers had to be scrutinized with respect to their mutual relations and their significance for other relationships in the international system, as well as for the major regional and global organizations concerned with peace and security.

Let us see what we have learned from this exercise and respond to the questions that were posed in chapter 1 on the efficiency of peacebuilding in comparison to victory consolidation to meet the requirements of quality peace.

With the quality peace notion as a starting point we could survey the various war outcomes in the armed conflicts, particularly since the end of the Cold War. This has generated clear findings, largely in favor of the ability of negotiated outcomes to provide for conditions of quality peace. This result, however, can only be seen as preliminary, suggesting hypotheses that require further elaboration. They point strongly in favor of an approach building on quality peace as a way to understand postwar conditions. The following twenty-five general conclusions are presented for further consideration by the academic and policy communities. In order to stimulate such an effect, they are put in a stronger form than is typical of academic presentations.

For Post–Civil War Situations:

1. A negotiated outcome provides a greater chance than any other outcome for respect of dignity for all inhabitants, including the losers, especially as opportunities are greater for democracy building and transparency.

2. In a post–civil war situation that attempts at democracy building, there is a lower risk of armed conflict recurrence in the long run than for cases of victory consolidation, implying the importance of an early construction of democratic institutions.

3. The integration of the opposing military forces is central for sustained peaceful conditions, making it the most important aspect of power-sharing agreements, thus going beyond disarming strategies.

4. There is more international commitment to conflicts that ended through negotiations than through victory, serving to strengthen accountability and transparency.

5. Victories have a higher chance of creating predictable conditions for the immediate future. Nondemocratic regimes display remarkable longevity. If, after some decades, they open up for democratization, this is normally

unrelated to the victory as such. It is likely that democratization would have followed earlier through a negotiated settlement.

6. Victorious governments tend to become more authoritarian, more adverse to international insight, and, thus, gradually undermine their own power.

For Postwar Condition in State Formation Conflicts:

7. For territorial internal conflicts, the postwar patterns are more mixed and depend on the type of state building that emerges following the ending of the war.

8. In cases where the war results in state separation, future relations are likely to remain highly contentious between the separated states. In many situations, the lack of reasonable cooperation can not only be attributed to the separation, but also to the lack of democracy and transparency. The expectations of reasonable working relations in the foreseeable future are low.

9. Solutions that were negotiated and result in autonomy within the existing state are more lasting, provide for more democratic conditions, and provide more respect for the dignity of the inhabitants on opposite sides of societal divides. The key requirement for this is the democratization of the whole society, in particular the center.

10. As is the case with civil wars, government victory over separatist rebels is associated with authoritarian tendencies in the country as a whole, before as well as after the victory.

11. Inter-state regional integration serves to improve the quality of the internal war outcomes, whether created by victory or negotiations.

For Postwar Conditions between States:

12. Quality peace in inter-state relations after war is often low. Territorial disputes remain difficult to settle, even in cases of negotiated outcomes.

13. There are only two cases of inter-state peacebuilding in recent times, the relations of France–Germany and Ecuador–Peru. It is hard to generalize from just these two cases.

14. One finding is, nevertheless, that it is likely that settling salient territorial disputes between states helps to create sufficient confidence for further international cooperation.

15. Furthermore, with more openness on each side, it is more likely that agreed solutions would be upheld.

16. It is difficult to create quality peace in a society following major power intervention, unless there is a strong asymmetry and a shared popular understanding of the aims of the intervention.

For The Role of World Order in Quality Peace

17. A closer look at the activity of major powers shows that the concept of world order is of significance, as the relations among major states permeate throughout the globe.

18. It is fruitful to see the aftermath of the Second World War as a world order built on the victors' search for consolidation and acceptance of *their* victory. The divergent consolidation policies were associated with considerable and renewed conflicts between the victors.

19. A policy of victory consolidation that provides for dignity to the loser, security for all parties, and continued and predictable international commitment comes closer to quality peace. Thus the democratic systems in West Germany and Japan were more efficient in establishing long-term peace than the communist systems in Eastern Europe.

20. The post–Cold War period is a world order building on principles that emphasize inclusiveness and self-restraint among major powers. It provides for more space for negotiated solutions and conditions associated with quality peace globally than the previous order.

For The Connections between Levels

21. This study shows an intimate connection between levels of international society. Solutions to internal conflicts often apply international and global dimensions, ultimately traceable to the global configuration of power and the world order of the time.

22. Wars are seldom only a matter for the warring parties. The more protracted a conflict, the more actors are likely to be involved. And the more actors involved, the more likely that the conflict becomes even more protracted. In these circumstances, negotiations have difficulties ending wars in a conclusive way, but so has victory.

For The Role of International Organization

23. There has been an increasing resort to international organizations and the UN in ending conflicts. There has not been an equal emphasis on postwar conditions, whether peacebuilding or victory consolidation. Thus recurrence of war has not decreased sufficiently.

24. There has recently been a decreasing reliance on international organizations in prevention, mediation, and peacebuilding in conflicts with heavy major power interest. The commitment of major powers to international organizations needs to be reaffirmed.

25. Unorthodox forms of cooperation between international organizations may further the ability of the international community to succeed in building quality peace.

8.2 The Value of Quality Peace

Setting criteria for postwar conditions beyond the obvious one of the absence of war (whether for a minimum of two, five, or ten years) turns out to be productive. This is the strength of thinking about quality peace as a matter not only of the termination of war, but also the provision of dignity and security in life for all inhabitants for the foreseeable future. For such conditions to be observed and developed there is a need for further study. This also includes the criteria applied; in this work they have been general in nature, and they require further refinement. Some areas can be indicated:

It would be interesting to go deeper into the issue of *dignity* and what it entails, in terms of acknowledgment of guilt, reconciliation, and the pursuit of war crimes. Repeatedly we have pointed to the rights of minorities as indicators of how a society deals with issues of discrimination and dignity. Even more significant, gender equality is a way of understanding dignity for all in a society.

Similarly the issue of *security* has been dealt with in a broad way and would need to be pursued with more vigor. Military budgets are not transparent or not even public in all cases. Arms trade, whether legal or illicit, continues to be difficult to control or scrutinize. Clandestine networks for funding wars need to be exposed. This would give data for further understanding, for example, of insecurities relating to armaments, disbanding of armed groups, and ex-combatants, and not the least the importance of security equality, where the role of women's security is also highlighted.

Also the criterion of *predictability* needs more investigation. Not the least economic development would be an important dimension of this, but it may also be a double-edged issue: More resources may make peace beneficial to the many, but some may benefit more than others. The nexus of peace, war, and corruption needs to be explored. The way a society redistributes resources is not only a matter of human rights, but also one of the predictability of peace. This makes a postwar society's ability to manage a change of power a most instructive indicator.

Thus we have only begun to understand deeper concerns associated with quality peace. It is imperative that more work be done along these lines. In due course, we may see the contours of a *theory of quality peace,* where the ways the former adversaries treat each other becomes crucial, whether in victory or in peace agreements. Respecting the role of the other could be key: In that perspective, the opponent also has some power to determine the outcome, even in the cases of losing. If the opponent accepts the new conditions, they are more likely to be sustained. But the conditions for such acceptance may rest on the victor's ability to treat the loser in a generous way.

An unexpected effect is the possibility of also using quality peace criteria for the evaluation of the *role of international institutions* in postwar conditions. We have seen that peace agreements often are highly internationalized in the sense that they involve neighbors, major powers, and/or international organizations. This is true whether the agreements deal with civil wars, state formation conflicts, or inter-state relations. There are often international commitments to certain outcomes. Victories provide other challenges, as many victorious actors do not want interference from the outside. This issue has to find a place within global or regional organizations. Certainly nongovernmental organizations have a particular role in this regard.

The notion of quality peace also turns out to have implications for *world order*. The way world power is distributed and the way the major powers perceive each other is important for the postwar conditions in seemingly local and "distant" conflicts. If there is an emphasis on victory, local conflicts will be fought with this outcome in mind, often with the support of one or the other major powers. If there is an emphasis on negotiated settlements, the parties in local conflicts will be encouraged to pursue such a strategy. The major powers can reward behavior that fits their strategic concerns.

Even *relations between major powers*, such as the United States, Russia, and China, could be evaluated in terms of their ability to contribute to quality peace. Regions with tension could similarly be assessed. Drawing on general findings as well as the Western European experience, the future of peace in East Asia may have to include, as a first step, solutions to territorial issues. In today's world it also means asking what can be done with respect to Eastern Europe, which now witnesses dismembered states with a plethora of enclaves ruled with a mixture of links to Moscow, open or clandestinely. And what would it take to unite the major powers in a shared approach to the states of Syria, Iraq, and Palestine, for the betterment of the conditions of all their inhabitants?

These are implications for pertinent issues that face humanity in concrete forms today. They may seem disconnected but in a world of quality peace, they are not. They all affect the future of our planet.

NOTES

Chapter 1

1. For a broad survey of concepts and research on strategic peacebuilding, see Lederach and Appleby 2010.
2. In doing so this volume parallels the edited volume on quality peace by Joshi, et al. 2015. A further volume on indicators is planned by Christian Davenport, Patrick Regan, and Erik Melander. The issues of quality have become increasingly important in social sciences. An important example is the notion of quality of government (Rothstein 2011).
3. There is now an increased interest in thinking about causes of peace, in contrast to the study of the causes of war (see Regan 2014).
4. There is a need to develop indicators for dignity as well as for quality peace. Schachter's list does not explicitly include gender, but much recent work points to its importance. He also neglects class dimensions. It is not the purpose here to develop new indicators, however. Rather, customary measurements will be used covering both the relations between the former warring parties and the society as a whole. The aim now is only to demonstrate the utility of the notion of quality peace for relations that are important in making war and building peace.
5. There is some debate on this concept in relation to human rights (Bagaric and Allan 2006) and from a public health perspective (Jacobson 2009), but little from a peace perspective. However, a recent contribution is Hicks, with examples from the use of the concept in conflict resolution experiences (Hicks 2011). The opposites to dignity are humiliation and discrimination, for which there are more measures available.
6. "Normalization" is a term used in divergent social settings. In disability research, normalization refers to making life as similar to the life of the non-disabled as possible, inspired by the work of Bengt Nirje. In studies of rape, it refers to the normalization of violence in a domestic relationship (e.g., a woman's or child's acceptance of it as "normal"). There is, however, very little on how the non-use of force is normalized in postwar situations.
7. This definition was originally presented to represent only peacebuilding in Wallensteen 2010: 50. Here, however, it is enlarged to cover victory consolidation as well, thus turning it into a definition of quality peace.
8. At the end of the Second World War there was a keen awareness of how key factors of unemployment, loss of income, financial imbalance, economic insecurity, and extremism together could result in revanchism, militarism, and risk-taking that again could put the entire planet at risk. The World Bank originally was called the International Bank for Reconstruction and Development, expressing exactly such sentiments, and thus pointing to elements in the present use of the concept of "peacebuilding."

9. Undoubtedly the history of peace research cannot be written without appreciating the work of Galtung. This notwithstanding, peace research now finds itself in a post-Galtung phase with respect to conflict analysis and public pronouncements.

10. The article in *Impact of Science on Society* 26 (1/2) is thirteen pages, obviously shorter than the chapter in Galtung's *Essays*, (Vol. 2, 282–304), but both are from 1976; thus it is hard to know which one is the original one. References are here to the chapter. The article is actually called "Three Realistic Approaches to Peace"; the chapter dropped the reference to "realistic."

11. There is a danger of cynicism in this approach. The parties themselves may well see their causes as just and defensible. However, if the international approach is to stop the war with peaceful means (arms embargoes, peacekeeping, etc.) it may be beneficial for both sides. In the Iran–Iraq War, however, major powers for a long time seem to prefer to have the both sides destroy one another. The danger of this approach is evident, particularly as one side in the end may have perceived itself as victorious and embarked on new adventures (Iraq), while the other may have seen the need for nuclear development (Iran).

12. Toft is probably the most recent author demonstrating the importance of victory (Toft 2010a, Toft 2010b) and we will return to her work in Chapter 2.

13. An insightful example is Ikenberry 2001. Oddly, Ikenberry refrains from defining victory. However, he has much to say, for instance, on types of order, not the least the "constitutional" order that is relevant in this context (e.g., in his second chapter). The classic writer on this topic, Hedley Bull (2002) defines "order" very carefully, but has little to say about "victory." His notion of "international society" is relevant, however.

Chapter 2

1. The exact share of conflicts without victory or peace agreement is 59% for the 1975–1988 period and 42% for the 1989–2010 period. In addition, there are some conflicts that saw both a peace agreement and a victory: there are three such observations for the first period and eleven for the second. All but one were in intra-state conflicts over government.

2. It is interesting to note that a special unit for peacebuilding ethics has been created at the Peace Research Institute in Oslo (PRIO) to observe this matter.

3. Paris has further significant observations, based on the remaining seven cases as well as the three additional cases that are introduced to demonstrate the utility of his framework: Kosovo (where peacebuilding is given high marks), East Timor (almost seen as a model case, see Paris 2004: 221), and Sierra Leone. All have incorporated a more institutional model for peacebuilding in line with his argument. All three appeared stable at the time (and, largely, remain so today). In line with the concern here we may note that two of the three additional cases are territorial, facing different peacebuilding problems than the others (Kosovo and East Timor compared to Sierra Leone).

4. South West Africa was the colonialist name of the territory that today is Namibia, as was initially used by the liberation movements. By 1990 SWAPO was already an established name and the organization has continued to use it, although it is officially known as the SWAPO Party of Namibia.

5. Transparency International Corruption Perception Index for the Public Sector http://cpi.transparency.org/cpi2011/results/, accessed December 2012.

6. For example, Freedom House in 2011 labeled both countries as "not free"— see http://www.freedomhouse.org/images/File/fiw/FIW2011_SSA_Map_1st%20draft.pdf.

7. See note 5.

8. Interestingly, Öberg and Melander (2009) find that "high bureaucracy quality" is associated with less conflict in autocratic societies, thus going against the notion of corruption as a factor containing conflict.

9. Doyle and Sambanis include more government conflicts than UCDP, where they tend to constitute around half of all conflicts. It could be the result of the authors including a

number of restarted conflicts that are defined as separate and new, in a way UCDP would not (e.g., a series of armed conflicts in Algeria, Burundi, Indonesia, etc.). Also, a number of territorial conflicts are not listed as UCDP would (e.g., in Burma, Ethiopia, India, Iran). This is of no concern here, as the focus is on the success rates.

10. With the "lenient" definition the success rate increases, particularly for government conflicts, where almost half are seen as successful (i.e., there is at least a higher degree of absence of violence).

11. Armed violence was limited at the moment of dissolution, and only the Chechnya and Nagorno-Karabakh conflicts enter the data. This furthermore should be compared to the amount of violence that was exerted when the union was created in the 1920s and reconstituted in the 1940s, notably in Ukraine, the Caucasus, and the Baltic countries. Many state structures have been created in blood and maintained with heavy force, something that is also incorporated into the parties' understanding of the conflict.

12. This means often a study of instability, rather than the war as such. There is a tradition of this, for instance demonstrating the impact of war on future economic growth. A recent example is Polachek and Sevastianova 2012.

13. In a rerun using UCDP data, Dahl and Hoyland do not find the same clear-cut results (see Dahl and Hoyland [2012]).

14. Monica Toft, MTcodebook, accessed September 29, 2011, at http://belfercenter.ksg. harvard.edu/files/

15. We should note that Barbara Walter (2010) reports no difference in war recurrence between these two types of outcomes. Walter argues instead that the key is constraints on the government (such as formal constitution and rules of war—see Walter 2010: 33). A possible conclusion is that the effects of the type of war endings gradually cease to be important, as a new status quo is established. Again we may wonder, however, if the time span is too short for a firm statement on this.

16. On human security, see for instance editions of the Human Security Report Project, http://www.hsrgroup.org/. In the UN Secretariat there is a Human Security Unit: http://www.unocha.org/humansecurity/chs/index.html.

17. As previously mentioned, this idea is pursued in a separate book project by Christian Davenport, Patrick Regan, and Erik Melander.

Chapter 3

1. The chapter has benefited from reactions in the research seminar at the Department of Peace and Conflict Research, Uppsala University, February 2012, by among others, Erik Melander and Kristine Höglund, as well as comments from Monica Toft and Madhav Joshi. The responsibility for the analysis, however, remains with the author.

2. Jason Quinn has calculated that the number of scholarly articles on the onset of civil wars published in the first decade of the 21st century is larger than the previous five decades combined. Unpublished presentation, Kroc Institute, September 6, 2012.

3. These calculations build on the work of Doyle and Sambanis 2000 and 2006, adding the distinction between different types of incompatibilities and this author's updating of the development in the successful cases.

4. This section draws on my work for the EU 7th Framework Program on "Just and Durable Peace by Piece," led by Associate Professors Karin Aggestam and Annika Björkdahl, Lund University, Sweden. Data collection and statistical work was done by Mihaela Racovirta of the Kroc Institute, University of Notre Dame, for which I am most grateful. <See http://cordis.europa.eu/project/rcn/88613_en.html, accessed 4/5/15. >

5. For more systematic data, see UCDP Conflict Termination Dataset, Version 2.1. 1946–2007, website: http://www.pcr.uu.se/research/ucdp/datasets/ucdp_conflict_termination_dataset/

6. For a discussion on the outcomes of the Rwandan *gacaca* proceedings for national reconciliation, see Brounéus 2007.

7. The fate of Rwanda's allies, notably Laurent Nkunda (leader of a rebel group in Eastern Congo called CNDP), who was arrested in Rwanda in 2011 remains unclear. For instance, will he be charged with systematic sexual violence against women in Eastern Congo? Nkunda's challenger, Bosco Ntaganda, is wanted by the ICC since 2008 for recruiting child soldiers. By 2012 he was clearly aligned with Rwanda as well as the government of DRC.

8. In September 2014, the president of Kenya, Uhuru Kenyatta, appeared in the ICC in The Hague, in a case dealing with the incidence of one-sided violence (massacres, mass violation of human rights) following the election outcome in Kenya in 2007. By UCDP standards, this is not an armed conflict. It was still significant that he appeared, leaving his official duties to the Vice President.

9. Flores and Nooruddin 2009 make a similar observation, however without a separation between Cold War and post–Cold War periods, which probably would have strengthened their results (cf. p 19). The authors point to another dilemma—namely that early democratization delays economic recovery, as there will be uncertainty about the long-term stability. In cases of outright victory (and often more authoritarian regimes), in other words, the country may be able to attract more outside investment and thus recover more quickly. These results also suggest the importance of international aid in the early stages after a war has ended (ibid. p 23).

10. Codebook and data were downloaded September 29, 2011, at http://belfercenter.ksg. harvard.edu/files/MTcodebook2010.pdf. Domain lately apparently changed to http:// www.bsg.ox.ac.uk/sites/blavatnik/files/documents/MTcodebook2010_0.pdf.

11. Note that Namibia in this book is not categorized as a civil war, but is found in the state formation category dealt with in chapter 4.

12. Joshi and Mason 2011 also report contrary findings. They note that Toft does not use a decay function, which would help in the methodological challenge.

13. Toft indicates that the different results could be dependent on the cases included, as, for instance, there is a difference between her dataset and that of Doyle and Sambanis (Toft 2010b: 57–58). If this is so, it requires a deeper analysis than pursued here.

14. There are benefits in comparing the two internally driven processes in Nepal and South Africa. In South Africa, the ANC rebel army was quickly integrated into the new defense forces, and the reduction of the size did not cause concern (Schoeman 2015).

Chapter 4

1. The categorization of conflicts into the two types of incompatibility, government and territory, was developed in the UCDP during the 1980s. A first peer-reviewed presentation is Wallensteen and Axell 1993. For a fuller explanation see Wallensteen 2015 and earlier editions.

2. Downloaded from UCDP Conflict database, customized report, September 2011. Note that there was one conflict with both a peace agreement and a victory, thus it is counted twice.

3. A peace agreement was signed in 2012 between one of these groups, MILF, and the government. Smaller groups objected, however.

4. Also the conflict between the government of the Philippines and MILF [Mindanao Islamic Liberation Front] in Mindanao has seen a series of agreements, many setbacks, and splinter groups. Still it was possible to arrive at a comprehensive peace agreement in 2014.

5. Partition is defined as "war outcomes that include both border adjustment and demographic changes" (Sambanis 2000: 445). One may actually ask whether the word partition is sufficiently neutral for an academic analysis as the term has a negative connotation of a territorial solution imposed from the outside.

6. A peculiar inclusion is the Republic of (South) Vietnam, which was merged with the North following the latter's victory in 1975. It was actually the undoing of a partition (done in 1954) rather than the start of partition. The war that led to the partition is not included, although it would have strengthened Sambanis's argument.

7. It is notoriously difficult to find comparable economic data on subregions of states. Thus the conclusions in the text have to build on estimates given by experts. Both Northern Ireland and Eritrea were economically more advanced than the rest of the state at the time of start of the armed struggle. For Northern Ireland also the comparison with the Republic of Ireland has been important. Thus during the 1990s and early 2000s Ireland was catching up strongly with the UK, before being severely hit by the financial crisis. Still Ireland's GNI/capita in current US dollars was higher than the United Kingdom already by 2003. Eritrea has remained somewhat ahead of Ethiopia, with a GNI/capita in current US dollars in 2009 of 429 compared to Ethiopia's 343. Remarkably, the aftermath of the inter-state war in 1998–2000 did not spark an economic crisis in either country; rather both reported growth rates. Source: http://data.un.org/CountryProfile.aspx?cr.

8. There are additional state formation conflicts, but they have been excluded as the outcomes have been unclear, agreements and their implementation difficult to document, and there was an early return to conflict. This refers to situations in Angola, Comoros, India, Mali, Niger, and Senegal. For all practical purposes, however, Table 4.1 can be regarded as a complete inventory of state formation conflicts that were active and ended in the period after 1989.

9. Doyle and Sambanis record this conflict as a success for international peacebuilding, as there was no return to war after two years (2000: 783–784). Sambanis 2000: 447 does not include this case at all, even though it would support many of his arguments on the dangers of partition.

10. Several campaigns for recognition have faltered. Somaliland has not been recognized at all, North Cyprus by one country (Turkey), Abkhazia and South Ossetia by a few (Russia and allies). This contrasts with Kosovo (some one hundred states have extended recognition) and Palestine (around 130 states) by 2014. Palestine actually achieved the special status as a "non-member observer state" with the UN in November 2012 with 138 votes in favor, 9 against and 41 abstentions. See http://www.un.org/press/en/2012/ga11317.doc.htm.

11. For a penetrating analysis, see International Crisis Group 2011.

12. A test of this leadership hypothesis is, of course, what will happen after the two men have departed. Ethiopia's leader Meles Zenawi died unexpectedly in 2012, opening up for a more liberal approach under his successor Hailemariam Desalegn, but with no immediate effect on bilateral relations.

13. An example is that Indonesia did not exploit the 2006 internal conflicts in Timor-Leste for its own agenda. Nonaction can also constitute a form of reassurance. Similarly, Timor-Leste did not allow bases for territorial opposition groups from Indonesia.

14. Objections were raised by Singapore, arguing that Timor-Leste was too poor and unstable. See *The Straits Times*, 5 May 2011.

15. See, for instance, http://www.diretube.com/ethiopian-news/eritrean-representative-thrown-out-of-igad-meeting-in-ethiopia-video_e219074e8.html.

16. The most celebrated autonomy from the 1920s is, undoubtedly, the Åland Islands, situated between Sweden and Finland, demilitarized since the mid-1850s and with self-rule to protect the right to speak Swedish since 1921. This solution was not an outcome of a war. Rather it was implemented as a preventive measure against any such possibility. It still yields insights into the durability of autonomy arrangements.

17. The agreement between Moldova and the Trans-Dniester Republic has not been implemented and is left aside here.

18. Finland actually exemplifies this as well: The Swedish-speaking minority not living on the Åland Islands has instead continuously played a constructive role in Finland's parliament and national political life.

19. Cornell (2002) finds some support for such notions in a study of Soviet-style autonomies. Commentators have also compared the Aceh solution to Papua in Indonesia, asking for similar policies (e.g., http://www.voanews.com/content/special-autonomy-works-in-indonesias-aceh-province-but-not-papua-136097288/168310.html., accessed on June 11, 2015.)

20. The Peace Accords Matrix at the Kroc Institute, University of Notre Dame, tracks the implementation is considerable detail. See https://peaceaccords.nd.edu/

21. See The Dayton Agreement, Annex 1-B Agreement on Regional Stabilization, Article IV, 3 http://peacemaker.un.org/sites/peacemaker.un.org/files/BA_951121_DaytonAgreement. pdf. Accessed on June 11, 2015. As well as on https://peaceaccords.nd.edu/accord/general-framework-agreement-peace-bosnia-and-herzegovina, accessed on June 11, 2015.

22. It was also cited as one of the motive for extending the Nobel Peace Prize to President Ahtisaari in 2008: http://www.nobelprize.org/nobel_prizes/peace/laureates/2008/press.html. Most recently accessed on June 11, 2015.

23. This was atypical, as other former Italian colonies were granted independence, notably Libya and Somalia.

24. In post–Saddam Hussein Iraq, the Kurdish leaders attempted something similar, with a Kurdish president for Iraq as a whole while at the same time elaborating on the autonomy of the Kurdish region in the north of the country. So far this seems more successful than in Sudan. An important difference is that the Kurdish leader Jalal Talabani was elected president in 2005. He was replaced with another Kurd in 2014.

25. There is an additional model for a minority to protect itself, namely holding national power. The white minorities in South Africa and Rhodesia tried this, and religiously based minorities are doing the same elsewhere, today most notably in Syria under the Assad regime. In an age building on democratic principles, media scrutiny, and mass mobilization, this is not likely to be a durable arrangement, however.

26. The following paragraphs build on the PNG Yearbooks done by Edward P. Wolfers and the works by Anthony Regan (2002, 2010), as well as on my own interviews in PNG in March 2010.

27. My own involvement in this in 1990 is recounted in Wallensteen 2011b.

28. These observations build largely on statements by participants in the workshop on village courts in Papua New Guinea, organized by PNG and international donors, Port Moresby, PNG, March 17, 2010.

29. In 1989, the mine in Bougainville generated 35% of PNG total exports, 15% of government revenue, and 8% of GNP (Batten 2010). For the 2010 budget, Bougainville was projected to internally raise $3.9 million of a total budget of $63.4 million (i.e., 6%). *Pacific Islands Report*, "Bougainville Passes $63 Million Budget" December 21, 2009, accessed at http://pidp.eastwestcenter.org/pireport/2009/December/12-22-12.htm.

Chapter 5

1. The experience of Germany and France as major powers will be dealt with in chapter 6.

2. There are many remarkable parallels in the US and FRG constitutions. Some have pointed to the role of the American political scientist and US advisor in Germany, James K Pollock, as a source for this.

3. The Nobel Peace Prize committee reminded the world of this when, somewhat belatedly, awarding the Prize to the European Union in 2012.

4. Armed conflicts not systematically covered include: Burkina Faso–Mali, Laos–Thailand, Chad–Nigeria, Chad–Libya, Cameroon–Nigeria, and Djibouti–Eritrea. Chad–Libya did result in a war, involved a large piece of territory, and was settled by international arbitration. It is worth more analysis as a case of conflict resolution, but has less to say about peacebuilding and quality peace.

5. Some sources claim that Germany also agreed to make French the first foreign language in Saarland schools. For an overview see http://www.cvce.eu/viewer/-/content/9dd5d241-4969-4a90-9685-ab4b5ecb63d0/en

6. On this settlement, see www.mundoandio.com

7. For news on boundary issues, see http://www.dur.ac.uk/ibru/news/boundary_news/.

8. The case of Yemen requires a real long-term perspective, from the border disputes in the 1970s, which also involved governance issues, to the unification in the 1990s, the emergence of al-Qaeda inspired movements in the 2000s, and the democratization movement as part of the Arab Spring of 2011. It begs the question of whether there was lasting termination, which is left outside this analysis.

9. For instance, the postwar conditions between Ethiopia and Eritrea are typically described as "fragile peace,"; see, for instance, Crisis Group 2008. *Beyond the Fragile Peace between Ethiopia and Eritrea: Averting New War.* Africa Report 141, accessed November 23, 2011 from http://www.crisisgroup.org/en/regions/africa/horn-of-africa/ethiopia-eritrea/141-beyond-the-fragile-peace-between-ethiopia-and-eritrea-averting-new-war.aspx.

10. Accessed on November 22, 2011: http://www.google.com/publicdata/explore?ds=d5bncppjof8f9_&met_y=ms_mil_xpnd_gd_zs&idim=country:ETH&dl=en&hl=en&q=ethiopia+military+expenditures#ctype=l&strail=false&bcs=d&nselm=h&met_y=ms_mil_xpnd_gd_zs&scale_y=lin&ind_y=false&rdim=country&idim=country:ETH:ERI&ifdim=country&hl=en&dl=en.

11. Accessed on November 23, 2011: http://www.un.org/en/peacekeeping/missions/past/unmee/.

12. The first case was probably the Versailles Treaty of 1919, which identified the German Emperor, William II as personally responsible, in Article 227(1). Typically this was after he had abdicated.

13. The Soviet perception was different, and more in the mode of traditional war reparations. Thus Finland had to pay compensation to the Soviet Union, and in East Germany entire industries were dismantled, shipped to the Soviet Union, and then set up again, a crude form of war reparations.

14. It is remarkable that Germany in 1953 agreed to restart to pay the post–World War I reparations once the country was reunited. This happened in 1990 and thus Germany continued to pay the final installments until October 2010. http://www.dailymail.co.uk/news/article-1315869/Germany-end-World-War-One-reparations-92-years-59m-final-payment.html and http://www.csmonitor.com/World/Europe/2010/1004/Germany-finishes-paying-WWI-reparations-ending-century-of-guilt/. Accessed on July 17, 2015.

15. The West suggested the extension of Marshall aid to Soviet-controlled countries, but in 1947 the Soviet leaders declined such support, describing aid as a vehicle for Western influence in Eastern and Central Europe.

16. Iranian Deputy Oil Minister, Mohammad Nejad-Hosseinian, *Teheran Times*, August 10, 2010. http://old.tehrantimes.com/index_View.asp?code=211165. Later the same year, the issue was also taken up by the Speaker of the Iranian Parliament, Ali Larijani. http://old.tehrantimes.com/index_View.asp?code=219904, accessed November 19, 2011.

17. The Paris Peace Agreement of 1973 actually stipulated US reparations to Vietnam. This provision was not adhered to.

18. Remarkably the actual process of reunification has not been studied. There seems to have been no deliberate policy of reconciliation. Amer 1991 dealt with the situation for ethnic Chinese in Vietnam, particularly in relation to the war in 1979. Beresford (1989) reports on the economic crisis in 1978–1979, where rice production was much lower than prior to 1975. In the period there was an exodus of people from the south ("the boat people"). The crisis led to repression as well as economic rethinking—see Beresford 1989: 5–6, 9, 112–116. Elliott 2012 points to a difference in economic policy, where the North sent out inspections to the South—see Elliott 2012: 45–46.

Chapter 6

1. Alternatives are also "planetary order" or "planetary system," but this links to environmental concerns rather than peace and security.

2. There are more than forty cases of military occupation since the end of the Second World War, almost one-third involving the victors. Some still continue, notably the Russian control over the Kuril Islands; some were ended as the Cold War ended (e.g., Soviet control over the Baltic states); see VanderZee 2012.

3. This development was more pronounced for Germany than for Austria, for instance. Austria was amalgamated with Nazi Germany in 1938, thus sometimes described as the first victim of aggression. Other accounts, however, suggest that Austrian officers willingly participated in Germany's actions during the Second World War. This was highlighted in the case of Kurt Waldheim, UN Secretary General and Austrian president, where his experiences in the Balkans were omitted from his official biography. For an account see http://www.britannica.com/EBchecked/topic/634429/Kurt-Waldheim, accessed November 17, 2012.

4. The difference between West Germany and Japan is worth a treatise of its own. For instance, the Korean War may have made the United States more in need of an ally and thus eased its pressure for deeper democratization in Japan. The lack of a strong opposition may also be part of the picture, where the conservative German governments continuously faced a credible and well-organized Social Democratic movement. Also, in the case of Germany, the US allies had more of a say, notably France, Britain, and the smaller neighbors. In Japan, the United States determined the policy on its own.

5. See, for instance, http://millercenter.org/president/events/07_18

6. There are explanations pointing to a) the burden of increased military spending (particularly weakening the Soviet economy), b) the effects of the Afghanistan war ("bleeding" the Soviet military), c) the effect of alternative thinking stemming from peace movements of the early 1980s (Soviet leader Gorbachev being interested in cheaper forms of deterrence), d) the need for reforms in the Soviet Union (Gorbachev's domestic agenda required reduced international tension) as well as e) the impact of popular culture from the West (rock and roll music and the Beatles have been mentioned).

7. The only transfer of territory is the US purchase of Alaska from Russia in 1867, which seemed a good deal for Russia at the time.

8. For the record, this was true for parts of these wars, as the United States entered World War I in April 1917, while Russia under Lenin withdrew from the war in March 1918 by making a separate deal with Germany. Also, the United States entered World War II after being attacked by Japan in December 1941, while the Soviet Union was attacked by Germany in June the same year.

9. The most symbolic expressions of this are probably the reunification of Germany in October 1990, the withdrawal of Soviet troops, and the restoration of Berlin as Germany's capital.

10. http://www.sweetliberty.org/issues/war/bushsr.htm, accessed November 14, 2012.

11. http://euobserver.com/13/27890, April 1, 2009, statement by Ambassador Dmitry Rogozin, accessed June 12, 2015.

12. It is interesting to see that the Chinese leadership under President Hu Jintao (2002–2012) constantly emphasized the need for "harmonious" development and coexistence in the region as a condition for China's economic growth. See, for instance, Foreign Minister Yang Jiechi in April 21, 2011 " Win-Win Cooperation for Harmonious Development," [http://www.fmprc.gov.cn/mfa_eng/wjdt_665385/zyjh_665391/t820486.shtml] which connects well with Hu's statements four year earlier, during his Africa tour [http://www.china.org.cn/english/infernational/197215.htm]. Similarly, the successor Xi Jinping since 2012 has repeatedly emphasized China's "path of peaceful development" (e.g., May 15, 2014, http://usa.chinadaily.com.cn/china/2014-05/16/content_17511170.htm). In most statements on this topic, an exception is made for the relations to Taiwan.

Chapter 7

1. The UN Charter became operative after it was ratified by a sufficient number of states. This happened on October 24, 1945, which became the internationally celebrated UN Day.
2. What became known as the Schuman Declaration, after the French foreign minister, was presented on May 9, 1950, which now has been declared as the founding date of the EU and is thus celebrated as the Day of Europe.
3. OIC originally meant the Organization of the Islamic Conference.
4. The expression now refers to the ASEAN official hymn, but had originally been used to describe the informal way of solving intra-ASEAN conflicts; see for instance, Askandar et al. 2002.
5. It could be argued that the assets held from the Ghadaffi regime in Libya in 2011 should not immediately have been returned to the new government. It could instead have given the international community leverage in furthering new more peace-inducing policies in the country. However, the Security Council did not use this particular opportunity to enhance postwar peace.
6. The Iraq War in 2003 saw some UN engagement, following a resolution in May 2003. However, the bombing of the UN headquarters in Baghdad on August 19, 2003 changed this. To local opposition, the difference between the UN and US was not obvious. On this see Annan 2012.
7. For an example of this heated debate see *The New York Times*, March 23, 2012: http://www.nytimes.com/2012/03/23/world/asia/rights-body-passes-measure-on-sri-lanka.html?_r=0 (accessed November 21, 2012).
8. Two documents were important in this regard. The High-Level Panel presented its report to the Secretary-General in 2004 with unusually blunt suggestions for reform and stimulated considerable discussion (United Nations 2004). It was followed by the report by the Secretary-General to the UN General Assembly in 2005, following up on a large number of the proposals.
9. Data are available from the author on request. The categories of funding used were state building, democracy building, security building, nation building and market building. The total sums dispersed included less than USD 40 million, up to 2009.
10. The source for the information on troop size is http://www.zif-berlin.org/fileadmin/uploads/analyse/dokumente/veroeffentlichungen/ZIF_World_Map_Peace_Operations_2012.pdf (accessed on October 22, 2012). The budget information comes from regular sources and concerns 2012–2013.
11. For the Schuman declaration see http://europa.eu/about-eu/basic-information/symbols/europe-day/schuman-declaration/index_en.htm, accessed on November 23, 2012.

REFERENCES

Abbink, John. 2003. "Ethiopia—Eritrea: Proxy Wars and Prospects of Peace in the Horn of Africa." *Journal of Contemporary African Studies* 21 (3): 407–425.

Ahrnens, Annette 2007. *A Quest for Legitimacy. Debating UN Security Council Rules on Terrorism and Non-Proliferation*, Lund, Sweden. Lund University Publications.

Alexander, Gerard. 2002. *The Sources of Democratic Consolidation*. Ithaca, NY: Cornell University Press.

Amer, Ramses. 1991. *The Ethnic Chinese in Vietnam and Sino-Vietnamese Relations*. Kuala Lumpur: Forum.

Amer, Ramses. 1997. *Border Conflicts between Cambodia and Vietnam*. IBRU Boundary and Security Bulletin Summer 1997, pp. 80–91. Accessed November 24, 2011. https://www.dur.ac.uk/resources/ibru/publications/full/bsb5-2_amer.pdf.

Annan, Kofi and Nader Mousavizadeh. 2012. *Interventions: A Life in War and Peace*. New York: Penguin Press.

Bagaric, Mirko, and James Allan. 2006. "The Vacuous Concept of Dignity." *Journal of Human Rights* 5 (2): 257–270.

Ballentine, Karen, and Jake Sherman. 2003. *The Political Economy of Armed Conflict: Beyond Greed and Grievance*. Boulder, CO: Lynne Rienner.

Barash, David P. 1991. *Introduction to Peace Studies*. Belmont, CA: Wadsworth.

Batten, Aaron. 2010. *Foreign Aid and the Fiscal Behaviour of the Government in Papua New Guinea*. Discussion Paper No. 114. Boroko, PNG: National Research Institute.

Beresford, Melanie. 1989. *National Unification and Economic Development in Vietnam*. New York: St. Martin's Press.

Blainey, Geoffrey. 1973. *The Causes of War*. New York: Free Press.

Boothby, Derek. 2004. "The Political Challenges of Administering Eastern Slavonia." *Global Governance* 10 (1): 37–51.

Brosché, Johan. 2009. "Sharing Power—Enabling Peace? Evaluating Sudan's Comprehensive Peace Agreement 2005." Uppsala, Sweden: Uppsala University, Mediation Support Unit, Department of Political Affairs, United Nations. Accessed May 10, 2015. http://peacemaker.un.org/resources/mediation-library/section?term_node_tid_depth=Case%20Studies.

Brounéus, Karen. 2008. *Rethinking Reconciliation*. Uppsala, Sweden: Uppsala University, Department of Peace and Conflict Research.

Brounéus, Karen. 2010. "The Trauma of Truth Telling: Effects of Witnessing in the Rwandan *Gacaca* Courts on Psychological Health." *Journal of Conflict Resolution* 54 (3): 408–437.

Bull, Hedley, and Andrew Hurrell. 2002. *The Anarchical Society: A Study of Order in World Politics*. 4th Edition. New York: Colombia University Press.

Bush, George 1991. Address before a Joint Session of the Congress on the State of the Union, January 29, 199. *The American Presidency Project.* Accessed November 29, 2014. http://www.presidency.ucsb.edu/ws/?pid=19253.

Call, Charles, ed. 2008. *Building States to Build Peace.* Boulder, CO: Lynne Rienner.

Caprioli, M. 2005. "Primed for Violence: The Role of Gender Inequality in Predicting Internal War." *International Studies Quarterly* 49 (2):161–178.

Cederman, Lars-Erik, Kristian Skrede Gleditsch, and Halvard Buhaug. 2013. *Inequality, Grievances, and Civil War.* New York: Cambridge University Press.

Chan, Steve. 2013. *Enduring Rivalries in the Asia-Pacific.* New York: Cambridge University Press.

Chernoff, Fred 2004. "The Study of Democratic Peace and Progress in International Relations." *International Studies Review* 6 (1): 49–77.

Clausewitz, Carl von [1832], 1984. *On War.* Princeton, NJ: Princeton University Press.

CMI, Crisis Management Initiative. 2012. *Aceh Peace Process Follow-Up Project.* Final Report, Helsinki. Accessed May 10, 2015. http://www.cmi.fi/images/stories/publications/reports/2012/aceh_report5_web.pdf.

Collier, Paul, et al. 2003. *Breaking the Conflict Trap: Civil War and Development Policy.* Washington, DC: World Bank.

Collier, Paul. 2007. *The Bottom Billion.* New York: Oxford University Press.

Collier, Paul. 2009. *Wars, Guns and Votes. Democracy in Dangerous Places.* New York: Harper Perennial.

Collste, Göran. 2010. "'. . . Restoring the Dignity of the Victims.': Is Global Rectificatory Justice Feasible?" *Ethics & Global Politics* 3 (2): 85–99.

Cornell, Svante E. 2002. "Autonomy and Conflict: Ethnoterritoriality and Separatism in the South Caucasus—Cases in Georgia." Report No. 61. Uppsala, Sweden: Uppsala University, Department of Peace and Conflict Research.

Curle, Adam. 1971. *Making Peace.* London: Tavistock.

Dahl, Marianne, and Björn Hoyland. 2012. "Peace on Quicksand? Challenging the Conventional Wisdom about Economic Growth and Post-Conflict Risks." *Journal of Peace Research* 49 (3): 423–429.

Deiwiks, Christa, Lars-Erik Cederman, and Kristian Skrede Gleditsch. 2012. "Inequality and Conflict in Federations." *Journal of Peace Research* 49 (2): 289–304.

DeRouen, Karl, Jr., Jenna Lea, and Peter Wallensteen. 2009. "The Duration of Civil War Peace Agreements." *Conflict Management and Peace Science* 26 (4): 367–387.

Deutsch, Karl W. et al. 1957. *Political Community and the North Atlantic Area.* Princeton, NJ: Princeton University Press.

Diamond, Larry. 2005. "Lessons from Iraq." *Journal of Democracy* 16 (1): 9–23.

Diamond, Larry, Marc Plattner, and Philip J. Costopoulos, eds. 2010. *Debates on Democratization.* Baltimore, MD: Johns Hopkins University Press.

Diehl, Paul F., and Gary Goertz. 2001. *War and Peace in International Rivalry.* Ann Arbor, MI: University of Michigan Press.

Dimitrova, Anna. 2013. "The Politics of Recognition in International Conflicts." *Journal of International Studies* 41 (3): 663–668.

Doyle, Michael W., and Nicholas Sambanis. 2000. "International Peacebuilding: A Theoretical and Quantitative Analysis." *American Political Science Review* 94 (4): 779–801.

Doyle, Michael W., and Nicholas Sambanis. 2006. *Making War and Building Peace: United Nations Peace Operations.* Princeton, NJ: Princeton University Press.

Easterly, William. 2006. *The White Man's Burden: Why the West's Efforts to Aid the Rest Have Done So Much Ill and So Little Good.* Oxford, UK: Oxford University Press.

Elliott, David W. 2012. *Changing Worlds: Vietnam's Transition from Cold War to Globalization.* New York: Oxford University Press.

Eriksson, Mikael. 2010. *Supporting Democracy in Africa: African Union's Use of Targeted Sanctions to Deal with Unconstitutional Changes of Government.* Stockholm, Sweden: Swedish Defence Research Agency (FOI).

Falk, Richard A., and Saul H. Mendlovitz. 1966. *The Strategy of World Order*. Vol. 1, *Toward a Theory of War Prevention*. New York: World Law Fund.

Fearon, James D. 1995. "Rationalist Explanations for War." *International Organization* 49 (3): 379–414.

Fearon, James D. 2004. "Why Do Some Civil Wars Last So Much Longer Than Others?" *Journal of Peace Research* 41(3): 275–301.

Flores, Thomas Edward, and Irfan Nooruddin. 2009. "Democracy under the Gun. Understanding Postconflict Economic Recovery." *Journal of Conflict Resolution* 53 (1). 3–29.

Fortna, Virginia Page. 2004. "Does Peacekeeping Keep Peace? International Intervention and the Duration of Peace after Civil War." *International Studies Quarterly* 48 (2): 269–292.

Fox, Sean, and Kristian Hoelscher. 2012. "Political Order, Development and Social Violence." *Journal of Peace Research* 49 (3): 431–444.

Franck, Tom M. 2002. *Recourse to Force: State Action Against Threats and Armed Attacks*. Cambridge, UK: Cambridge University Press.

Frost, Lillian 2010. "The Iraq-Kuwait Border Issue: A Step In The Right Direction Or More Empty Rhetoric?" *Spotlight*. 9/13/2010. Washington, DC: The Stimson Center. Accessed November 20, 2011. http://www.stimson.org/spotlight/the-iraq-kuwait-border-issue-a-step-in-the-right-direction-or-more-empty-rhetoric-/.

Galtung, Johan. 1976. "Three Approaches to Peace: Peacekeeping, Peacemaking and Peacebuilding."" In *Peace, War and Defence: Essays in Peace Research*, Volume 2, by Johan Galtung, pp. 282–304. Copenhagen: Ejlers.

Gawerc, Michell I. 2006. "Peace-Building: Theoretical and Concrete Perspectives." *Peace & Change* 31 (4): 435–478.

Geller, Daniel S., and J. David Singer. 1998. *Nations at War: A Scientific Study of International Conflict*. Cambridge: Cambridge University Press.

Gent, Stephen E. 2011. "Relative Rebel Strength and Power Sharing in Intrastate Conflicts." *International Interactions* 37 (2): 215–228.

Gibler, Douglas M. 2007. "Bordering on Peace: Democracy, Territorial Issues, and Conflict." *International Studies Quarterly* 51 (3): 509–532.

Gibler, Douglas M. 2012. *The Territorial Peace: Borders, State Development and International Conflict*. Cambridge, MA: Cambridge University Press.

Gilliam, Michael, and Stephen J. Stedman. 2003. "Where Do the Peacekeepers Go?" *International Studies Review* 5 (4): 37–54.

Gizelis, Theodora-Ismene. 2009. "Gender Empowerment and United Nations Peacebuilding." *Journal of Peace Research* 46 (4): 505–523.

Gleditsch, Nils Petter. 2008. "The Liberal Moment Fifteen Years On." *International Studies Quarterly* 52 (4): 691–712.

Goldstein, Joshua S., and Jon C. Pevehouse. 2013. *International Relations*. 10th Edition. Boulder, CO: Pearson.

Gurr, Ted R. 2000a. *Peoples versus States: Minorities at Risk in the New Century*. Washington, DC: United States Institute of Peace Press.

Gurr, Ted. R. 2000b. "Ethnic Warfare on the Wane." *Foreign Affairs* 79 (3): 52–64.

Gurses, Mehmet, and T. David Mason. 2008. "Democracy out of Anarchy: The Prospects for Post–Civil-War Democracy." *Social Science Quarterly* 89 (2): 315–336.

Gurses, Mehmet, and Nicolas Rost. 2013. "Sustaining the Peace after Ethnic Civil Wars." *Conflict Management and Peace Science* 30 (5):469–491.

Hadenius, Axel, ed. 1997. *Democracy's Victory and Crisis*. Cambridge: Cambridge University Press.

Harbom, Lotta, Stina Högbladh, and Peter Wallensteen. 2006. "Armed Conflict and Peace Agreements." *Journal of Peace Research* 43 (5): 617–631.

Harbom, Lotta, and Peter Wallensteen 2005. "Armed Conflict and Its International Dimensions 1946–2004." *Journal of Peace Research* 42 (5): 623–635.

Harzell, Caroline A. 2009. "Settling Civil Wars: Armed Opponents' Fate and the Duration of the Peace." *Conflict Management and Peace Science* 26 (4): 347–365.

Harzell, Caroline, Matthew Hoddie, and Donald Rothchild. 2001. "Stabilizing the Peace after Civil War." *International Organization* 55 (1): 183–208.

Hayner, Priscilla B. 2011. *Unspeakable Truths: Transitional Justice and the Challenge of Truth Commissions*. 2nd Edition. New York: Routledge.

Hegre, Håvard, Tanja Ellingsen, Scott Gates, and Nils Petter Gleditsch. 2001. "Toward a Democratic Civil Peace? Democracy, Political Change, and Civil War, 1816–1992." *American Political Science Review* 95 (1): 33–48.

Herz, Monica, and João Pontes Nogueira. 2002. *Ecuador vs. Peru: Peacemaking Amid Rivalry*. International Peace Academy Occasional Paper Series. Boulder, CO: Lynne Rienner.

Hettne, Björn. 1999. "Globalization and the New Regionalism: The Second Great Transformation." In *Globalism and the New Regionalism*, by Björn Hettne, Andras Inotai, and Osvaldo Sunkel, pp 1–25. New York: St. Martin's.

Hicks, Donna. 2011. *Dignity: The Essential Role It Plays in Resolving Conflict*. Foreword by Archbishop Desmond Tutu. New Haven, CT: Yale University Press.

Hobbes, Thomas [1651], 1991. *Leviathan*. Cambridge, UK: Cambridge University Press.

Hoddie, Matthew, and Caroline Hartzell. 2005 "Signals of Reconciliation: Institution-Building and the Resolution of Civil Wars." *International Studies Review* 7 (1): 21–40.

Högbladh, Stina. 2006. "Finding a Peace That Will Last—Examining Peace Processes and Peace Agreements." Paper presented at the annual ISA Convention, San Diego, California, March 22–25.

Högbladh, Stina. 2012. "Peace Agreements 1975–2011—Updating the UCDP Peace Agreement Dataset." In *States in Armed Conflict 2011*, edited by Therése Pettersson and Lotta Themnér, pp 39–56. Research Report 99. Uppsala, Sweden: Uppsala University, Department of Peace and Conflict Research.

Höglund, Kristine. 2008. *Peace Negotiations in the Shadow of Violence*. Leiden, The Netherlands: Martinus Nijhoff.

Höglund, Kristine, and Camilla Orjuela. 2011. "Winning the Peace: Conflict Prevention after a Victor's Peace in Sri Lanka." *Contemporary Social Science* 6 (1): 19–37.

Huisman, Pieter, Joost de Jong, and Koos Wieriks. 2000. "Transboundary Cooperation in Shared River Basins: Experiences from the Rhine, Meuse, and North Sea." *Water Policy* 2 (1–2): 83–97.

Ikenberry, G. John. 2001. *After Victory: Institutions, Strategic Restraint, and the Rebuilding of Order after Major War*. Princeton, NJ: Princeton University Press.

International Crisis Group. "Reconciliation in Sri Lanka: Harder than Ever." Asia Report No 209. 18 July 2011. Accessed May 12, 2015. http://www.crisisgroup.org/~/media/Files/asia/south-asia/sri-lanka/209%20Reconciliation%20in%20Sri%20Lanka%20-%20Harder%20than%20Ever.pdf

Jacobson, Nora. 2009. A Taxonomy of Dignity. *BMC International Health and Human Rights* 9 (3). doi:10.1186/1472-1698X-9-3.

Jacquin-Berdal, Dominique. 2005. "Introduction." In *Unfinished Business: Eritrea and Ethiopia at War*, edited by Dominique Jacquin-Berdal and Martin Plaut, ix–xxi. Lawrenceville, NJ: Red Sea Press.

Jarstad, Anna, and Desiree Nilsson. 2008. "From Words to Deeds: The Implementation of Power-Sharing Pacts in Peace Accords." *Conflict Management and Peace Science* 25 (3): 206–223.

Johansson, Emma, Joakim Kreutz, Peter Wallensteen, Christian Altpeter, Sara Lindberg, Mathilda Lindgren, and Ausra Padskocimaite. 2010. "A New Start for EU Peacemaking? Past Record and Future Potential." UCDP Paper No 7. Uppsala, Sweden: Uppsala University, Uppsala Conflict Data Program, Accessed May 12, 2015. http://www.pcr.uu.se/digitalAssets/21/21951_UCDP_paper_7.pdf.

Joshi, Madhav, and John Darby. 2013. "Introducing the Peace Accords Matrix (PAM): A Database of Comprehensive Peace Agreements and Their Implementation, 1989–2007." *Peacebuilding* 1 (2): 256–274.

Joshi, Madhav, John Darby, and Peter Wallensteen, eds. 2015. *After the End of Civil War: Finding the Dimensions of Quality Peace* (forthcoming).

Joshi, Madhav, and T. David Mason. 2011. "Civil War Settlements, Size of Governing Coalition and Durability of Peace in Post-Civil War States." *International Interactions* 37 (4): 388–413.

Joshi, Madhav, Sung Yong Lee, and Roger Mac Ginty. 2014. "Just How Liberal is the Liberal Peace?" *International Peacekeeping* 21(3): 364–389.

Keating, Tom, and W. Andy Knight, eds. 2004. *Building Sustainable Peace*. Tokyo: United Nations University Press.

Kelsen, Hans. 1948. "Collective Security and Collective Self-Defense Under the Charter of the United Nations." *The American Journal of International Law* 42 (4): 783–796.

Keynes, John Maynard. 1920. *The Economic Consequences of the Peace*. New York: Harcourt Brace Howe. Also available online: accessed November 17, 2011. http://www.gutenberg.org/files/15776/15776-h/15776-h.htm.

Kissinger, Henry. 2014. *World Order*. New York: Penguin.

Kostić, Roland. 2007. "Ambivalent Peace: External Peacebuilding, Threatened Identity and Reconciliation in Bosnia and Herzegovina." Department of Peace and Conflict Research, Uppsala University.

Krauthammer, Charles. 1990. "The Unipolar Moment." *Foreign Affairs* 70 (1): 23–33.

Kreutz, Joakim. 2010. "How and When Armed Conflicts End: Introducing the UCDP Conflict Termination Dataset." *Journal of Peace Research* 47 (2): 243–250.

Last, Alexander. 2005. "A Very Personal War: Eritrea Ethiopia 1998–2000." In *Unfinished Business: Eritrea and Ethiopia at War*, edited by Dominique Jacquin-Berdal and Martin Plaut, 57–86. Lawrenceville, NJ: Red Sea Press.

Lata, Leenco. 2003. "The Ethiopia-Eritrea War." *Review of African Political Economy* 30 (97): 369–388.

Lederach, John Paul. 1997. *Building Peace: Sustainable Reconciliation in Divided Societies*. Washington, DC: United States Institute of Peace Press.

Lederach, John Paul, and R. Scott Appleby. 2010. "Strategic Peacebuilding: An Overview." In *Strategies of Peace. Transforming Conflict in a Violent World*, edited by Daniel Philpott and Gerard F. Powers, 19–44. New York: Oxford University Press.

Lind, Jennifer. 2009. "Apologies in International Politics." *Security Studies* 18 (3): 517–556.

Lindemann, Thomas. 2011. "Peace Through Recognition: An Interactionist Interpretation of International Crises." *International Political Sociology* 5 (1): 68–86.

Long, William J, and Peter Brecke. 2003. *War and Reconciliation: Reason and Emotion in Conflict Resolution*. Cambridge, MA: MIT Press.

Lund, Michael S. 1996. *Preventing Violent Conflicts: A Strategy for Preventive Diplomacy*. Washington, DC: United States Institute of Peace Press.

Mac Ginty, Roger. 2011. *International Peacebuilding and Local Resistance: Hybrid Forms of Peace*. New York: Palgrave MacMillan.

MacMillan, Margaret. 2003. *Paris 1919: Six Months That Changed The World*. New York: Random House.

Mansfield, Edward D., and Jack L. Snyder. 2005. *Electing to Fight: Why Emerging Democracies Go To War*. Cambridge, MA: MIT Press.

Maoz, Zeev, and Bruce M. Russett. 1993. "Normative and Structural Causes of Democratic Peace, 1946–1986." *American Political Science Review* 87 (3): 624–638.

Martins, Vasco. 2011. "The Côte d'Ivoire Crisis in Retrospect." *Portuguese Journal of International Affairs* 5 (Spring/Summer): 72–84.

Matheson, Michael J. 2009. "Eritrea-Ethiopia Claims Commission: Damage Awards." ASIL Insights 13:13. Washington, DC: American Society of International Law. Accessed November 20, 2011. http://www.asil.org/insights090904.cfm.

McGrath, John J. 2006. *Boots on the Ground: Troop Density in Contingency Operations.* Global War on Terrorism Occasional Paper 16. Fort Leavenworth, Kansas: Combat Studies Institute. Accessed October 7, 2012: http://www.cgsc.edu/carl/download/csipubs/mcgrath_boots.pdf

Melander, Erik. 2005a. "Gender Equality and Intrastate Armed Conflict." *International Studies Quarterly* 49 (4): 695–714.

Melander, Erik. 2005b. "Political Gender Equality and State Human Rights Abuse." *Journal of Peace Research* 42 (2): 149–166.

Melander, Erik 2010. *Amnesty, Peace and Human Development in the Aftermath of Civil War.* Paper presented at the 2010 annual convention of the International Studies Association, February 17–20, New Orleans, LA.

Mendeloff, David 2004. "Truth-Seeking, Truth-Telling and Postconflict Peacebuilding: Curb the Enthusiasm?" *International Studies Review* 6 (3): 355–380.

Merikallio, Katri, 2008. *Making Peace: Ahtisaari and Aceh.* Helsinki, Finland: WSOY.

Metternich, Nils W. and Julian Wucherpfennig. 2011. "Institutional Change We Can Believe in: Democratization, Commitment and Civil War Recurrence." Paper for the Security, Peace and Conflict Workshop, Duke University, Durham, NC, March 23, 2011. Accessed September 2011. http://web.duke.edu/~gelpi/nmjw_spc.pdf.

Mitchell, Sara McLaughlin, and Brandon Prins. 1999. "Beyond Territorial Contiguity: Issues at Stake in Democratic Militarized Interstate Disputes." *International Studies Quarterly* 43 (1): 169–183.

Mitrany, David. 1948. "The Functional Approach to World Organization." *International Affairs* 24 (3): 350–363.

Morgan, Patrick M. 1997. "Regional Security Complexes and Regional Orders." In *Regional Orders: Building Security in a New World,* edited by David A. Lake and Patrick M. Morgan, 20–45. University Park, PA: Pennsylvania State University Press.

Nilsson, Marcus. 2012. "Reaping What Was Sown: Conflict Outcome and Post–Civil War Democratization." *Cooperation and Conflict* 47 (3): 350–367.

Öberg, Magnus, and Erik Melander. 2009. "Autocracy, Bureaucracy and Civil War." Paper presented at the 5th ECPR General Conference, Potsdam, September 10–12, 2009.

Olsson, Louise. 2009. *Gender Equality and United Nations Peace Operations in Timor-Leste.* Leiden, The Netherlands: Martinus Nijhoff.

Olsson, Louise. 2011. "Security Equality: The Protection of Men and Women by Peace Operations." Paper presented at the annual convention of the International Studies Association, Montreal, Canada, March 16, 2011.

Omitoogun, Wuyi. 2003. *Military Expenditure Data in Africa: A Survey of Cameroon, Ethiopia, Ghana, Kenya, Nigeria, and Uganda.* SIPRI Research Report No. 17. Oxford, UK: Oxford University Press. Accessed May 13, 2015. http://books.sipri.org/files/RR/SIPRIRR17.pdf

Paris, Roland 2004. *At War's End: Building Peace after Civil Conflict.* Cambridge, MA: Cambridge University Press.

Paris, Roland. 2010. "Saving Liberal Peacebuilding." *Review of International Studies* 36 (2) 337–365.

Peace Accords Matrix. Kroc Institute for International Peace Studies, University of Notre Dame. Accessed May 12, 2015. https://peaceaccords.nd.edu/.

Philpott, Catherine R., and Matthew J. Hornsey. 2011. "Memory for Intergroup Apologies and its Relationship with Forgiveness." *European Journal of Social Psychology* 41 (1): 96–106.

Pierson, Paul. 2000. "Increasing Returns, Path Dependence and The Study of Politics." *American Political Science Review* 94 (2): 251–268.

Plaut, Martin. 2005. "Background to War: From Friends to Foes." In *Unfinished Business: Eritrea and Ethiopia at War,* edited by Dominique Jacquin-Berdal and Martin Plaut, 1–22. Lawrenceville, NJ: The Red Sea Press.

Polachek, Solomon W., and Daria Sevastianova. 2012. "Does Conflict Disrupt Growth? Evidence of the Relationship Between Political Instability and National Economic Performance." *The Journal of International Trade and Economic Development*. 21 (3): 361–388.

Pridham, Geoffrey, ed. 1990. *Securing Democracy: Political Parties and Democratic Consolidation in Southern Europe*. London: Taylor and Francis.

Regan, Anthony J. 2002. "The Bougainville Political Settlement and the Prospects for Sustainable Peace." *Pacific Economic Bulletin* 17 (1): 114–129.

Regan, Anthony J. 2010. *Light Intervention: Lessons from Bougainville*. Washington, DC.: US Institute of Peace Press.

Regan, Patrick M. 2014. "Bringing Peace Back In: Presidential Address to the Peace Science Society, 2013." *Conflict Management and Peace Science* 31(4): 345–356.

Richmond, Oliver P. 2006. "The Problem of Peace: Understanding the 'Liberal Peace.'" *Conflict, Security, and Development* 6 (3): 291–314.

Richmond, Oliver. 2009. "A Post-Liberal Peace: Eirenism and the Everyday." *Review of International Studies* 35 (3): 557–580.

Rothstein, Bo. 2011. *The Quality of Government: Corruption, Social Trust, and Inequality in International Perspective*. Chicago: The University of Chicago Press.

Russett, Bruce M. 1993. *Grasping the Democratic Peace: Principles for a Post–Cold War World*. Princeton, NJ: Princeton University Press.

Russett, Bruce, and John R. Oneal. 2001. *Triangulating Peace: Democracy, Interdependence, and International Organizations*. The Norton Series in World Politics. New York: W.W. Norton.

Sambanis, Nicholas. 2000. "Partition as a Solution to Ethnic War: An Empirical Critique of the Theoretical Literature." *World Politics* 52 (4): 437–483.

Sambanis, Nicholas. 2010. "How Strategic is UN Peacebuilding?" In *Strategies of Peace: Transforming Conflict in a Violent World*, edited by Daniel Philpott and Gerard F. Powers, 141–168. New York: Oxford University Press.

Sambanis, Nicholas, and Branko Milanovic. 2014. "Explaining Regional Autonomy Differences in Decentralized Countries." *Comparative Political Studies* 47 (13):1830–1855.

Sarkees, Meredith Reid, and Frank Wayman. 2010. *Resort to War: 1816–2007*. Washington, DC: CQ Press.

Schachter, Oscar. 1983. "Human Dignity as a Normative Concept." *American Journal of International Law* 77 (4): 848–854.

Schahczenski, Jeff. 1991. "Explaining Relative Peace: Major Power Order, 1816–1976." *Journal of Peace Research* 28 (3): 295–309.

Schoeman, Maxi. 2015. "How Noble the Impulse, How Harsh the Realities? Twenty Years of South African Peacemaking and Peacebuilding in Africa." *Current Affairs* 2015. Uppsala: Nordiska Afrikainstitutet (forthcoming).

Schori, Pierre. 2015. "ECOWAS and the AU in Cooperation with the UN: The Case of Côte d'Ivoire." In *Regional Organizations and Peacemaking: Challengers to the UN?* edited by Peter Wallensteen and Anders Bjurner, 160–178. London: Routledge.

Senese, Paul D., and John A. Vasquez. 2008. *The Steps to War: An Empirical Study*. Princeton, NJ: Princeton University Press.

Sinclair, Timothy J. 1996. "Beyond International Relations Theory: Robert W. Cox and Approaches to World Order." In *Approaches to World Order*, edited by Robert W. Cox and Timothy Sinclair, 3–18. Cambridge, UK: Cambridge University Press.

SIPRI (Stockholm International Peace Research Institute) *Yearbook 2012*. Stockholm and Oxford: Oxford University Press.

Slaughter, Anne-Marie. 2004. *A New World Order*. Princeton, NJ: Princeton University Press.

Snyder, Jack L. 2000. *From Voting to Violence: Democratization and Nationalist Conflict*. New York: Norton.

Staub, Ervin. 2011. *Overcoming Evil: Genocide, Violent Conflict and Terrorism*. Oxford: Oxford University Press.

Staub, Ervin. 2013. "A World Without Genocide: Prevention, Reconciliation and the Creation of Peaceful Societies." *Journal of Social Issues* 69 (1): 180–199.

Stedman, Stephen J. 1997. "Spoiler Problems in Peace Processes." *International Security* 22 (2): 5–53.

Stedman, Stephen J. 1998. "Conflict Prevention as Strategic Interaction: The Spoiler Problem and the Case of Rwanda," In *Preventing Violent Conflicts: A Strategy for Preventive Diplomacy*, edited by Peter Wallensteen, 67–86. Uppsala University: Department of Peace and Conflict Research.

Stewart, Frances. 2002. *Horizontal Inequalities: A Neglected Dimension of Development*. Oxford: Centre for Research on Inequality, Human Security and Ethnicity, University of Oxford.

Stoltenberg, Thorvald. 2001. *Det handler om mennesker*. Oslo, Norway: Gyldendal.

Styan, David. 2005. "Twisting Ethio-Eritrean Economic Ties." In *Unfinished Business: Eritrea and Ethiopia at War*, edited by Dominique Jacquin-Berdal and Martin Plaut, 177–200. Lawrenceville, NJ: The Red Sea Press.

Suksi, Markku. 2013. "Explaining the Robustness and Longevity of the Åland Example in Comparison with Other Autonomy Solutions." *International Journal on Minority and Group Rights* 20 (1): 51–66.

Svensson, Isak, and Peter Wallensteen. 2010. *The Go-Between: Jan Eliasson and the Styles of Mediation*. Washington, DC: United States Institute of Peace Press.

Themnér, Lotta, and Peter Wallensteen. 2014. "Armed Conflicts, 1946–2013." *Journal of Peace Research* 51 (4): 541–554.

Toft, Monica. 2010a. "Ending Civil Wars: A Case for Rebel Victory?" *International Security* 34 (4): 7–36.

Toft, Monica. 2010b. *Securing the Peace: The Durable Settlement of Civil Wars*. Princeton, NJ: Princeton University Press.

Toft, Monica. MT Codebook. Accessed September 29, 2011. http://belfercenter.ksg.harvard.edu/files/.

Tønnesson, Stein. 2011. "The East Asian Peace Since 1979: How Deep? How Can It Be Explained?" Upppsala Universit: Department of Peace and Conflict Research. http://www.pcr.uu.se/research/eap/About_us/ Accessed on June 12, 2015.

Tønnesson, Stein, Erik Melander, Elin Bjarnegård, Isak Svensson, and Susanne Schaftenaar 2013. "The Fragile Peace in East and South East Asia." *SIPRI Yearbook 2013: Armaments, Disarmament and International Security*. Oxford University Press, 28–40.

Travlos, Konstantinos. 2013. "From Warmongers to Peace Builders. Major Power Managerial Coordination and the Transformation of International Relations, 1715–2001." Ph.D. diss., University of Illinois.

UN Secretary-General. 1992. "An Agenda for Peace: Preventive Diplomacy, Peacemaking and Peace-keeping." A/47/277–S/24111 .17 June 1992. Accessed May 13, 2015. http://unrol.org/files/A_47_277.pdf

UN Secretary-General 1995. "Supplement to An Agenda for Peace: Position Paper of the Secretary-General on the Occasion of the Fiftieth Anniversary of the United Nations." A/50/60–S/1995/1. 3 January 1995. Accessed May 13, 2015. http://www.un.org/documents/ga/docs/50/plenary/a50-60.htm.

United Nations 2004. "The Secretary-General's High-Level Panel Report on Threats, Challenges and Change, A More Secure World: Our Shared Responsibility." New York: United Nations. Accessed May 13, 2015. http://unrol.org/doc.aspx?n=gaA.59.565_En.pdf.

United Nations. Security Council, Resolution 598. 20 July 1987. Accessed May 13, 2015. http://www.parstimes.com/history/un_598.html.

Uppsala Conflict Data Program. Department of Peace and Conflict Research. Conflict Encyclopedia. www.ucdp.uu.se.

Valeriano, Brandon, and Kwang Theo. 2009. "The Tragedy of Offensive Realism: Testing Aggressive Power Politics Models." *International Interactions* 35 (2): 179–206.

VanderZee, Lenore 2012. "Understanding Occupation: Introducing a New Data Set of Military Occupations." Paper presented at the annual convention of the International Studies Association Meeting, San Diego, CA, April 1–4, 2012.

Vasquez, John A. 1995. "Why Do Neighbors Fight? Proximity, Interaction and Territoriality." *Journal of Peace Research* 32 (3): 277–293.

Vasquez, John A., ed. 2012. *What Do We Know about War?* 2nd Edition. Lanham, MD: Rowman and Littlefield.

Vasquez, John A., and Marie T. Henehan. 2001. "Territorial Disputes and the Probability of War, 1816–1992." *Journal of Peace Research* 38 (2): 123–138.

Väyrynen, Raimo. 2003. "Regionalism: Old and New." *International Studies Review* 5(1): 25–51.

Wallensteen, Peter. 1981. "Incompatibility, Confrontation and War: Four Models and Three Historical Systems, 1816–1976." *Journal of Peace Research*, Vol. 18 (1): 57–90.[Reprinted Wallensteen 2011a: *Peace Research: Theory and Practice,* 33–73. London: Routledge]

Wallensteen, Peter 1984. "Universalism vs. Particularism. On the Limits of Major Power Order." *Journal of Peace Research* 21 (3): 243–257. [Reprinted Wallensteen. 2011a: *Peace Research: Theory and Practice,* 74–92. London: Routledge.]

Wallensteen, Peter. 2007 [2002]. *Understanding Conflict Resolution: War, Peace and the Global System.* London: SAGE..

Wallensteen, Peter. 2008a. "Global Governance and the Future of United Nations," In *Human Values and Global Governance: Studies in Development, Security and Culture,* Vol. 2., edited by Björn Hettne, 198–219. New York: Palgrave-Macmillan.

Wallensteen, Peter. 2008b. "International Response to Crises of Democratization in War-Torn Societies." In *From War to Democracy: Dilemmas of Peacebuilding,* edited by Anna K. Jarstad and Timothy D. Sisk, 213–238. Cambridge, UK: Cambridge University Press.

Wallensteen, Peter 2010. "Strategic Peacebuilding: Concepts and Challenges." In *Strategies of Peace: Transforming Conflict in a Violent World,* edited by Daniel Philpott and Gerard F. Powers, 45–64. New York: Oxford University Press.

Wallensteen, Peter. 2011a. *Peace Research: Theory and Practice.* London: Routledge.

Wallensteen, Peter. 2011b. "The Strengths and Limits of Academic Diplomacy: The Case of Bougainville." In *Peace Research: Theory and Practice,* by Peter Wallensteen, chapter 17. London: Routledge.

Wallensteen, Peter. 2012. "Future Directions in the Scientific Study of Peace and War." In *What Do We Know about War?* edited by John A Vasquez, 257–270. 2nd Edition. Lanham, MD: Rowman and Littlefield.

Wallensteen, Peter. 2015. *Understanding Conflict Resolution: War, Peace and the Global System.* Fourth edition. London: SAGE.

Wallensteen, Peter, and Karin Axell. 1993. "Armed Conflict at the End of the Cold War, 1989–1992." *Journal of Peace Research* 30 (3): 331–346.

Wallensteen, Peter, and Anders Bjurner, eds. 2015. *Regional Organizations and Peacemaking: Challengers to the UN?* New York: Routledge.

Wallensteen, Peter, Karl DeRouen, Jr., Jacob Bercovitch, and Frida Möller. 2009. "Democracy and Mediation in Territorial Civil Wars in Southeast Asia and the South Pacific." *Asia Europe Journal* 7 (2): 241–264.

Wallensteen, Peter, and Helena Grusell. 2012. "Targeting the Right Targets? The UN Use of Individual Sanctions." *Global Governance* 18 (2): 207–230.

Wallensteen, Peter, and Patrik Johansson. 2004. "Security Council Decisions in Perspective." In *The UN Security Council. From the Cold War to the 21st Century,* edited by David Malone, 17–33. Boulder, CO: Lynne Rienner.

Wallensteen, Peter, and Patrik Johansson. 2014. The United Nations Security Council in State-Based Armed Conflicts, 2003–2012. *SIPRI Yearbook 2014: Armaments, Disarmament and International Security*, 56–69. New York: Oxford University Press.

Wallensteen, Peter and Patrik Johansson. 2015. "The UN Security Council: Decisions and Actions." In *The UN Security Council in the 21st Century*, edited by Sebastian von Einsiedel, David M. Malone, Bruno Stagno Ugarte. Boulder, CO: Lynne Rienner.

Wallensteen, Peter, Kjell-Åke Nordquist, Björn Hagelin, and Erik Melander. 1994. *Toward a Security Community in the Baltic Region: Patterns of Peace and Conflict*. 1995 edition. Updated 2001 by Claes Levinsson and Witold Maciejewski. Uppsala, Sweden: Baltic University.

Wallensteen, Peter and Margareta Sollenberg. 1998. "Armed Conflict and Regional Conflict Complexes, 1989–1997," *Journal of Peace Research* 35 (5): 593–606.

Walter, Barbara F. 2010. "Conflict Relapse and the Sustainability of Post-Conflict Peace." Working Paper. World Bank Development Report. Accessed September 2011. documents. worldbank.org/curated/en/2010/09/14265914/conflict-relapse-sustainability-post-conflict-peace.

Weaver, Carol. 2011. "Black Sea Regional Security: Present Multipolarity and Future Possibilities." *European Security* 20 (1): 1–19.

Wehr, Paul, and John Paul Lederach. 1991. "Mediating Conflict in Central America." *Journal of Peace Research* 28 (1): 85–98.

Weller, Marc, and Stefan Wolff, eds. 2005. *Autonomy, Self-Governance, and Conflict Resolution: Innovative Approaches to Institutional Design in Divided Societies*. New York: Routledge.

Wennman, Achim, and Jana Krause. 2009. *Resource Wealth, Autonomy and Peace in Aceh*. Centre on Conflict, Development and Peacebuilding. CCDP Working Paper. Geneva, Switzerland: The Graduate Institute of International and Development Studies.

Wolfers, Edward P. 2006. "Bougainville Autonomy—Implications for Governance and Decentralisation." State, Society, and Governance in Melanesia. Public Policy in Papua New Guinea—Discussion Paper Series 2006 No 5. Canberra, Australia: Research School of Pacific and Asian Studies, Australian National University. Accessed May 13, 2015. http://ips.cap.anu.edu.au/sites/default/files/wolfers_web_NRI_05_2006.pdf.

Wolfers, Edward P. 2007. "Bougainville: Meeting the Challenge of Peacebuilding and Autonomy." In B. Gomez (ed) *Papua New Guinea Yearbook 2007*. Port Moresby: The National and Cassowary Books, 98–113.

Wolff, Stefan. 2013. "Conflict Management in Divided Societies: The Many Uses of Territorial Self-Governance." *International Journal on Minority and Group Rights* 20(1): 27–50.

"World Bank Development Report 2011: Overview." In *World Bank Development Report 2011: Conflict, Security and Development*, 1–52. Washington, DC: World Bank. Also available online http://documents.worldbank.org/curated/en/2011/01/14281992/world-development-report-2011-conflict-security-development-overview.

World Summit Outcome 2005. United Nations General Assembly, 14–16 September 2005. Accessed May 13, 2005. http://www.un.org/ga/59/hl60_plenarymeeting.html.

INDEX

Abbink, John, 121

Abkhazia conflict (Georgia): international community's refusal to recognize rebels in, 116, 119; Russia's support for rebels in, 49, 116, 136; as a state formation conflict, 114, 116

absence of war: between Cold War superpowers, 173; in formerly war-torn countries, 16; negative peace defined as, 3, 16, 141

Aceh region (Indonesia): autonomy arrangements in, 103, 114, 124, 127, 129–30, 135, 137; economic rights in, 129; elections in, 129; Indonesian government institutions in, 135; peace agreement and disarmament in, 127–28; quality peace in, 129–30; South Asia tsunami (2004) and, 129; traditional sultanate in, 127

Adenauer, Konrad (Federal Republic of Germany), 140–41

Afghanistan: al-Qaeda in, 22, 184; China and, 18; civil war in, 77–78, 98, 144, 151, 163; peacebuilding in, 99, 151; regional security and, 8, 121, 154; Russia and, 78, 181, 184; Soviet Union and, 21, 143–44, 150–52, 155, 159, 202; The Taliban and, 22, 77–79, 163; terrorism and, 8; United Nations and, 77, 99; United States and, 18, 22, 78, 181, 184; victory consolidation in, 22

Africa. *See also specific countries and regions*: Cold War in, 177; decolonization in, 176; diaspora communities from, 18; ethnic conflict in, 1; France and, 188; global systems and, 168; Great Britain and, 188; international market forces entering, 24; major powers and, 195–96; Soviet withdrawals from, 185; United Nations' post-conflict roles in, 195–96, 200; world order and, 168

African National Congress (ANC, South African political party), 89

African Union (AU), 189, 191

An Agenda for Peace (Boutros-Ghali report to UN Security Council, 1992), 11–12

aggression: arms purchases as intended deterrent against, 52; collective security against, 201–2; recognition of, 131, 156

agreements. *See* peace agreements

Ahtisaari, Martii (Finland), 39, 128–29

aid and assistance: civil war and, 52, 81, 90; critiques of, 27; Marshall Plan and, 157, 159; peace agreements and, 90; peacebuilding and, 47, 81; repression and, 52; scholarly trends regarding, 34; South Asia tsunami (2004) and, 129

Åland Islands (Finland), 126, 215n16

Albanians, 1, 124

Algeria, 98, 176

al-Qaeda: in Afghanistan, 22, 184; bin Laden's death and, 78; global threat from, 163; international campaign against, 184; United Nations and, 199

Amin, Idi (Uganda), 144

amnesty, 50, 65, 91

Angola: Cabinda separatist region in, 43, 109; civil wars in, 16, 21, 41, 43–44, 98; Cold War and, 21; constitution in, 42; corruption in, 42, 44; decolonization and liberation movement in, 176; economic growth in, 44; elections in, 41–44; military spending in, 43; oil in, 44; peace agreement in, 42–43; peacebuilding in, 38, 41–45, 62, 99; peacekeeping in, 41–42; peacemaking in, 181; power-sharing in, 42–44; United Nations and, 41, 44–45, 99; victory consolidation in, 41–45, 65

Annan, Kofi (United Nations), 199

Apartheid (South Africa), 41, 69, 122, 124

CPSIA information can be obtained
at www.ICGtesting.com
Printed in the USA
BVHW030027020320
573769BV00002B/24